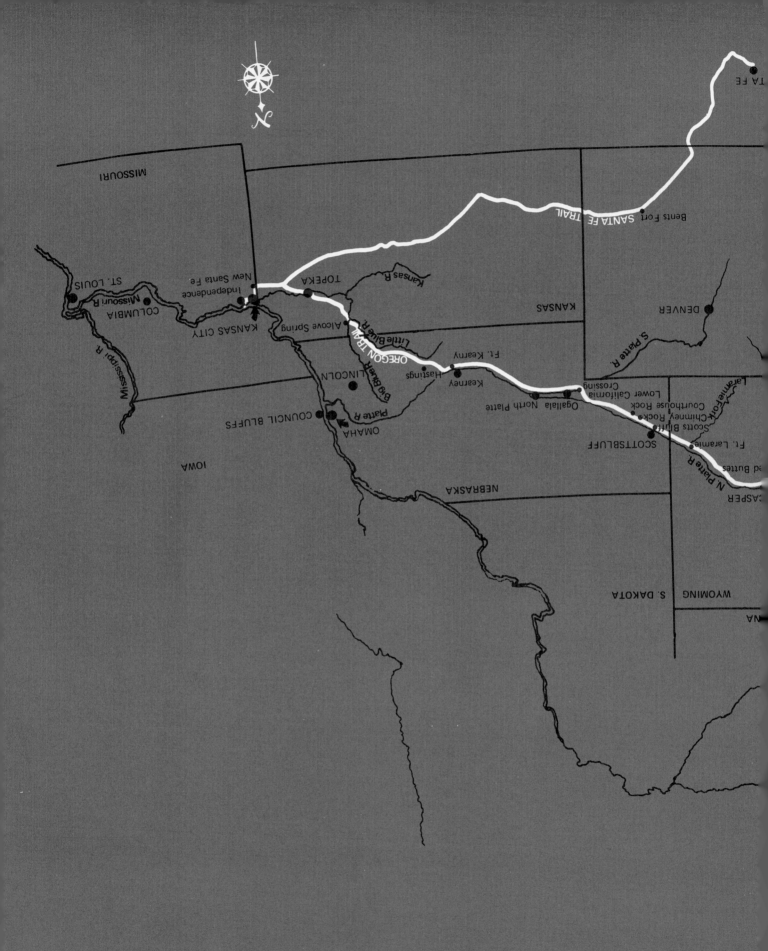

MAPS OF THE OREGON TRAIL

Other books by the author

The Old Cathedral
1965 (2nd edition, 1980)

The Story of Old Ste. Genevieve
1967 (2nd edition, 1973; 3rd edition, 1976)

The Oregon Trail Revisited
1972 (2nd edition, 1978)

History of the Hazelwood School District
1977

Legacy: The Sverdrup Story
1978

Leif Sverdrup: Engineer Soldier at his Best
1980

MAPS OF THE OREGON TRAIL

GREGORY M. FRANZWA

THE PATRICE PRESS
GERALD, MISSOURI

Library of Congress
Cataloging in Publication Data

Franzwa, Gregory M.
  Maps of the Oregon Trail.
  1. Oregon Trail — Maps. I. Title.
G1422.07F7 1982   911´.78   82-675039
ISBN 0-935284-30-3 — Cloth   AACR2
ISBN 0-935284-31-1 — Looseleaf
ISBN 0-935284-32-X — Paper

Published by:
The Patrice Press
Box 42 · Gerald, MO 63037

Printed in the United States of America

To Jane
who kept us all
together

CONTENTS

FOREWORD

In 1804 Meriwether Lewis and William Clark, acting on orders from President Thomas Jefferson, led their "Voyage of Discovery" from St. Louis to the Pacific Northwest. News of their epochal venture was slow in reaching the hearths of the common man. In the ensuing three decades the Mountain Men, traveling much the same route in search of beaver peltry, also told of the land behind the shining mountains. Again, it was slow to reach the general populace.

Not until 1841, and the arrival of the vanguard migration to the West, could the nation begin to understand that this might be a place of settlement, a place to live and raise their families. Before the next two decades had passed, Americans made that leap across half a continent, traveling over a network of old Indian paths which had become known as the Oregon Trail. They came first by the dozens, then by the hundreds, then by the tens of thousands. As they traveled, they pressed that trail into a highway, seemingly never to disappear.

But disappear it did — all but an estimated 15 percent of it is gone or radically altered in character. So have so many of the historic sites associated with the great trace — the forts, the Pony Express and Overland Stage stations, the road ranches, even the lonely wayside graves. A part of our history — a priceless heritage — is on the verge of disappearing from the face of the earth.

For the past generation and a half, a lonely cadre of scholars has been searching, both in the field and in archival repositories, for the disappeared elements. They worked on their own time, and at their own expense, to attempt to relocate the hallowed road and its story spots. The first of the guide books of this century appeared just 10 years ago. Now we have a book of maps to guide the motorist to the trail from the Missouri River to my own state of Oregon. We can even walk part of the way along the designated hiking segments, and our own feet can literally retrace the footsteps of the intrepid pioneers who settled our land.

As governor of the State of Oregon, I invite my fellow citizens of this state to retrace the path taken by their ancestors as they crossed our beautiful land. And we ask them, too, to extend the hand of friendship and welcome to those from other states, keeping alive the spirit of friendship and hospitality extended by our pioneer forefathers.

Victor Atiyeh
Governor of Oregon

vii

PREFACE & ACKNOWLEDGMENTS

The Oregon Trail was memorialized in 1978 when the Congress of the United States designated it as a National Historic Trail. It became the responsibility of the National Park Service to prepare a comprehensive report to Congress on the entire length of the trail, for submission late in 1981. The second book of their three-volume report was a compilation of maps, on which the trail and some alternates appeared, along with 125 historic sites and seven hiking segments totaling 318 miles. The goal is to preserve significant remnants of the trail and those historic sites not already protected, before all are erased from the face of the earth by time and ''progress.''

The Patrice Press, the nation's most active publisher of books on the Oregon Trail, elected to publish this consumer version of that volume of maps. It contains all the data included in Aubrey L. Haines' classic, *Historic Sites Along the Oregon Trail* (Patrice, 1981) and some listed in my own book, *The Oregon Trail Revisited* (Patrice, 1972).

In 1974 we received a call from James A. Michener to ask our help in debugging a chapter intended for his book, *Centennial*. Shortly after the book came out we received a check from the author. It was promptly returned. Here's why.

Our research work on the Oregon Trail started in 1968 and has never stopped. We have written thousands of letters and all have been answered. Our files hold dozens of hours of tape recordings from trail experts on certain aspects of the overland experience. Some dropped whatever they were doing to draft thumbnail map sketches to clear up trouble spots. We have been helped by such magnificent men as the late Paul C. Henderson and the late Ray Allen Billington. Tens of thousands of people bought our books and thus helped sustain the research program. People like Nancy Ehrlich, archivist of the Jackson County Historical Society, sent books at their own expense. People like Vicki Clark of the Wyoming State Archives photocopied books they couldn't send, just to help out. People like Estaline Carpenter of Fairbury, Nebraska, provided aerial photographs to prove out rut swales. Dozens of others provided typescripts of unpublished and unrecorded overland diaries from their ancestors. In all those years, and for all those hours of help, not one solitary soul asked for one cent of remuneration. Estaline even gave us a jar of jam.

So that's why Jim Michener got his check back. And as the personal

requests came in from our readers, they too were answered to the best of our ability, and without charge. As the man says, we are all in this together.

We are not about to stop leaning on our resources either, because we feel those people want us to continue to publish and make the fruit of the study available to all. In the preface to *The Oregon Trail Revisited* we asked the readers to report any changes since publication — or just plain errors — so that subsequent editions could be improved. A correction file more than three inches thick was used to update the first edition. We hope readers of this book also will help readers of future editions by reporting changes. We are not at all confident that we have shown all the rut swales, for example. If more exist, we want to know about them.

There would be no room for maps if we attempted to include the names of all who have helped find and identify these ancient routes, but we shall name a few and hope all those not mentioned will understand.

One of the most important is Helen Henderson. Her husband Paul died in 1979 after a lifetime of scholarly research and cartography on the Oregon Trail, but Helen continues to help whenever asked, and that is often. Her most valuable service these days, however, is guarding that priceless archival collection which she and her husband gathered over more than half a century of detective work on the trail.

Aubrey L. Haines contributed heavily to the work, largely through his NPS-sponsored research for *Historic Sites Along the Oregon Trail*. Merrill J. Mattes, whose *The Great Platte River Road* stands as one of the masterpieces of trail literature, has never hesitated to question and to probe, and although his service has been almost as long as the Hendersons', he hasn't begun to slow down. Dr. Merle Wells, Idaho's State Historic Preservation Officer, continues as that state's most knowledgeable person on the Oregon Trail west of Casper, and he and his colleague, Larry Jones, share their knowledge freely.

Reg Duffin, the talented Englishman who researches with exhausting thoroughness, so desired to see us issue a memorable volume that he volunteered to prepare several maps just for this book. Bob Knecht of the Kansas State Historical Society sent volumes of historic maps for our study, and Wendell Frantz of the Nebraska State Historical Society, forwarded a number of scholarly articles which helped clear up some mysteries. Troy and Billie Gray of Dallas used *The Oregon Trail Re-*

visited as a guide to where they, as readers, should not go because of the dangerous terrain. And promptly went there. They have traversed the Sublette Cutoff and several related roads in their entirety, alone, in a ¾-ton pickup truck. Their advice on this volume has been invaluable.

Two men from the National Park Service — Stanford Young and Dr. John A. Latschar — walked a great deal of the trail personally, responding to counsel fed into their work by Haines, Charles W. Martin, Mattes, Wells and the author. They returned with lots of current, dependable information and proceeded to teach the old hands a thing or two. The two men established the seven hiking segments shown in this book, certainly a major contribution.

We owe much to our editor, Arielle North, who continues to check our English with patience and kindness.

There was no question about the picture that we wanted on the front of this book. There is just one photo of the Oregon Trail which stands out above all others — a shot of Mitchell Pass taken in 1973 by Mortimer S. Sumberg of Ridgewood, New Jersey. A framed copy hangs in the Henderson living room in Bridgeport, Nebraska, and another is in our study. When we asked for permission to use it, Mort had the original here in a matter of days.

Finally, we express our gratitude to those who examined all or portions of this work critically before it was sent to the printer: Alice Antilla, Chester and Karen Buck, Duffin, Laura Franzwa, Troy and Billie Gray, Latschar, Martin, Mattes, Bob and Bertha Rennells, Jim Weeks and Wells. All of them took hours from their work or leisure time to debug the maps and accompanying text, thus helping minimize error in the first edition.

Noble authors, after thanking their resource people, usually freak out on a humility trip by adding something like this: ". . . however, responsibility for any error is entirely my own." The hell with that. If they missed it, blame *them*.

— Gregory M. Franzwa
April 15, 1982

ONE GIANT STEP

AN INTRODUCTORY ESSAY

Had there ever been anything like it in the Old World, it had long since been forgotten. The frontier experience of the 19th century seemed to be uniquely American, and uniquely 19th century too, for that matter. Who, in this day and age, could imagine a man settling on a tract of ground, clearing it with backbreaking labor, erecting his own buildings on it with his own bare hands and with no help, breaking the tough sod with primitive farm implements, nursing that farm to the point where it would sustain his family, and then chucking the whole works just because somebody staked out a mile away and did the same thing? Today he seems crazy — paranoid about preserving his terrible aloneness.

It wasn't a trait exclusive to the region known today as the Midwest, but more settlers of that type were there than anywhere else. They and their ancestors had followed that pattern since coming to America. They jumped successively from the Eastern Seaboard over the Alleghenies and into Ohio, maybe Kentucky, into Arkansas, Indiana, Illinois, Wisconsin, Iowa, and especially into Missouri. And there they stopped. It no longer was a matter of packing up and moving a few days to the west. Now there was the barrier of the Great Plains, or the Great American Desert as it was then known. It stretched westward for 2,000 miles, and at the time was thought incapable of supporting more than greasewood, buffalo and hordes of savage Indians.

But all the land wasn't like that. That was merely what was in between — in between where they were, which would never do, and where they were going. There happened to be a strip of land near the western ocean which offered a better climate, a more fertile soil, and an opportunity to satisfy that westering urge just one last time. That was the lure, and the restless transplanted Midwesterner sat there in a blue funk until the light turned green. That happened in the 1840s.

The light was hardly an incandescent blaze. It started as a flicker — news of a trading caravan, perhaps, which had rolled wagons over the fabled South Pass. Then a couple of missionaries, who took their wives over the continental divide — one of them achieving pregnancy in the process. Then, in 1841, a single caravan became the vanguard of the 300,000 people who would follow in the next two decades. There were only 58 settlers in the Bidwell-Bartleson company. At Sheep Rock, about four

miles past the fantastic Soda Springs, the party split. Twenty-four headed south down the Bear River, bound for California but not having the foggiest notion of how to get there. (That they did, and all safely, is but one of the wonders of those 20 years.) The other 34 continued along the trace to the valley of the Willamette River, south of the Columbia River.

That was the beginning, a mere trickle. The so-called Great Migration took place two years later, when 875 farmers went to Oregon and another 38 went to California. Then it became a small stream, with as many as 4,000 going west in 1847, when it was learned the unpleasantness with Mexico was over. The shocking tragedy of the Donner Party during the winter of 1846-47 dissuaded no more than a few. By the end of 1848, 11,500 had moved to the West Coast. They were sending letters back to the home folks urging them to come too. They said that the danger of the Indians along the way had been vastly exaggerated — that was true. They said the trip would be easy — that wasn't. Usually the advice was sound and the expansion of the truth was harmless.

Newspaper editors printed their letters home and the phenomenon began to feed upon itself. Guide books began to appear, to be snatched up eagerly by those who dreamed of the West. Emigrating societies formed, met regularly through the winter, and moved to the jumping-off places in the spring to outfit and await the greening of the prairies.

Who were these people? Well, for the most part, they were farmers. A few artisans went along too. They were substantial people, most of them. By the time they sold their farms, machinery, draft animals and household goods, they had a sizeable amount of cash to invest in the trip and their new homes. Their outfit wouldn't be terribly costly — one or two small, sturdy wagons, six to 10 head of oxen, a milk cow or two. Most of the time heavy items like household furniture, kitchen ranges, or pianos would be freighted to the West Coast by clipper, around the Horn to California or Oregon. A few packed stuff like that in the wagons; it usually ended up at trailside along the way.

They were religious people — most of them Protestant. Some were so religious that they refused to travel on Sunday. Not a bad idea, for six days of tough going was debilitating to the oxen, and the day of rest could do wonders for tired feet — human as well as bovine. Still, the right kind of driving boss could pace his caravan so that the wagons could roll every day without doing any damage.

For most, there were forced layovers, and they were frequent enough without the religious influence. A broken axle in the morning could hold a wagon back until noon, and when one wagon stopped, they all did. In the early years the Indians never attacked a sizable train, but a straggler could be in big trouble. The most frequent cause of a forced layover was illness or an accident. Cholera, that wretched scourge of the 19th century, could hit a perfectly robust person after breakfast, and he would be in his grave by noon. Many would linger for weeks in the jouncing wagons. When it was obvious the victim wouldn't last the day, the train held up to await the end. The burials were sometimes right in the trail, and the next morning each wagon rolled over the grave, tamping it down and erasing the scent. The practice was effective — wolves wouldn't open a grave they couldn't smell, and Indians wouldn't go after a cheap scalp if they didn't know where it was.

The character of the westering experience changed dramatically after the discovery of gold in 1848 on the American River east of Sutter's Fort, in present-day Sacramento. The American of mid-century had heard some tall tales before, but when the news was confirmed by the president of the United States all skepticism disappeared. It should have. The find was real, and it certainly was true that an incredible fortune in gold was simply lying in the bottoms of the shallow streams. Men dropped everything to prepare hurriedly for the trip, and by the time 1849 ended there were 25,000 more people in California. (Only 2,700 had gone there in all previous years.)

These were not just Midwestern farmers — they were from all over the United States, and from the big cities too. They were almost universally without their families, their intent being to go to the diggings, make their pile, and come home and live off their affluence.

A few did just that. Most had to settle for the adventure of a lifetime. Many remained on the West Coast to become successful citizens, finding their gold in mercantilism, shipping or agriculture.

The gold rush didn't end in 1849. As a matter of fact, 55,000 people went to California the next year and 50,000 in 1852. The process had the effect of accelerating the movement to Oregon, and in 1852 alone 10,000 made the jump to the Pacific Northwest. Thus, the restless population of the eastern half of America terminated the frontier in one giant step — a 2,000-mile, 20-year vault from the Missouri River to the coastal valleys of the West. By the time it began to slack off, during the awful Indian problems of the 1860s, 300,000 people had moved west, and the United States had geographical unity, stretching from sea to shining sea, with no intrusive ownership by any foreign nations. The seeds of world power were sown in those years.

The route identified in this book is the one determined through the research of the National Park Service in its 1981 study. It starts at the old Independence Landing north of Independence, Missouri. Here the emigrants left the steamboats after a five- or six-day trip from St. Louis. They wound up the hill and came down the old road to the bustling square in the little town.

Most camped within a mile or two of the square, buying what they needed to take along during their four- to five-month trip. The fields surrounding the jumping-off towns were ablaze with campfires during every night in April, as the process continued and as the warm spring rains started the bluestem up through the prairie thatch. Those with horses or mules left first. Their buck-toothed animals had no trouble finding the short grasses. But the majority — those with powerful and during able oxen — had to wait a couple of weeks longer, because cattle have different dentition than horses.

The first days on the move were spent searching for the proper organization. That generally had been accomplished by the time they arrived at the Kansas River, the first major crossing, in what is now downtown Topeka. Watch was posted every night, because the travelers were approached every day by begging Indians who would not be so polite under cover of darkness. The wagons were drawn in a circle every night, too, not so much to guard against Indian attack as to form a corral for the loose stock. Emigrants rarely rode in the bumpy, springless wagons, and rarely slept in them either. There were tents for that purpose. The more organized trains even had latrine tents, especially for the ladies. Otherwise, the girls and their billowing skirts formed a protective screen. They would go behind this screen, one at a time, *al fresco*.

Eighteen to 20 miles a day over the prairie lands was considered a fairly good clip. To accomplish this the pioneers were awakened shortly before daybreak by the sound of a bugle or a gunshot from the guard. They prepared breakfast, yoked their oxen and usually were able to begin the day of travel within two hours or less. By the mid-1840s the campgrounds were listed in the guidebooks, and the trains usually had a particular destination for the one-hour "nooning" as well as the overnight camp. The daily pull usually was over by 6 o'clock. After dinner came a time of great socialization. Campfires blazed, fiddles and jew's harps came out, and evenings were filled with singing and storytelling. The travelers made friendships during those nights which held fast for the rest of their lives, as did the memories.

Soon the wagon trains left the valley of the Little Blue River and arrived at the Platte River — called the "Coast of the Nebraska" by John Charles Fremont. The pioneers followed the flat valley west and watched the land change before their eyes. Prairie became sand hills; sand hills became foothills and picturesque rock/clay formations.

Many crossed the South South Platte River west of present Ogallala — now the stream is a sluggish rivulet but then it was a rushing torrent a half-mile wide. They mounted a high plateau and caught their breath on the brow of the steepest hill many had ever seen. They locked the wheels and hung onto check ropes, but the wagons still dragged everybody down the slope now called "Windlass Hill" and into picturesque Ash Hollow. As they followed the south bank of the North Platte River, they marveled at Courthouse and Jail Rocks. Beyond this was Chimney Rock, which had been in view for over 30 miles. In each case the heated air off the sand acted as a magnifier and the rocks appeared to be much closer than they really were. Then, as now, the traveler had to touch as well as see, and sometimes what seemed to be a half-hour joyride really took a half-day. But they got there, most of them, and had little trouble scratching their names in the soft brule clay.

They saw the formidable mass of Scotts Bluffs choking off the route along the river, and prior to 1851 they detoured several miles to the south to cross the bluffs via Robidoux Pass. There they met the raunchy French traders by that name, members of the Joseph Robidoux clan from St. Joe — and their equally raunchy Sioux wives. Here, besides blacksmithing services, were two of the finest springs along the Oregon Trail, both of which still flow. There was more. As they crested the pass there unfolded before them a panorama that gained mention in countless diaries. There on the horizon was the purple shadow of Laramie Peak, fully 120 miles to the west. The pulse of the emigration was quickening, and the journals reflected that with enthusiasm.

The teamsters drove harder now as they neared Fort Laramie, the first real semblance of civilization since leaving Fort Kearny, 331 miles to the east. A trading post since 1834, this became an Army post in 1849, as pressure built for protection of emigrant caravans from the Indians. The sutler maintained an abundant stock in the post store, where supplies could be replenished at outrageous prices. The post commissary also furnished supplies to destitute emigrants, when available.

The so-called Black Hills (of Wyoming, not South Dakota) were getting steeper, the scenery wilder. Soon they entered what they called the "red earth country," where the soil and the rocks reveal high concentrations of ferric oxide. Then to the Ayres Natural Bridge, where little La Prele Creek rushes beneath an arch of stone. A long journey away from the Platte ended when they rejoined the flat river bottom east of present Casper, Wyoming. There were the bridges and the ferries — several of them during the 1850s — that carried the south bank emigration to the

4

north and away from the Platte River which had sheltered them for hundreds of miles.

Now they were in hostile land. Water which looked so refreshing turned out to be deadly poison, laced with alkali. Oxen had to be beaten to keep them away from it. The pools were well labeled by the rotting carcasses of animals which partook, and died on the spot. Soon the emigration arrived at a stream which would delight and bedevil them for another week, the Sweetwater River, fateful tributary of the North Platte. They climbed the gentle granite slopes of Independence Rock — a thrill to this day — and patiently hammered their names into its flanks. Much of that elegant graffiti survives today.

Another six miles brought them to Devil's Gate, a narrow cleft through which the Sweetwater roared. The caravans passed just to the south, but the curious emigrants had to touch this one too. Some climbed to the top and peered into the frightful chasm. A few lost their footing and their lives. Ahead loomed another curiosity too remote to touch: Split Rock, a mountain with a cleft in its peak.

Soon a decision had to be made. The wagonmasters could choose the main trail, which required three crossings of the Sweetwater in a sheer-walled gorge about a mile and a half long. Or they could take the so-called "deep sand route" to the south. Most opted for the Three Crossings.

The wonders didn't cease. At the Ice Slough they stuck their arms down through a foot-thick layer of watery peat and pulled up thin sheets of ice. The nights were cool anyway, but the very idea of fresh ice in July at a place like this was fascinating, and some kept it in blankets right over the South Pass.

That wasn't far, but first they had to pick their way through a veritable Maginot line called the Rocky Ridges. The boulder field stretches for several miles and was a hellish test for the wheels. It still is. Soon things flattened out, and the appearance of two low mounds to the left of the trail gave indication that the fabled South Pass was not far away. They continued to look for it and soon came to a large spring. They were dumbfounded at this, for here was the Pacific Spring. They had traversed South Pass without knowing it. The gentle saddle is nearly 29 miles wide and only a trained surveyor could perceive the continental divide at that point.

There were more wonders just beyond the pass. First came the Plume Rocks, strange shapes near the crossing of the Dry Sandy. All too often the stream was just that — dry. So the teamsters sometimes dug holes on the stream was just that — dry. So the teamsters sometimes dug holes on the far bank of the draw, and enough water managed to well up in those cavities to quench the thirst of man and beast. Some of the troughs are still in evidence 130 years later. Six miles further another decision had to be made. Should the traveler continue to the southwest, away from his ultimate destination to the northwest, and follow the Blacks Fork River for its water and grass? Or should he cut off some 75 miles of travel and move straight west across the bitter desert on the road founded by old Caleb Greenwood, but known as the Sublette Cutoff? That meant a stretch of about 50 miles with no water at all. Travelers had to start moving at sundown, travel all night, and all the next day to hit the Green River.

The hurrying hordes of the gold rush did that, but earlier travelers bound for Oregon usually went the safe way, to decrepit Fort Bridger. Then they turned north to cross over the Bear River Divide and into what is now Idaho. They cleared the Georgetown Summit to arrive at what many felt was the most fantastic sight of all — the Soda Springs. Waters laden with iron and carbon dioxide bubbled from the earth in fields of hollow cones. One, Steamboat Spring, spewed its contents periodically in geyser-like fashion, puffing like a steamboat as it did it. The once-pastoral and sedentary travelers, who by this time were getting bored because they thought they had seen everything, grabbed their diaries and scribbled furiously.

A few more miles down the trail and those headed for California in 1849 and later had to make another decision. They could cut off a few miles (or so they thought) by moving straight west over the new Hudspeth Cutoff to intersect the California Trail down from Fort Hall. It looked good on paper but the saving in miles was minimal and the road was terrible. Few saved anything. The main Oregon Trail continued to the northwest through some bleak land, but with occasional patches of water and grass.

Then came Fort Hall, built in 1834 by Nathaniel Wyeth. Here the earlier travelers were introduced to the considerable hospitality of the Hudson's Bay Company, a British outfit that had every reason to shun the emigrants. Their very presence could (and in fact did) cost the crown the territory. Aside from discouraging the further passage of wagons, which they truly believed to be impossible, they were usually hospitable to the travelers.

Fort Hall was on the Snake River, about as different from the Platte as day from night. The Snake was a hellion of a stream, unnavigable by boat or raft. Furthermore, it didn't have the decency to leave a gentle valley, as the Blue, Platte, and even Sweetwater rivers did. The Snake cut through jagged scoria in chasms impossible to reach by the livestock. Even man had trouble scrambling down to the rushing waters. It wasn't as if there were a choice — the route along the Snake was the only way to go, so here they went. They crossed the Raft River, and there a final decision had to be made — to California or Oregon. Those going to Oregon continued to the west. The people bound for California had to turn south.

Fort Hall to them seemed to have been a terribly long shunt to the north, but again, it had proved to be the only practical way to go. It was safe, sure, relatively easy, and about as fast as the so-called shortcuts.

The Oregon-bound people passed the frightening Caldron Linn, noted in the diaries of the Astorians a generation earlier, and then veered farther and farther away from the Snake as they searched for a passage over a dumpy little stream called Rock Creek. It might not rival the Snake, but its chasm did. They crossed in present Twin Falls, and several miles later came back to the bank of the Snake River. Soon they found new wonders to excite them. There were rapids, noisy ribbons of white water crashing against mid-stream boulders and speaking eloquently of why rafting was impossible. Then came Salmon Falls, and soon thousands of springs were seen bubbling out of sheer gorge walls and cascading in slender white ribbons down to the Snake below. They saw waterfalls, they saw whirlpools, they saw everything an angry river was capable of doing. And then they left it, temporarily. They crossed the desert due west for nearly 20 miles, emerged over the brow of a hill to see the river once again. In it were three islands, side by side, and the path for fording that river was clear. They rolled to a point opposite the downstream end of the nearest and largest island, forded a shallow slough and then came up to the head of that island. They forded above the head of the center island, and then on to the last one. Then they moved to the north bank, across the deepest and fastest part of the Snake. Even though the stream had been divided into fourths, it was still a dangerous passage, and many paid with their lives. Most made it safely.

But in a few of the years, when the water was especially high, even that crossing was too perilous, and the decision was made to continue along the south bank of the river into present-day Oregon. Most did not. Most crossed here, moved northwestward to the lovely linear oasis of the Boise River. They then followed it to a safe ford at Canyon Hill and moved on to the Snake once more. There they found the second of the three Hudson's Bay installations along their way, Fort Boise.

They forded here in the early days, and in later years screamed bloody murder as the ferrymen gouged them at the rate of $8 per wagon. The travelers mounted Keeney Pass, crossed the Malheur River and struck out through the desert for one last glimpse of the Snake, at a place appropriately called "Farewell Bend."

Throughout their three months or more of travel, they were constantly fearful of being delayed to the point where passage through the formidable Blue Mountains would be impeded by snow. They now closed on that day of reckoning. As they rounded towering Flagstaff Hill, the pastoral Baker Valley unfolded below them. And then, far ahead, they saw the ominous blue shadow on the horizon. There were the Blue

Mountains.

For all the dread, they were surprisingly easy. Lives were lost to be sure, but lives were lost all along the trail. There were no disasters for those who stuck to the established trail. They coursed down Ladd Canyon Hill and into that intermontane saucer called *le grand ronde* by the French mountain men working for the Northwest Company. They camped at the sylvan Emigrant Springs, moved over what later became known as Deadman Pass, and rolled down Emigrant Hill to find themselves out of the Blues, and out of danger at last.

But they were not out of work — not by a long shot. Men and women who were pink and flaccid when they left the States now were bundles of sinew and gristle, with skin like leather and calluses on their calluses.

They still had to cut the dugways down to and up from stream crossings. They still had to lift the heavy ox yokes every morning and night. They still had to adz out an axle or wagon tongue when the old ones gave out. But they had their new strength, so tasks seemed easier. Their on-trail experience gave them better methods of doing things.

Attitudes became buoyant. Hearts sang with gratitude for having been spared during the hazardous crossing, and with hope that their luck would hold the rest of the way. For most of them, it did.

It seemed, though, that the trail goal was tantalizingly out of reach. For months they had heard about the Columbia, the Great River of the West, and they were so near. Yet, the trail refused to take them there. They were unable to see it or hear it for days as it was just out of reach to the north. The Oregon Trail paralleled it. They were seven miles south of the Columbia Gorge when they came to the John Day River, the stream named for one of the Astorians of 1812-15 who at that point lost his mind and had to be returned to the mouth of the Columbia.

At McDonald Ford, they found the John Day to be calm and shallow although there was white water both upstream and downstream. Many walked across without getting in over their shoetops. Another day's travel found them moving to the northwest once again, and as they crested a range of brown hills they caught their breath as they saw the majestic Columbia before them, at present-day Biggs, Oregon. They descended to the riverbank and followed it downstream. Soon they had to ford the mouth of another of Oregon's wild rivers, the Deschutes. In one more day they would be at The Dalles, the last decision point.

It was at these rapids that the emigrants could choose to pay raftsmen to ferry them down the Columbia to the Willamette, or pay the tolls for travel over the Barlow Road, after 1845. In later years, most chose the latter. Those who didn't took to the Columbia River at the mouth of Chenoweth Creek and floated down to the Cascades of the Columbia. There they disembarked to portage past the rushing waters, mounted the

rafts again after the danger was passed, and marveled at the spectacular scenery as they floated down the broad river toward their new home.

Some landed on the north bank to make the acquaintance of the kindly Dr. John McLoughlin, chief factor of the Hudson's Bay Company's Fort Vancouver. The "White Eagle of the Columbia" was the ultimate host. His sympathy was with the courageous Americans, and they sorely needed that — plus his groceries.

Others continued another five miles downriver and then turned up the Willamette. The going was slower now as they hugged the bank through what is now downtown Portland. For 23 miles they moved upstream, and then they saw the settlement of Oregon City and the Falls of the Willamette, which barred further passage upriver.

Those on the Barlow Road had tougher going. From The Dalles they had to negotiate the Tygh Grade, which was bad enough. But there was something worse. The towering cone of Mount Hood was before them and rarely out of their vision. They knew the road went through, but it was hard to imagine how it could circumnavigate that immense snow-capped peak.

They were well to the south of the cone, however, before they hit the tollgate and turned to the west. They now could see the solution, but it still didn't seem easy. Sure enough, it wasn't. Barlow Pass was a grind, but those who had read the trail guides knew the worst was yet to come. That was Laurel Hill. Here was a declivity the likes of which they had never seen before. This made "Windlass Hill" at Ash Hollow look like a sandpile. Down at the bottom of the first leg lay the wreckage of wagons which had slipped their restraints and had come crashing to the ledge in splinters. There were the remains of a few animals mixed in. But again, most made it safely with locked wheels, trailing a motley array of travelers trying to pull back on the ropes, digging in their heels, and sliding out of control down the chute.

They came to the Zig Zag River — no one wondered how it got its name — after passing the western tollgate, and then the Sandy. There was one last nasty stretch, known as the Devil's Backbone, but the excitement at nearing the destination was such that no one particularly noticed it.

They crossed the Clackamas River and were a half-day away. If it was late in the season they would have been met a few days earlier by the relief parties sent out from the settlements to help the newcomers. Most didn't need it. They needed tranquilizers. They rolled into little Oregon City in utter jubilation. The beasts which had survived the trek, and many did, were almost members of the family. Reunions with friends, neighbors and relatives who had come out in prior years were commonplace every fall, but always occasions of intense joy. Hospitality was extended to total strangers. The established citizens were almost as pleased to see the newcomers as the newcomers were to see them. Additional population meant additional safety and added leverage too, in their demands on Congress for statehood and military assistance.

So that was the classic pattern, repeated year after year after year. Soon there was no more room along the Willamette, so they settled to the east and the west, but especially to the north, into that magnificent wilderness which became the State of Washington.

And with that settlement, and the California gold rush too, three generations of the American wanderlust finally came to an end. It seemed almost a Calvinistic predestination that they should be there, at the end of the land, and once they realized that the frontier was gone they began to devote energy formerly used in relocating to making a living. The hard work produced those magnificent farms and cities. Parents who made the trip became grandparents and found themselves objects of awe. Little boys and girls who once headed out the coal chute when they saw grandpa coming with another trail story suddenly realized that they really were

heroes. The old folks became recognized in their time. They were invited to meetings of pioneer societies and seated at places of honor. Their speeches of 30 years later hardly compared with their diaries written during the actual crossing, and it seemed that those who needed to embellish the least did it the most.

But who cared? They, common men and women, wore the Apollonian wreath. They had a grand time in doing what they did, and at the time it certainly didn't seem sacrificial. But from the perspective of their grandchildren they were supermen, giving their all so that future generations could live in the Pacific Northwest.

They are all gone now. Some folks still live off the fortunes amassed by those who arrived first, but most find the fortune of their heritage quite adequate. The memory of those early travelers is revered. They will never be forgotten.

THE MAPPING OF THE OREGON TRAIL

A study of this nature would be incomplete without some mention of the sources of the data it contains. The means of establishing the route of the trail are varied indeed. The best way is to go out and look at it, on the face of the earth, and where there are not a lot of intersecting ranch roads this is easy enough. Most of the original pristine trace, however, simply doesn't exist anymore. Since most of the trail followed arid river valleys, there was complete inundation when reclamation techniques were used to bring the land to productivity. If the trail wasn't flooded, then it was obliterated by the annual tilling of the ground which had been reclaimed. A good base of the study is the United States survey, which was one of the preconditions for admission to the union of states. Surveyors went into the field with optical instruments and chains and measured the land in accordance with the public land system of the United States. This system divided the state into townships, six miles east and west and six miles north and south. The townships are numbered east or west of principal meridians of longitude, and north or south of parallels of latitude. Each of the numbered one-mile squares within a township is called a section, and for purposes of legal description each of the sections is divided into subsections of one-sixteenth section. There are half-sections, referred to as N½, S½, E½ or W½. The usual division, though, is the quarter-section: SE¼, NE¼, SW¼ or NW¼. Each of those quarters is further divided into sixteenth-sections, indicated as NE¼ of the SW¼, or SE¼ of the SW¼, for examples. Those divisions measure 440 yards on a side.

Section

Township

9

When those surveyors went into the field they noted two things principally: rivers and roads. In the early days there usually was but one road in the areas of interest to this study, and that was the Oregon Trail. They plotted the point where the road entered each section of the grid, what it did within that square mile of land, and where it emerged. These old maps survive. Contemporary highway maps show that identical grid, unchanged from the first survey, warts and all. They show what is there now, however, including houses, present river channels, diversion canals, and the various types of roads. It is a simple matter, given the constant of the public land system grid, to transpose the route of the trail from the original survey to the contemporary map. Sometimes this falls on a dotted line, indicating that a primitive road is there, and it is often a good bet that this is the Oregon Trail in one form or another, usually merely graded. It is also an indication that the road, if it may be called that, is in use today as a ranch road or a jeep trail.

Sometimes the red line falls over a pair of dark gray lines — that is a divided interstate highway and this means the trail is gone. (It does compliment the skill of our forebears, however, who had the uncanny ability to sense just the right way to go from one place to another.)

Sometimes states were admitted to the union at a late date, long after the trail had become virtually extinct. Wyoming and Idaho, for example, came in in 1890, when only occasional wagon trains were in transit to the West. This is where the emigrant diaries serve a valuable purpose. The speed of the caravans was generally known, the creeks had been identified during the early years of the emigration, and good detectives like Paul Henderson, Merrill Mattes and Merle Wells were able to fit the pieces of the puzzle together and establish which of the ranch roads was the trail.

Latter day devices have been used to great effect in establishing the bona fide rut swales. The airplane and the helicopter have been the most helpful. Infrared photography is showing considerable promise.

Most trail scholars prefer to work with maps published by the U.S. Geological Survey, at a scale of 1:24,000, or about 2½" : 1 mile. These are valuable because they contain complete topographical information and thus often show why the emigrants went the way they did. We rejected their use in this book for several reasons. First, they are in several colors, and to reproduce them in black and red only would cause great problems for the lithographers. Second, the scale is much too large, and the book would have to have five times as many pages (and cost perhaps three times as much).

In two areas there was no choice — suitable state highway maps of Jackson County, Missouri, and the City of Topeka, Kansas, simply don't exist, and the USGS quads had to be used. In some instances elsewhere the cities are shown in greatly enlarged detail on state highway department city maps. These are included to help the visitor find the route of the trail as it winds through the city streets. There will be errors here because the intensive development of the cities has eradicated all trace of the trail in most cases, and the route had to be extrapolated from less-detailed survey maps.

Most of the way the trail is platted on the standard ½" : 1 mile maps issued by the various state highway departments and updated every few years. Only a 7¾" x 10¼" segment of each map is shown on each of these 130 map pages. The names and subdivisions of the maps appear on the edges of the maps in this book. 1981 prices are listed. The complete maps may be ordered in the same scale from these agencies:

U.S. Geological Survey, Box 25286, Denver Federal Center, Denver, CO 80225, $2 per sheet.

Kansas Department of Transportation, Bureau of Transportation Planning, 8th Floor, State Office Building, Topeka, KS 66612, 35¢ per map or 3/$1; cities the same, except Topeka and Kansas City (Kansas), which are 2" : 1 mile and are priced at $2 per map.

Nebraska Department of Roads, Box 94759, Lincoln, NE 68509 (402) 477-6012, all maps 40¢ per sheet, but several counties are subdivided into several sheets.

Wyoming Highway Department, Billing Section, Box 1708, Cheyenne, WY 80001, county maps $1.25 per sheet, but all counties have multiple sheets. City of Casper is $2.50 for 1" : 1,000'.

Idaho Transportation Department, Box 7129, Boise, ID 83707 (208) 334-2569, county maps are 60¢ per sheet, but most counties have multiple sheets. City of Twin Falls is 16" x 21" and 50¢; City of Boise is on four sheets of that size, at 50¢ per sheet.

Oregon Department of Transportation, Map Distribution Unit, Room 17, Transportation Building, Salem, OR 97310 (503) 378-6254, county maps are 45¢ per sheet, but most counties have multiple sheets. La Grande, Pendleton, The Dalles and Oregon City are 30¢ each. Add $1 for mail orders.

CODES TO THE MAPS

The following is the code block to the Oregon Transportation Department maps, and agencies of the other states generally follow the same code pattern:

The material appearing in red in this book incorporates few codes. The wider of the two lines is the route which has been determined (rather arbitrarily at times) to be the principal route of the Oregon Trail. All other routes are indicated by lines half that width. The trail line is dotted when pristine or significant rut swales are visible today. This is the area which demands more field work and the area where the reader may be of maximum benefit to the effort by notifying the publisher of additional areas of visible ruts. Major stream crossings are shown with an X. A bridge is shown by two parallel lines. The beginning and end of a hiking segment is marked with large arrows and smaller arrows are used along the way.

The lines were laid on the red overlay with what is known as ''crepe tape.'' This is a very flexible graphic arts tape. Flexible as it is, it can't bend in perfect harmony with the sometimes hairpin turns taken by the emigration. Even the cartographers of the base maps can't do that, but they can come closer than we can. Thus, when the red line is shown overlying a twisting segment of the road in gray, and where it doesn't exactly line up with that segment, presume that in actuality the trail and the twisting dark gray lines of the base map are one and the same.

LEGEND

- PUBLIC USAGE—PRIVATE ROAD
- IMPASSABLE ROAD
- PRIMITIVE ROAD
- UNIMPROVED ROAD
- GRADED AND DRAINED ROAD
- SOIL SURFACED ROAD
- GRAVEL NOT GRADED OR DRAINED ROAD
- GRAVEL GRADED AND DRAINED ROAD
- PAVED ROAD, LOW TYPE
- PAVED ROAD, HIGH TYPE
- MULTIPLE LANE — DIVIDED ROAD
- ONE WAY ROAD
- FEDERAL AID PRIMARY HIGHWAY
- FEDERAL AID SECONDARY HIGHWAY
- ORE ROUTE—US ROUTE
- DISTANCE BETWEEN POINTS
- MINOR STRUCTURE
- BRIDGE—GRADE SEPARATION
- BRIDGE, COVERED
- FERRY, F F-FREE T F-TOLL
- DAM
- DAM, ROAD ON TOP
- DAM WITH LOCKS
- TUNNEL
- CATTLE UNDERPASS
- GATE
- INTERMITTENT STREAM
- STREAM
- RIVER N-NAVIGABLE
- DOCK, PIER, OR LANDING
- LAKE, POND, OR RESERVOIR
- DRAINAGE DITCH
- IRRIGATION DITCH
- PROMINENT MOUNTAIN, BUTTE, OR PEAK
- RAILROAD
- RAILROAD STATION
- RAILROAD GRADE CROSSING
- RAILROAD ABOVE ROAD
- RAILROAD BELOW ROAD
- AIRFIELD—AIRPORT
- LANDING AREA OR AIRSTRIP
- AIRFIELD, MILITARY

- SEAPLANE BASE, CIVIL
- AIRWAYS LIGHT BEACON
- WEATHER OBSERVATION STATION
- STATE CAPITOL
- COUNTY SEAT
- CITY OR LOCALITY

IN USE   NOT IN USE
- DWELLING, OTHER THAN FARM
- FARM UNIT
- GROUP OF DWELLINGS
- PUBLIC BUILDING, T-TOWNHALL G-GRANGE
- SCHOOL
- CHURCH
- CEMETERY
- FIRST AID STATION
- HOSPITAL
- RADIO STATION, WITH CALL LETTERS
- POST OFFICE OR (†) ATOP ANY BUILDING
- BUSINESS ESTABLISHMENT
- FACTORY OR INDUSTRIAL PLANT
- SAWMILL
- GRAIN ELEVATOR
- WAREHOUSE
- STOCK LOADING PEN
- POWER PLANT—HEATING PLANT—PUMP HOUSE
- POWER SUBSTATION
- TRANSMISSION LINE
- WATER TANK—OIL TANK—GAS TANK
- DISPOSAL, D-DUMP S-SEWAGE I-INCINERATOR
- ROAD MATERIAL STOCK PILE SITE
- GRAVEL OR CINDER PIT — QUARRY
- MINE
- CAMP AREA OR LODGE
- PARK OR CLUB, SP-STATE MP-MUNICIPAL WP-WAYSIDE RC-RIFLE AP-ATHLETIC GC-GOLF YC-YACHT EC-EQUESTRIAN
- FAIRGROUNDS OR RACE TRACK
- DRIVE-IN THEATER
- MILITARY INSTALLATION
- FOREST RANGER STATION
- OBSERVATION OR LOOKOUT TOWER
- FISH HATCHERY
- BENCH MARK
- TRIANGULATION STATION

ADVICE TO TRAVELERS

With this book in hand, the traveler may literally write his own ticket to what he sees. His most strenuous exertion might be to stop at the I-80 rest area near North Platte and walk a few yards up O'Fallon's Bluff, or take the guided tour of Fort Laramie. The explorer may do this in the middle of the winter in the family car if he wants to. But generally, the traveler will want to move out on June, July or August. Certain parts of the trail, such as South Pass, are sodden even in June. Along other stretches it rarely rains, but when it does — look out. The dust turns to a quagmire and some ranchers even fear for their loose stock. A normal car doesn't have a chance.

The best vehicle for those who want to move off the paved or graveled roads is one with four-wheel drive (known as a "4x4"). No seasoned explorer would attempt places like the Sublette Cutoff or the Rocky Ridge in a normal family car. There are even a few roads in Kansas that turn to skating rinks after a brief shower. The car should be equipped with a compass — that is imperative. An air conditioner is a big help, for the dust is simply awful. The emigrants didn't believe it, and today's traveler won't either. It is very uncomfortable, and a good air conditioner can turn what would be a nightmare into a thrilling ride.

Recreational vehicles are all right, but they can be a real pain in the neck on some stretches of the trail. It is best to leave trailers in a campground and do the exploration only with a car. Those going on the hairy trips should consider a light motorcycle for emergency exits, in the event of axle failure or a punctured oil or transmission pan.

In some places the trail may be approached only by canal access roads. There extreme caution is urged. There are no fences or guard rails. Those irrigation canals often carry the entire volume of a river with great speed and between sheer walls. Once in, never out.

Travelers are urged not to trespass on private lands. Of course public roads are on public property, and those who stick to the roads will not be in trouble. The trail itself, however, is a different story. Ranchers were not born hostile, but when they learn that their herd has been systematically carted off in innocent-looking pickup campers or motor homes they can become irritable. In fact they have been known to ping away with their .30-30's at any pickup camper seen on their land. Those who would rather not appear in the cross hairs may want to obtain permission first. Many ranchers share the sense of history of the travelers, and are pleased to open their land for visitation. Some like to accompany explorers to point out the sights. Visitors are always cautioned to reclose any gates after they pass through. A little courtesy and common sense is all most ranchers ask.

Visitors are welcome to hike on the hiking segments designated in this book, and also are encouraged to drive in the ruts. This keeps the track open and easily identified — it will be beneficial if not done to excess.

Even though the emigrants left their names on the great register rocks, the visitor is admonished not to. The emigrant had good reason to do this — to let those traveling in future caravans know he at least got that far. Today's traveler may send postcards.

The adventurers of midsummer should bring light clothing, but those camping out should know that western nights can be cold, especially in the high country. High top boots which cover at least the ankle are required. This not only will help prevent sprains but will make it tough on rattlesnakes too. They are there, and they can be most unpleasant. Ticks and mosquitoes are no less noisome than they were to the emigration. Repellent is effective against the latter; nothing works against the former. Nightly picking sessions, however, can be interesting.

For supplemental reading, it is suggested that the traveler go through Irene D. Paden's *Wake of the Prairie Schooner* (marketed by The Patrice Press) prior to leaving home. Bernard DeVoto's *The Year of Decision, 1846* and *Across the Wide Missouri* are classics, as is Francis Parkman's *The Oregon Trail*. The best book of all, from a scholastic standpoint, is John D. Unruh's monumental *The Plains Across*. An indispensable volume for understanding the trail east of South Pass is Merrill J. Mattes' magnificent *The Great Platte River Road*.

There are three publications by The Patrice Press which ought to be on any such trip: *The Oregon Trail Revisited*, by the author; *Historic Sites Along the Oregon Trail*, by Aubrey L. Haines; and this one.

MAPS OF THE OREGON TRAIL

This is an example of the type of map published by the United States Geological Survey (USGS). It is drawn from aerial surveys on a scale of 1:24,000, or about 2½":1 mile. The Cement City Road leads to within a few yards of the site of old Wayne City — the Independence Landing. However, the river is almost totally out of view due to the trees and underbrush between it and the road. The best vantage point is the overlook on the road leading down into the Missouri Portland Cement Company plant. Nancy Ehrlich, archivist of the Jackson County Historical Society, has developed a good case for the thesis that the travelers went down to Independence Square by the route here labeled "Santa Fe Trail," rather than the River Road.

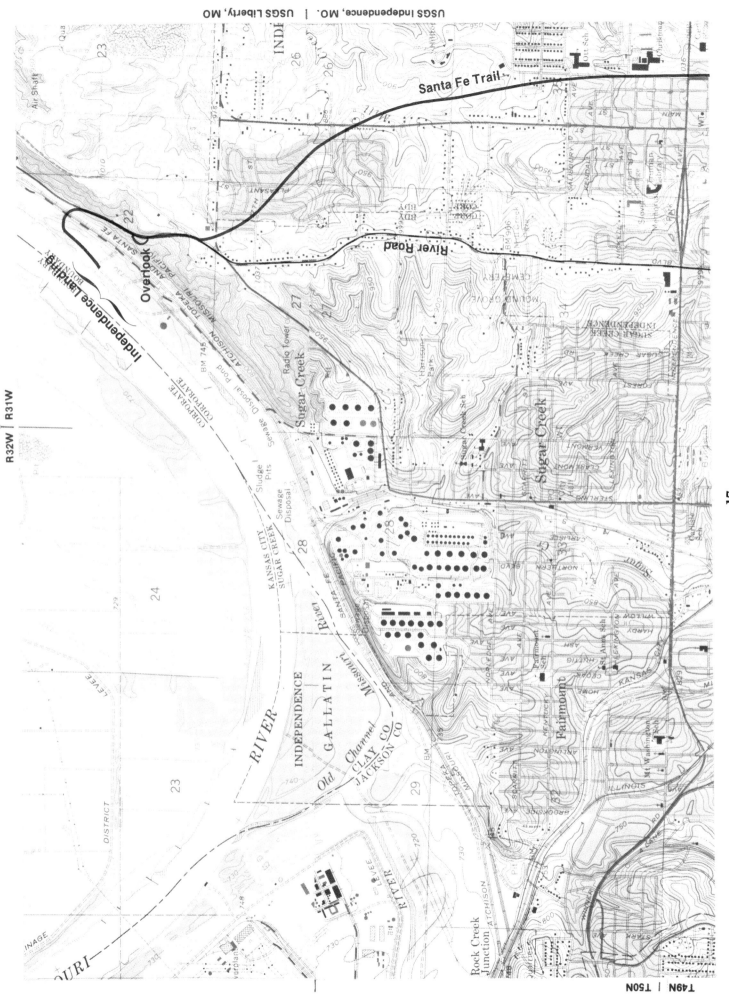

18

In the early years the travelers moved to the southwest over the Santa Fe Trail to get to the Oregon Trail, but jumping off by way of Westport gained more favor with each passing year. The alignment of the old trail coincides with the present-day streets in many areas. The curving of the Independence-Westport Road is most apparent in viewing it to the west across 23rd Street.

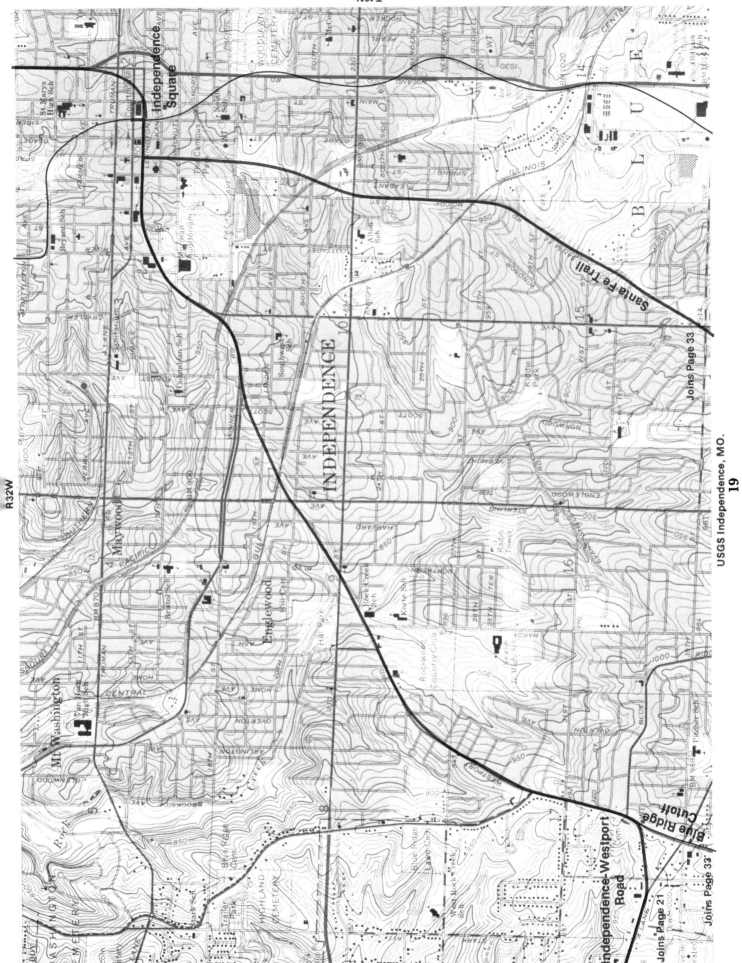

R32W

T49N

Joins Page 33

Joins Page 21

Joins Page 33

USGS Independence, MO.

19

There are still traces of rock leading west from the Big Blue River — almost surely the graded remnants of the original Independence-Westport Road. It takes about eight minutes to hike the hill from the corner of 27th and Topping, and it is well worth it. In the heyday of the trail there would have been dugways leading down to the water, and then back out again on the west bank.

21

Joins Page 19

Joins Page 25

Westport gained favor largely because of its landing. Unlike the Independence Landing, there wasn't a miserable, twisting pull up to the prairie. The site of the 1826 Chouteau's Landing is just off this map to the northeast, but is only an approximation based on a lifelong study of the location by the late Dean Earl Wood. The route of the "Old Fur Road to the Mountains" is also based upon his work. Westport Landing became the original "Kanzas" or "Kansasville," which evolved into Kansas City.

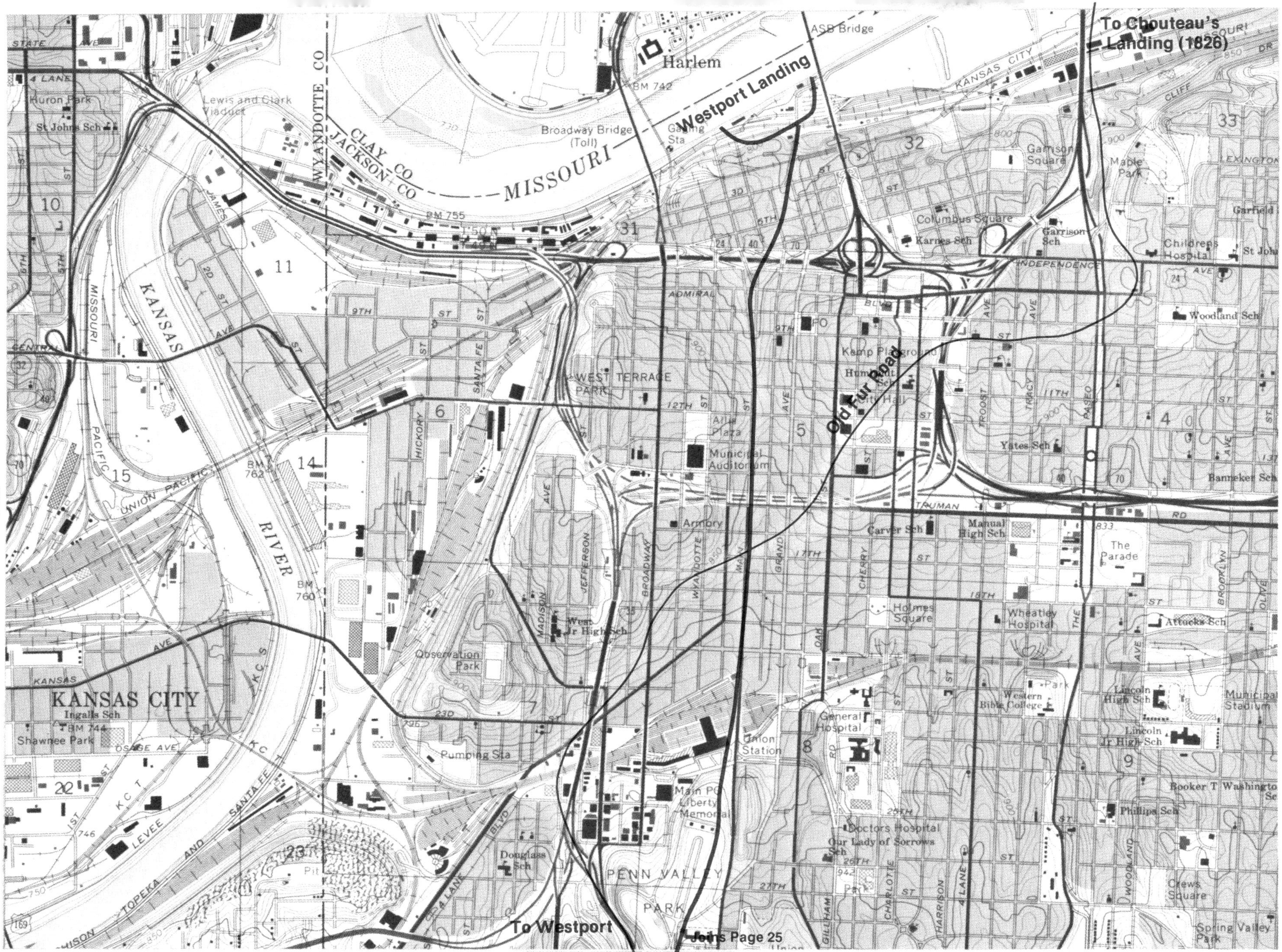

USGS Kansas City, Mo.-Kans.

The boundaries of old Westport are those shown in the 1877 Atlas of Jackson County, recently reprinted by the Jackson County Historical Society. The streets then, as now, aligned with the old trail. The order of the County Court to pave Wornall Road in 1846 leads to the assumption that it would have been used to carry those outfitting in Westport to the Santa Fe Trail. The old town, long submerged in the Kansas City metropolis, is now enjoying a revitalization and today features many fine gift shops, restaurants and saloons.

T11S | T10S

R25E | R33E

25

USGS Kansas City, Mo.-Kans.

Joins Page 41 WYANDOTTE CO. JOHNSON CO.

Joins Page 27

Lawrence-Westport Road

To Shawnee Mission

Joins Page 27

Wornall Road

Westport Landing Road

Old Fur Road

Joins Page 23

Independence-Westport Road

Joins Page 21

WESTPORT

KANSAS
MISSOURI

JACKSON CO.

University of Kansas
Medical Center

Westwood

Westwood Hills

Mission Woods

Roanoke

Hyde Park

Nelson Art Gallery

Art Institute

Metropolitan Junior College

Broadway

Main

Gillham

Holmes

Campbell

Tracy

Paseo

Euclid

Brooklyn

Olive

Prospect

Brush Creek

3 4

27

26

35

19

18

30

29

20

21

28

17

16

34

Those journeying from Westport prior to 1847 probably would have taken the route identified here as the Olathe Cutoff. Surveyed in 1855, it was extrapolated from original maps in the possession of the Kansas State Historical Society.

Chestnut Ave
Brooklyn Park
OLIVE HILLS
AVE
BROOKLYN AVE
PROSPECT
4 LANE

33

55TH

54TH ST

EUCLID AVE

St Teresa Sch

4

Pershing Sch

Nazarene Seminary

Research Hospital

MEYER

BLVD

Mill Creek

Blue Hills Country Club

Dunn Park

THE PASEO

9

Blenheim Park

9

CHESTNUT AVE

PO

Temple Seminary

OLIVE

Blenheim Sch

OLIVE

BROOKLYN

St

WAYNE

Marlborough Sch
BM 982

32

Nelson Sch

Rockhurst College

4 LANE

55TH ST

56TH ST

57TH ST

TROOST AVE

ROCKHILL RD

HOLMES

St Peters Sch

Hogan High Sch

Troost Sch

Shopping Center

TRACK

Baptist Hospital

FOREST HILL CEMETERY

Calvary Cemetery

Forest Hill Cem

Holmes Park

Rose Hill Cem

GREGORY

4 LANE

950

Nichols Sch

73D

72ND

St Elizabeth Sch

5

Park

St Mary's Sch
Bingham

27

Joins Page 25
Joins Page 29

Wornall Road

31

MEMORIAL PARK

LOOSE

To Westport

College of St Teresa

Bryant Sch

WYANDOTTE ST

BROOKSIDE BLVD

KANSAS CITY

PUBLIC SERVICE

WORNALL RD

Border Star Sch

Southwest High Sch

PENNSYLVANIA AVE

SUMMIT ST

MAIN ST

63D ST

ARMOUR BLVD

OAK ST

HOLMES

TROOST

6

5

8

8

7

7

Cook Sch

To New Santa Fe

Olathe Cutoff

Kansas Missouri

JACKSON CO
JOHNSON CO

STATE LINE

CORP LINE

KANSAS CITY

T49N
T48N

PARKWAY

WARD PARKWAY

WARD PARKWAY

FAIRWAY

SHAWNEE MISSION

Mission Hills Country Club

Brush Creek

Mission Hills

Kansas City Country Club

10

11

14

15

BELINDER RD

FAIRWAY RD

MISSION RD

MISSION DR

HIGH DR

WINDSOR DR

63D ST

68TH ST

69TH ST

BELINDER RD

Indian Hills Country Club

Bollinger Sch

PRAIRIE VILLAGE

PRAIRIE VILLAGE

23

22

Park

MISSION RD

TOMAHAWK RD

CHEROKEE

Joins Page 25
Joins Page 41

Travelers moving due south from old Westport would have experienced a major chore in fording the Dyke Branch of the Blue River. They were only a half-mile from the border of the United States (in those years).

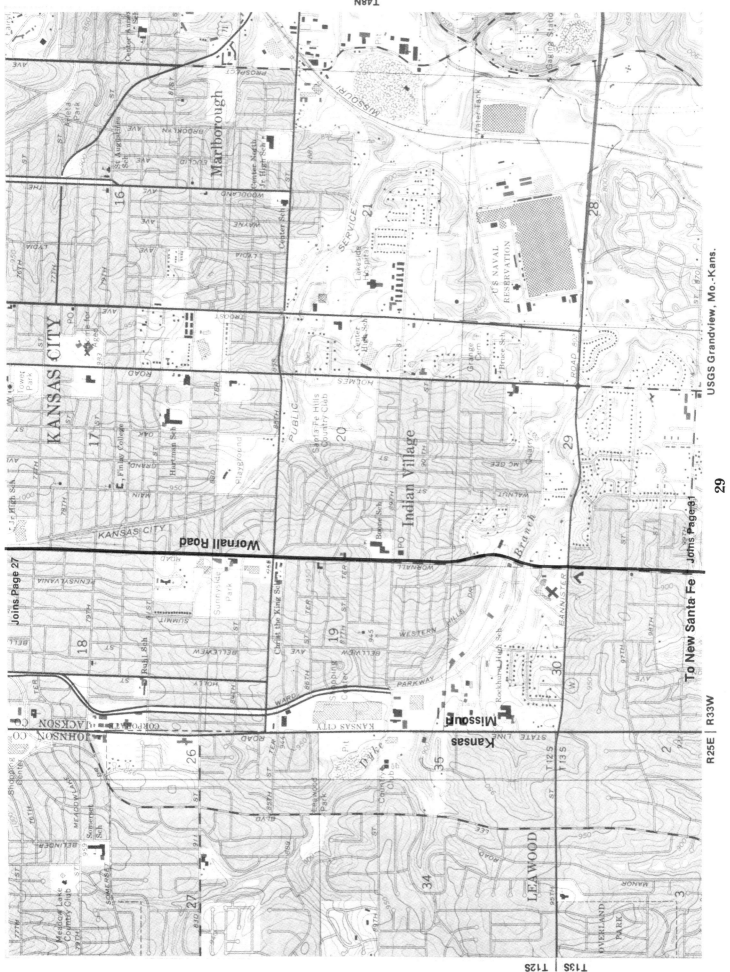

USGS Grandview, Mo.-Kans.

R25E | R33W

Jim Bridger was one of the greatest of the mountain men, scouts and traders. His days in the West ended when his sight began to fail. He bought a store in Westport (which houses a fine restaurant today) and this farm at the settlement known as Dallas. He died and was buried on the farm, later reinterred in the Mount Washington Cemetery by his friend, Gen. Granville M. Dodge. The swale in Minor Park is easily visible from Red Bridge Road. The Red Bridge itself stood just a few yards north of the present crossing of the Blue River. The Santa Fe Trail west of Avila College now is paved, but follows exactly the original route.

USGS Grandview, Mo.-Kans.

31

The Santa Fe, like most trails, rode the ridges, and most of the way this can be seen by looking past the houses flanking the street. This is especially evident along the Blue Ridge Cutoff.

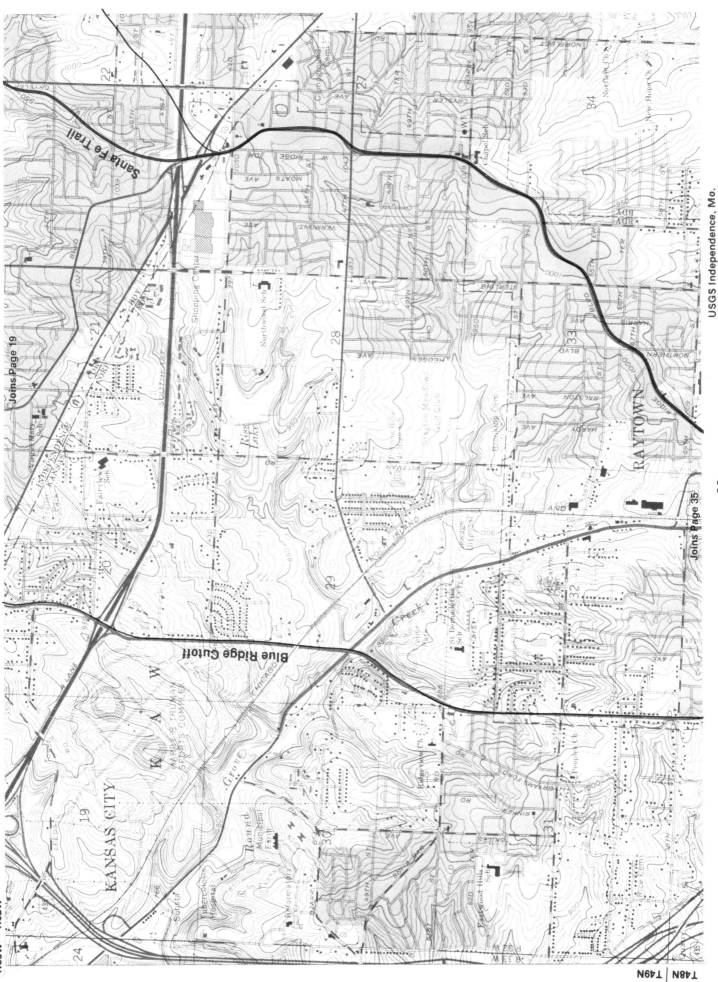

Santa Fe Trail

Blue Ridge Cutoff

KANSAS CITY

RAYTOWN

USGS Independence, Mo.

Joins Page 35

T49N | T48N

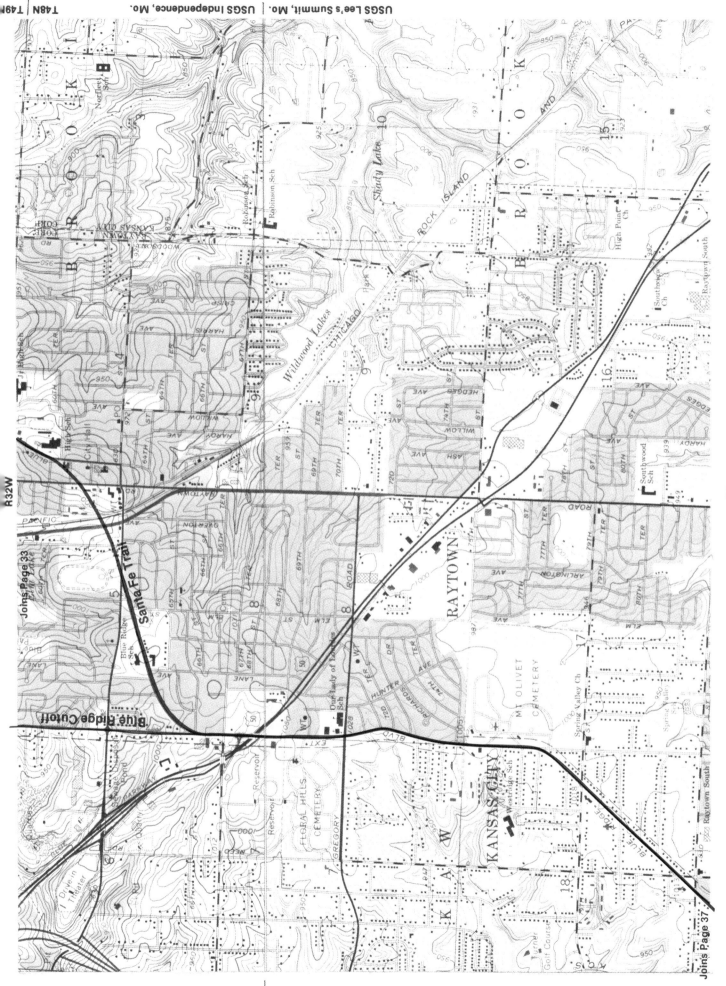

Joins Page 33

Joins Page 37

Knobtown

Creek

White Oak

Quarries

Flannery Cem

Military Country Club

Fairway Ranch Land na Strip Vale

BOUNDARY

CORPORATE

KANSAS CITY

Ganzer Cem

RAYTOWN

ROAD

STREET

Girls Camp

AVE

Basonia Ch.

BANNISTER

Union Point Sch

Oliver Cem

ELM

LANE

Sewage Disposal Ponds

AVE

Jr High Sch

SPRING VALLEY RD

STARK

87TH

BOOTH

TER

LANE

LEWIS AVE

STARK AVE

WALLACE

AVE

MARSH

MANCHESTER AVE

Ervin Jr High Sch

Athletic Field

Truman Sch

BM 1012

REED

Santa Fe Trail

Joins Page 35

Joins Page 39

GREENWOOD BLVD

ROAD

22 21 34 28 33 21 20 29 32 19 30 31

Pursuing a trail through a scrambled interstate highway interchange, on foot or driving, is little short of madness. The best way through this is to follow Bannister west to Grandview, then southeast through the subdivision south of the Circumferential Freeway.

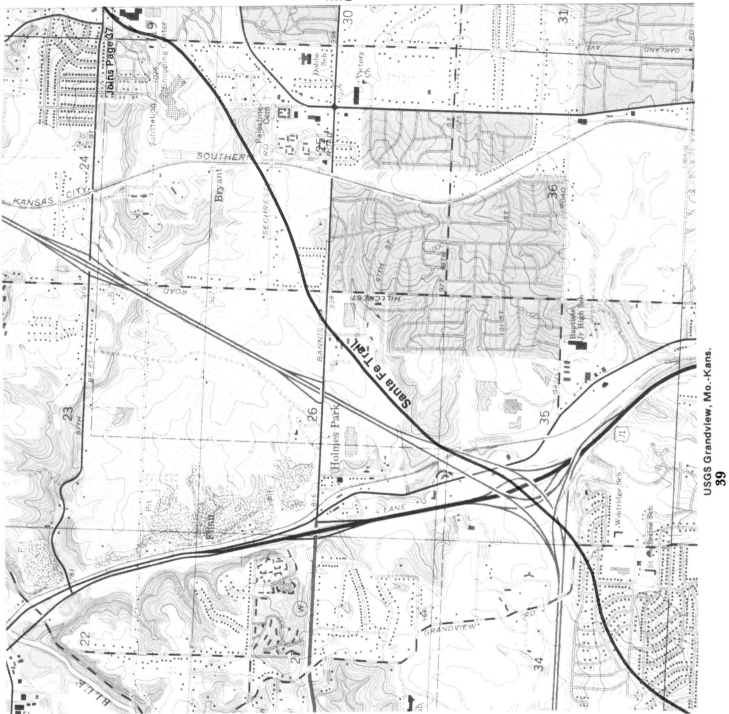

USGS Grandview, Mo.-Kans.

The routing through Kansas was taken directly from the U.S. Surveys, shot in 1855, 1856 and 1857. In those years there was still an enormous amount of traffic on the trails west of Jackson County, although the Omaha/Council Bluffs and St. Joseph jumping-off places had gained supremacy. The Lone Elm Campground usually was the first or second night's resting place. The famous junction, at least in later years, was only a few miles beyond. The site is now on the west border of a tree farm and no trace is visible. The land is perfectly flat, so in each succeeding year the junction crept closer to Gardner. At one point, according to Irene Paden, it was in the schoolyard in that town. Many diarists reported that there was a small signboard at the junction of the two trails which carried the simple legend, "Road to Oregon." This is the first example of the ¼":1 mile maps used from here on (except in Topeka). They are prepared county by county by the various state highway departments. This map joins the USGS map shown on page 31, not at the edge of that map but at the state line.

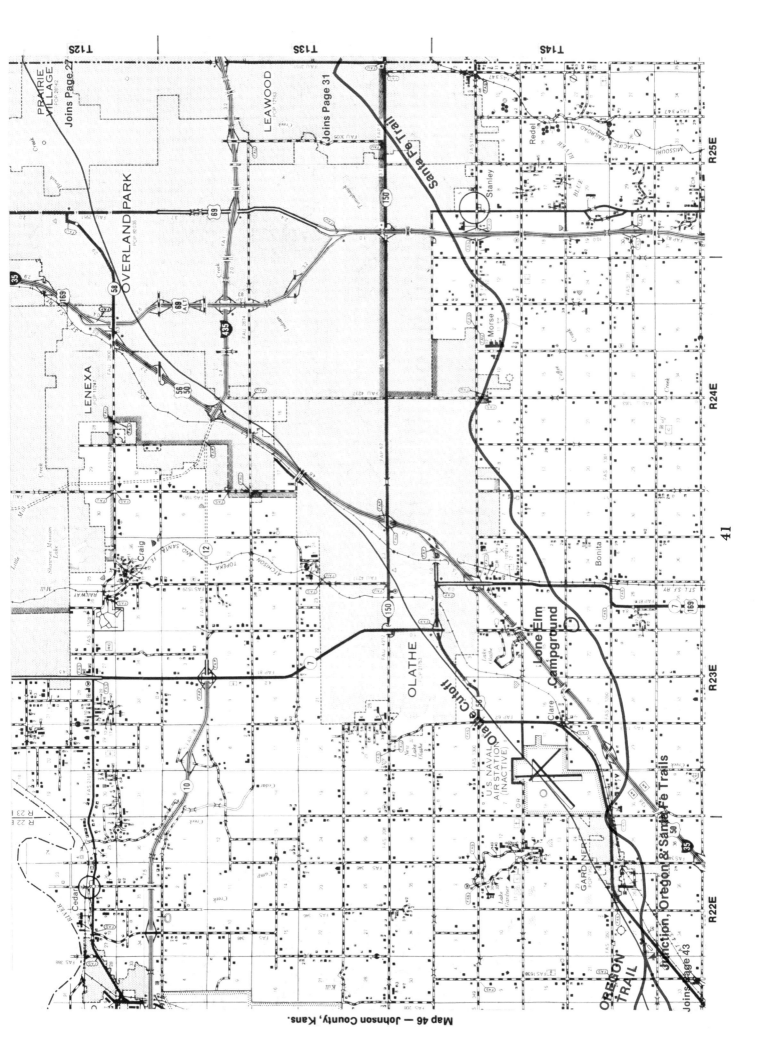

Map 46 — Johnson County, Kans.

Irene Paden dwells on the Blue Jacket Crossing, but Mattes has looked in vain through hundreds of diaries for mention of the crossing. It isn't on the main trail. That route carried the emigration past the spectacular Blue Mound, which rose dramatically from the prairie and often was climbed by the travelers for the view from the top. It was treeless in trail days, as was the surrounding prairie. It has occasionally been used as a ski hill in recent years. The Wakarusa River isn't big but it was a tough one to cross, due to its steep banks.

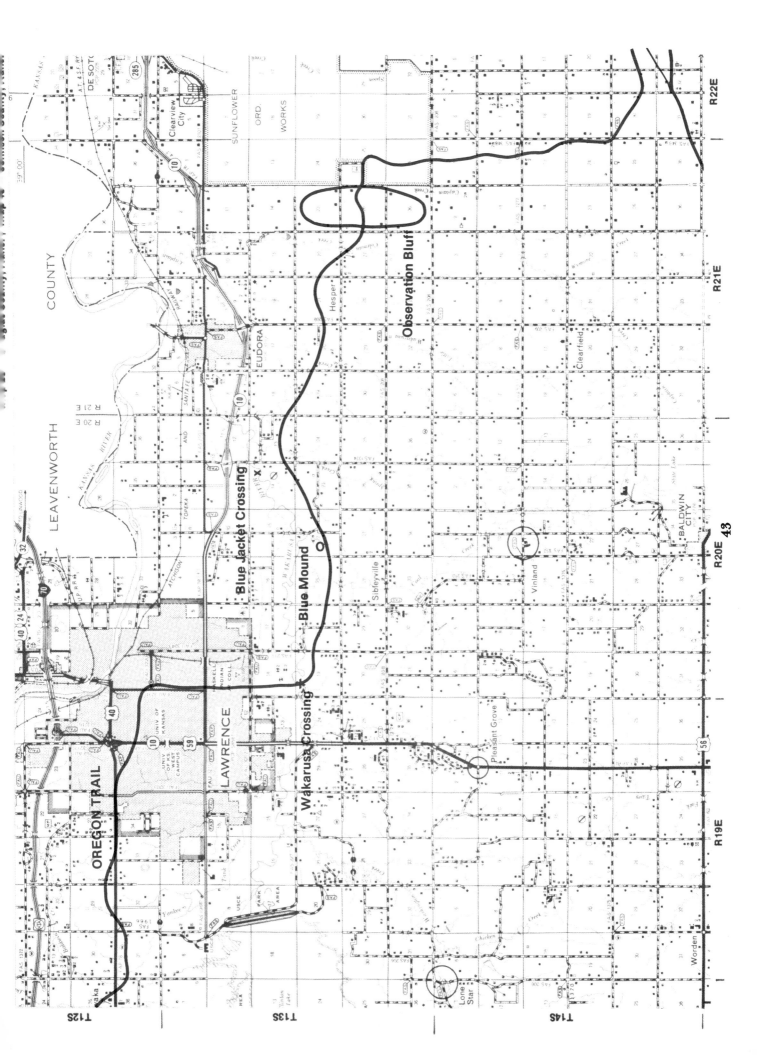

OREGON TRAIL

Wakarusa Crossing

Blue Mound

Blue Jacket Crossing

Observation Bluff

LAWRENCE

EUDORA

LEAVENWORTH

COUNTY

43

44

The U.S. Survey does not include the route through Topeka. The only guide extant is from the Kansas State Historical Society, and even that document is disputed. Some travelers went to the south to cross at old Uniontown, but the majority crossed in what is presently downtown Topeka.

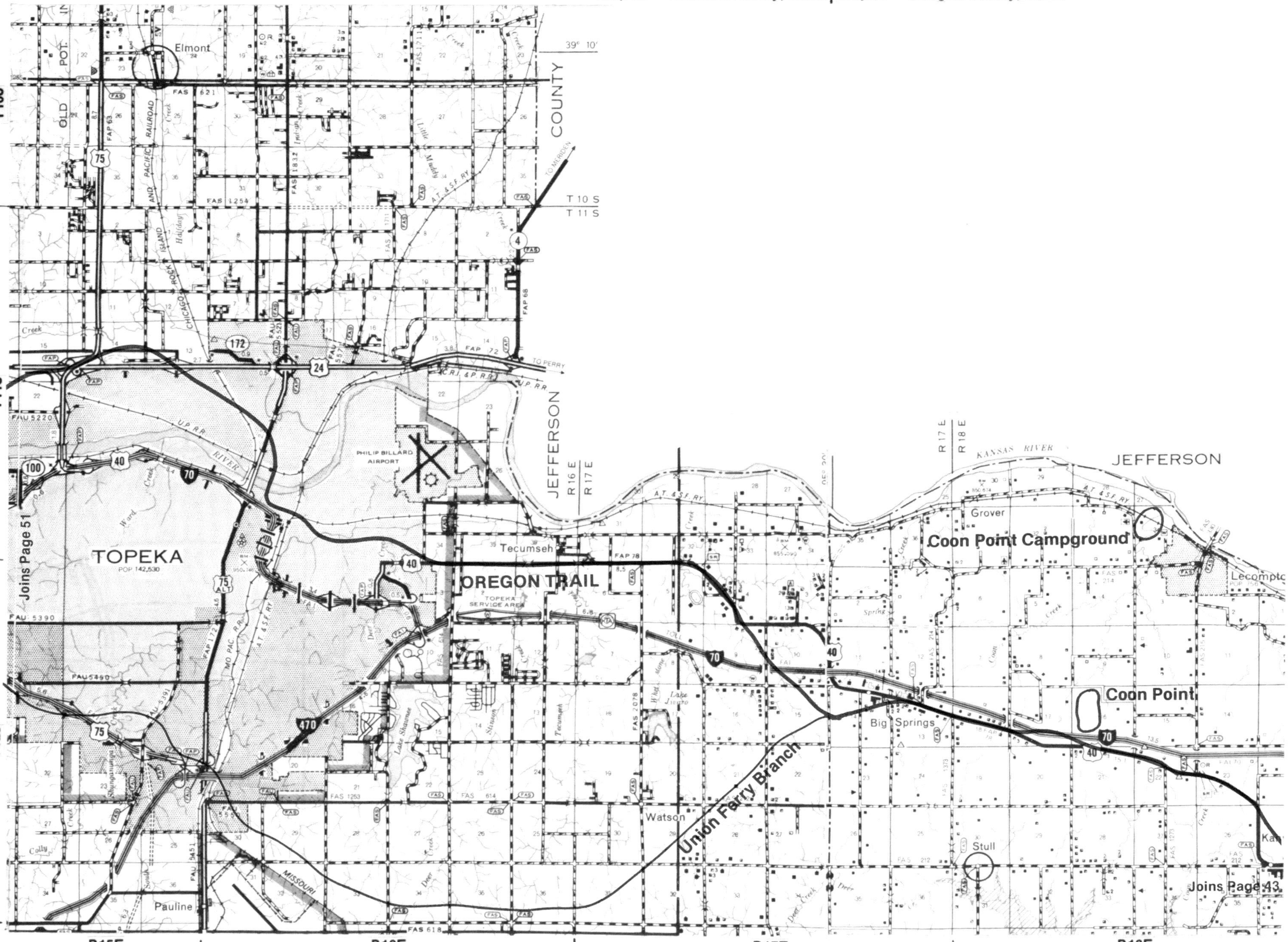

Map 63 — Shawnee County, Kans. | Map 23 — Douglas County, Kans.

JEFFERSON

Coon Point Campground

Coon Point

Joins Page 43

JEFFERSON

COUNTY

OREGON TRAIL

Union Ferry Branch

45

TOPEKA
POP. 142,530

Joins Page 51

R15E   R16E   R17E   R18E

T10S   T11S   T12S

46

The USGS quad of Topeka shows the tough crossing of Shunganunga Creek, often mentioned by emigrants. The exact spot of crossing, and the probable location of the Papin Ferry, has been extrapolated from the so-called Ross Map, archived at the Kansas State Historical Society.

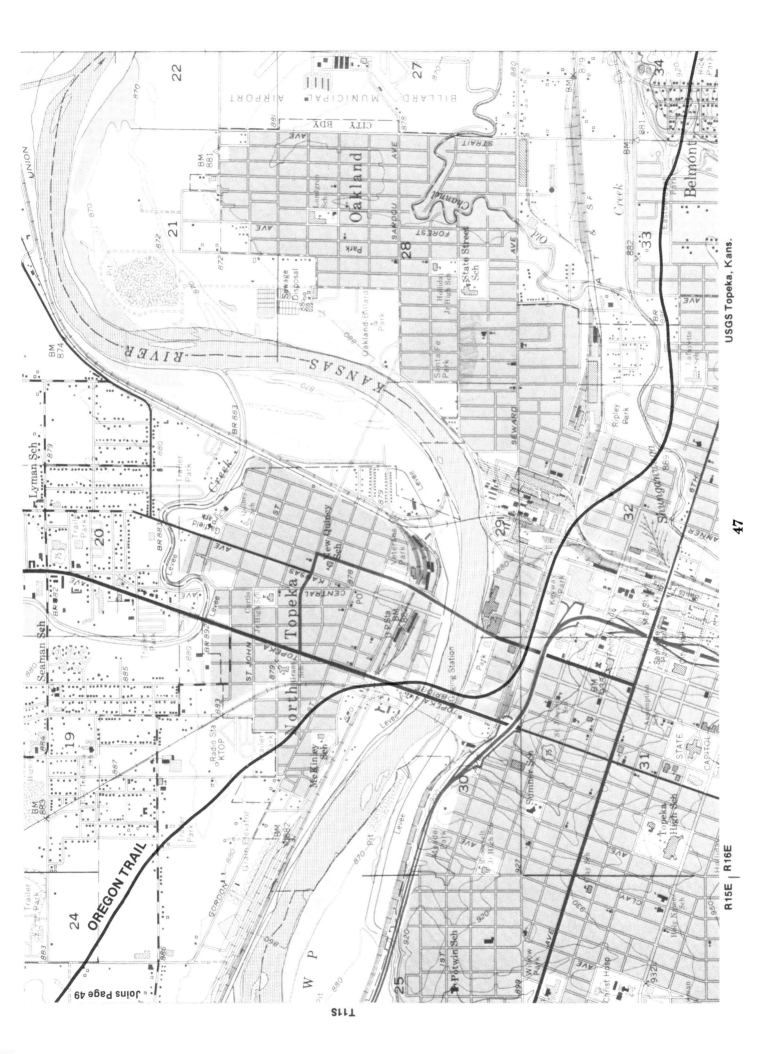

USGS Topeka, Kans.

R15E | R16E

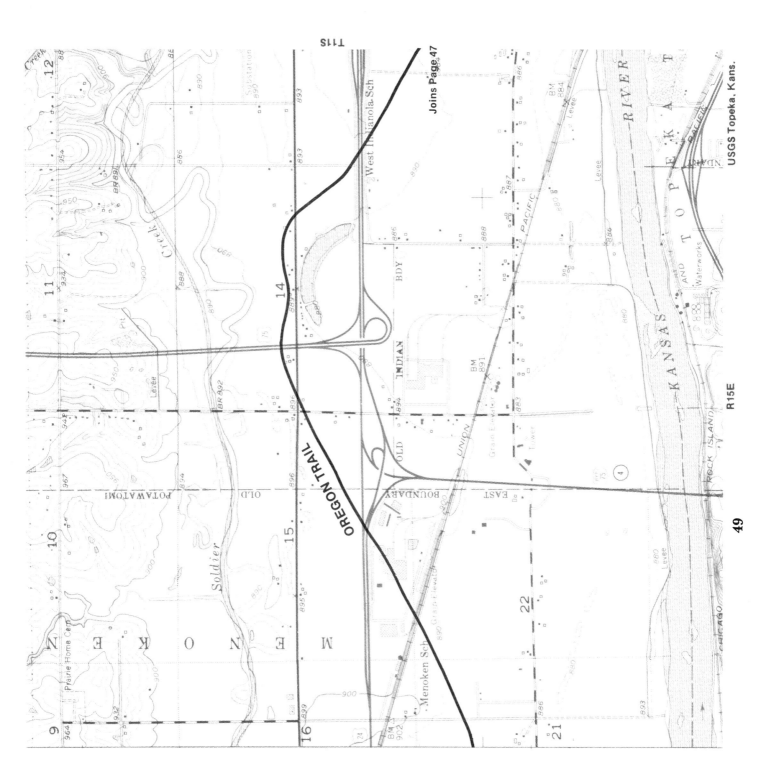

Joins Page 47

OREGON TRAIL

USGS Topeka, Kans.

R15E

49

The twisting gravel road leading northwest out of St. Marys is a direct descendant of the Oregon Trail. It has been graded and graveled, and possibly is a bit less bumpy. The rocks are big and loose, and the road should be driven with caution.

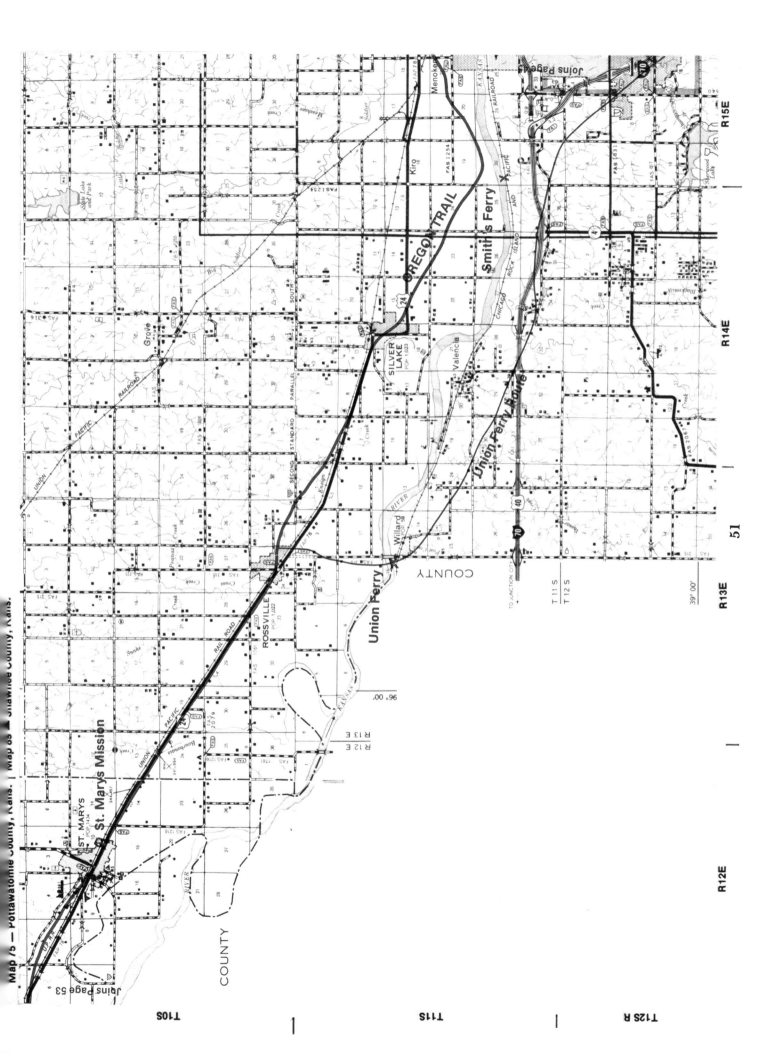

Map 75 — Pottawatomie County, Kans. | Map 63 ▲ Shawnee County, Kans.

51

Joins Page 53
Joins Page 49

The north half of Section 24 is believed to hold the bodies of 45 to 50 cholera victims from 1849. David de Wolfe passed here on May 31 and wrote:

"May 31st got an early start, was joined by another Company from Illinois consisting of horse teams, they had thirteen men we crossed a small stream the name not known we next crossed the little Vermillion which has very steep banks and rapid current. We crossed without much difficulty. On the bank of this stream there was 6 graves, all died with the Colery and out of a company of seven from Tenn. We travelled this day on a fine level prairie covered with beautifull flowers. We encampt on the bank of the Vermillion having travelled 18 miles."

The headstone of T.S. Prather and two unidentified stones are all that remain today. These are now protected by a new and unsightly chain link fence. In the gully to the west of Highway 99, just north of the Westmoreland rest area, is a stone incised: "Here lies an early traveler who lost his life in quest of riches in the west." The body actually is beneath the west edge of the pavement, east of the stone. One Scotts Spring is about 30 yards southwest of that marker. Another is about 120 yards east of the rest area. The trail forded Rock Creek exactly below the present bridge. There are ruts visible from Highway 99 about a half-mile south of the rest area — fragments only, and only on the west side of the highway. Other depressions course over the top of a rise east of there, out in the field. The map at left was prepared especially for this volume by Reg P. Duffin.

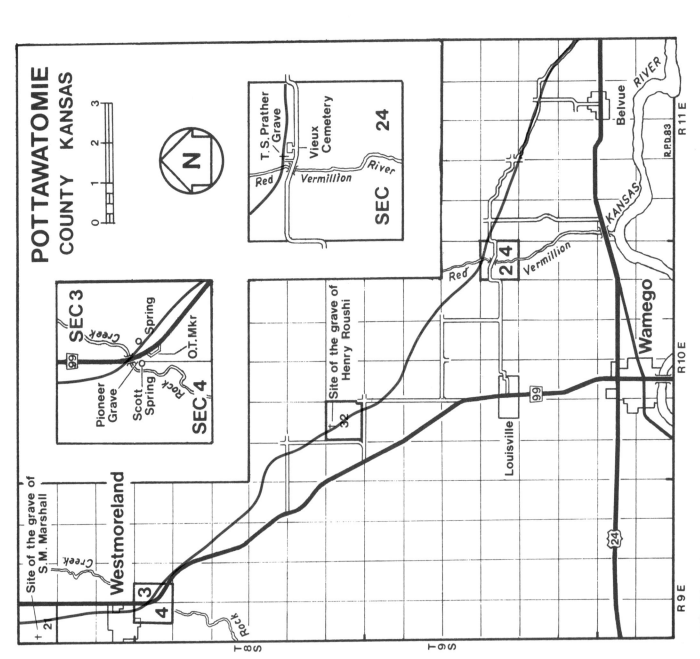

POTTAWATOMIE
COUNTY KANSAS

0 1 2 3

N

SEC 3
SEC 4
99
Pioneer Grave
Scott Spring
Rock Creek
O.T. Mkr
Spring
Creek

T.S. Prather Grave
Red Vermillion River
Vieux Cemetery
SEC 24

Site of the grave of S.M. Marshall
Creek
Westmoreland
3
4
Rock Creek
+ 2

Site of the grave of Henry Roushi
32

Louisville
99
Red
Vermillion
24

Belvue
RIVER
KANSAS RIVER
R.P.D.83
R 11 E

Wamego
R 10 E

24

R 9 E

T 8 S
T 9 S

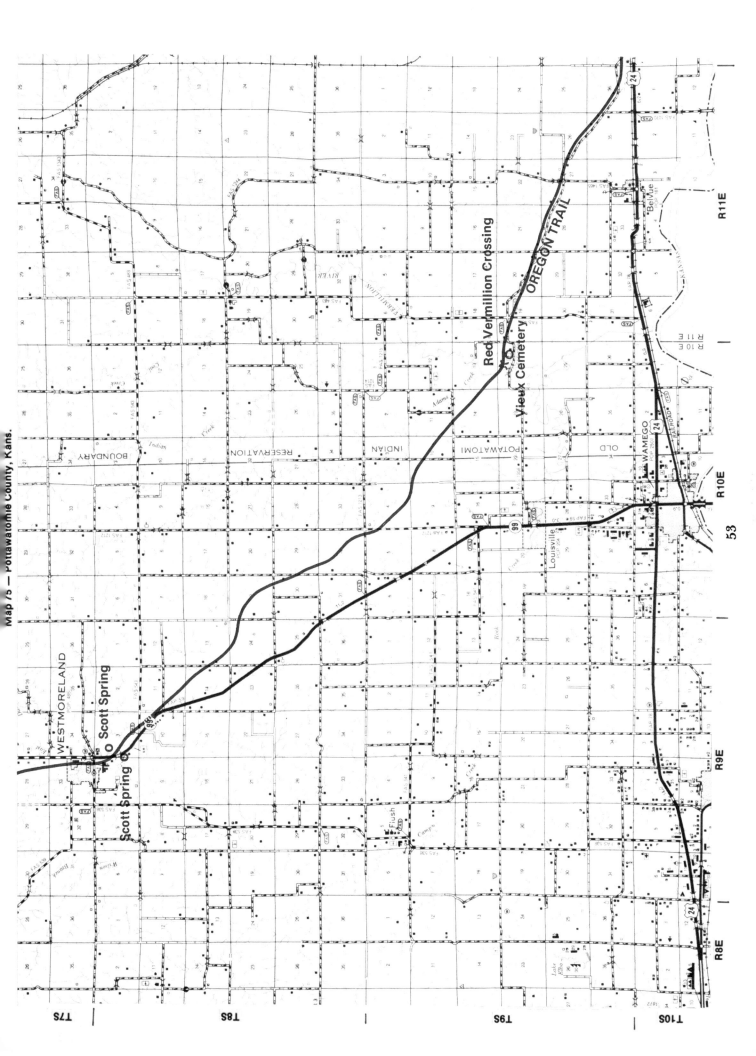

Map 75 — Pottawatomie County, Kans.

The access roads northwest of Blaine are very slippery and muddy for a day or two after a rain. They should not be traveled except after a dry spell. Little streams flow right across the roads in many places, but the bottom usually is quite firm at these points.

Two Marshalls are buried in this vicinity — which one this is has yet to be learned. The unmarked grave is about ¼ mile south of the road.

Map 75 — Pottawatomie County, Kans. | Map 58 — Marshall County, Kans.

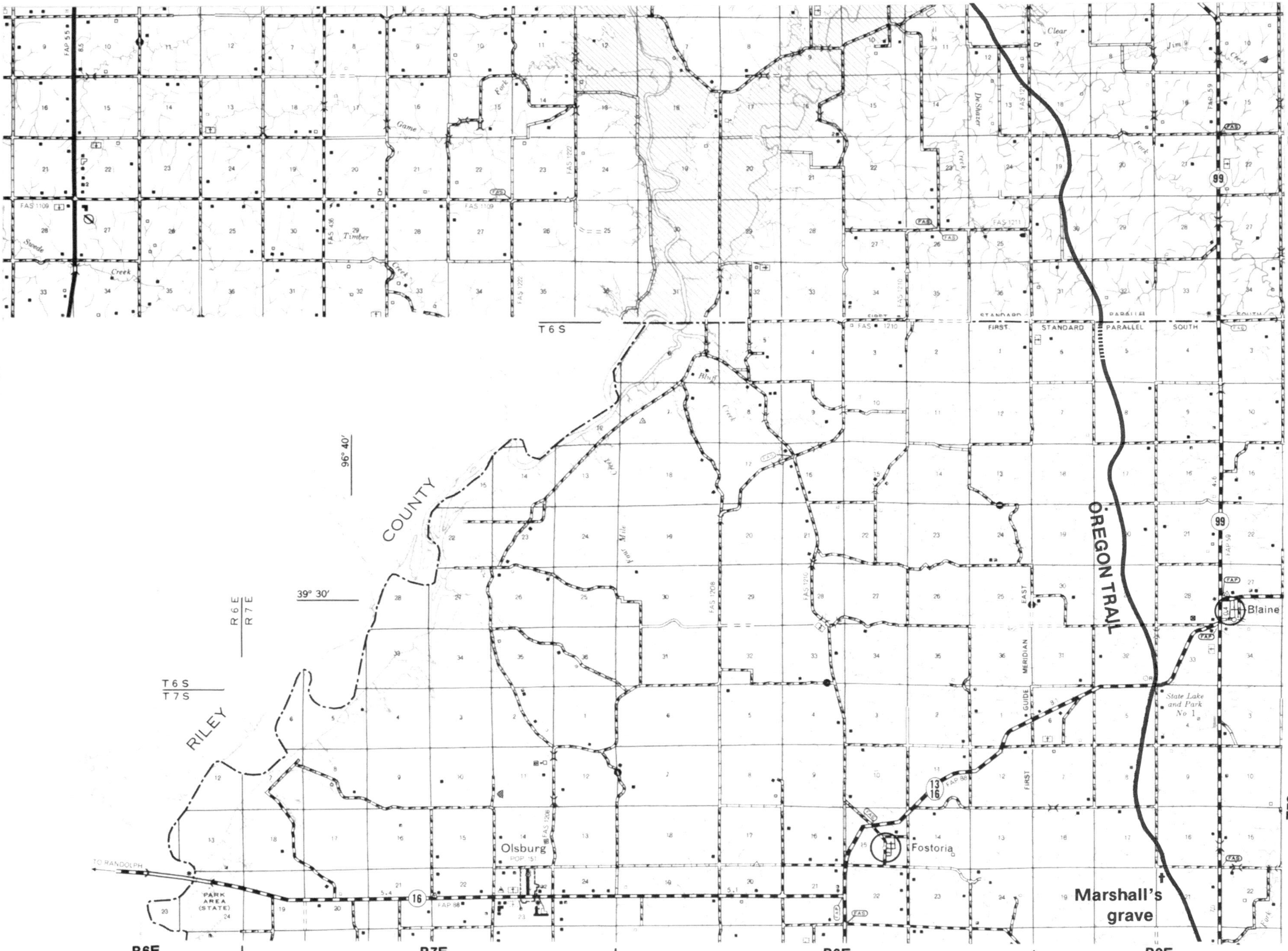
OREGON TRAIL
Marshall's grave
Blaine
Fostoria
Olsburg
POP 151
State Lake and Park No 1
RILEY
COUNTY
PARK AREA (STATE)
TO RANDOLPH
FIRST STANDARD PARALLEL SOUTH
FIRST GUIDE MERIDIAN EAST
Clear
Jim
Creek
DeShazer
Fork
Game
Timber
Swede
Bluff
Four Mile
T5S
T6S
T7S
T 6 S
T 6 S / T 7 S
R6E
R7E
R8E
R9E
R 6 E / R 7 E
96° 40′
39° 30′

The Alcove Spring is listed even on today's maps as a state park, but it isn't and is not open to the public. It used to be, but it was littered by so many crumb bums that it had to be locked up. It is one of the most sylvan and romantic spots on the Oregon Trail and certainly deserves state park status. The heavy line is the route surveyed in 1856, but Troy Gray feels the road to the south was heavily used too. From the intersection of highways 71 and 9 he caught a good view of the old swale going up the hill. The owner, Mrs. Stella Hammett, lives in Blue Rapids and enjoys having decent people visit the spring, but permission must be obtained first. The famous "JFR" rock is down at the edge of the water in the alcove — a reminder of the early pleasant days of the Donner Party of 1846. Several other names are there too. When the travelers reached the area in the upper left corner of the map they reported looking from one trail to a line of white tops on the other side as the St. Joe and Independence roads neared their point of convergence. (The USGS's Marysville quad mislocates the Alcove Spring one mile north of where it really is. The Blue Rapids quad lists it correctly.)

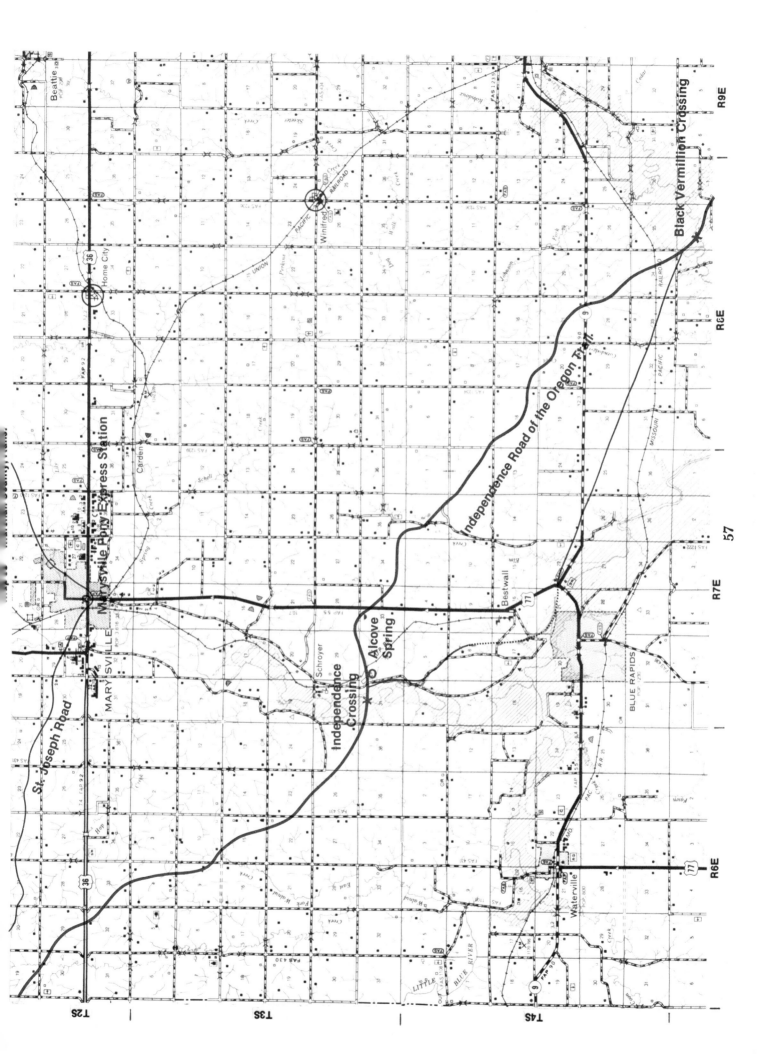

Black Vermillion Crossing

Independence Road of the Oregon Trail

St. Joseph Road

Marysville Pony Express Station

Independence Crossing

Alcove Spring

57

R6E   R7E   R6E   R9E

T2S   T3S   T4S

Beattie

Home City

Winifred

MARYSVILLE

Carden

Schroyer

Bestwall

BLUE RAPIDS

Waterville

LITTLE BLUE RIVER

36

77

9

The Hollenberg Ranch house, a Kansas State Historic Site, is the only example of an unmoved, unrestored Pony Express station, and stands today in almost the identical condition it was in during the stagecoach days. It is manned by an expert guide. The rut swales to the northwest are faint and intermittent, and hardly worth hiking to see. The line at the top of this map is the Kansas-Nebraska border.

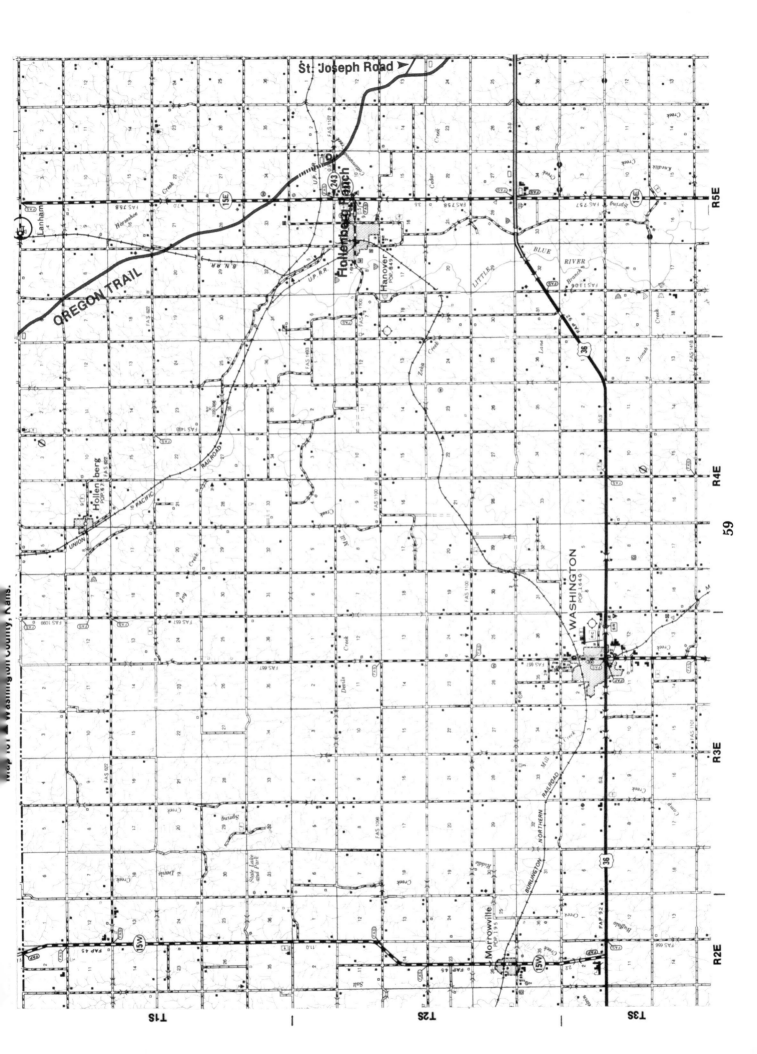

St. Joseph Road ►

OREGON TRAIL

Hollenberg Ranch

Hanover
POP. 849

Lanham

Hollenberg
POP. 67

UNION PACIFIC RAILROAD

WASHINGTON
POP. 1,640

Morrowville
POP. 195

State Lake and Park

BURLINGTON NORTHERN RAILROAD

36

US 36

59

The location of Fremont Springs will forever be a source of debate among trail authorities. For that matter, so will lots of Pony Express and Overland Stage station sites. The basis for locating Pony Express sites in Nebraska and eastern Wyoming is the booklet, *The Pony Express: Across Nebraska From St. Joseph to Fort Laramie*, by Merrill J. Mattes and Paul Henderson (1960). The Oketo Cutoff resulted from a financial dispute between Ben Holladay and civic leaders of Marysville. Holladay rerouted his stagecoach line to bypass Marysville in 1862. The controversy was resolved and the Oketo abandoned the following year. Quivera Park is the location of inscriptions of the names of Kit Carson and John C. Fremont, neither of which has been authenticated. The George Winslow grave is on private property and is maintained by an owner who really cares about this dramatic spot. There is a gate to close, and it is only common courtesy to ask permission to visit the grave and the shallow rut swales nearby. Certainly the most dramatic Oregon Trail site in southeastern Nebraska is the Rock Creek State Park. The park has two angry rut swales, helped along by erosion. The two maps on page 62 were prepared by Reg P. Duffin of La Grange Park, Illinois. The text below the rule, however, refers to the regular map on page 63.

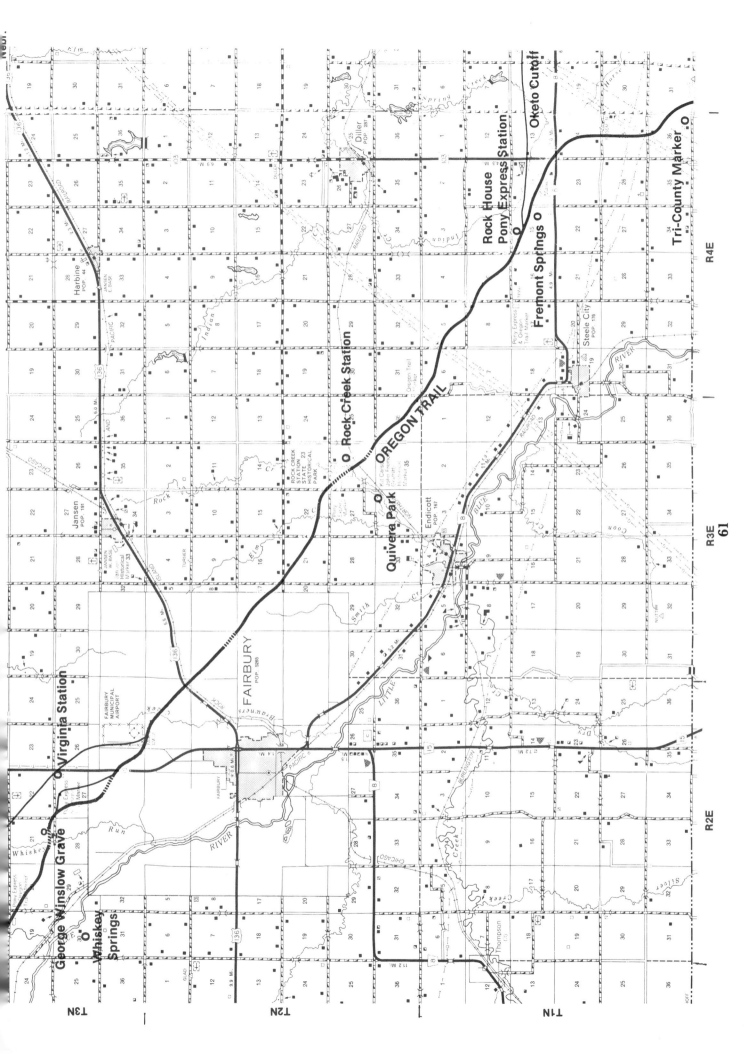

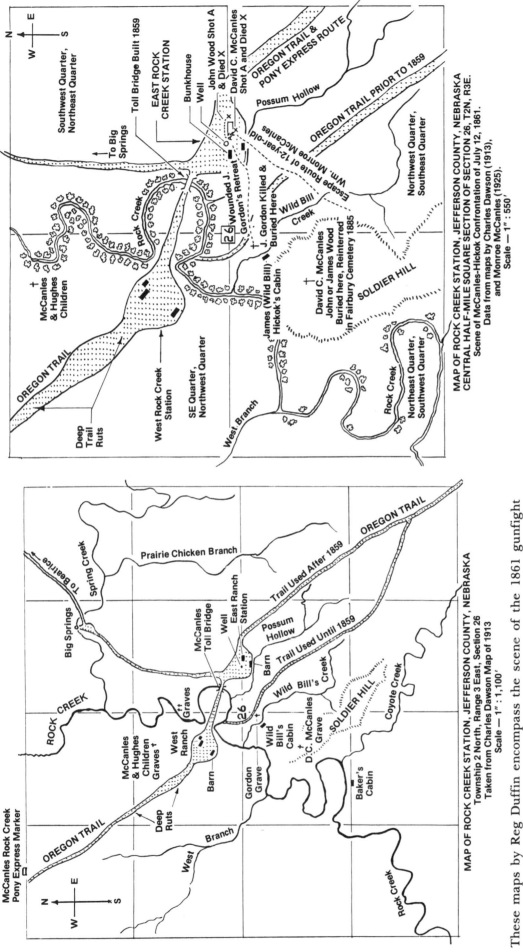

MAP OF ROCK CREEK STATION, JEFFERSON COUNTY, NEBRASKA
CENTRAL HALF-MILE SQUARE SECTION OF SECTION 26, T2N, R3E.
Scene of McCanles-Hickok Confrontation of July 12, 1861.
Data from maps by Charles Dawson (1913),
and Monroe McCanles (1925).
Scale — 1″ : 550′

MAP OF ROCK CREEK STATION, JEFFERSON COUNTY, NEBRASKA
Township 2 North, Range 3 East, Section 26
Taken from Charles Dawson Map of 1913
Scale — 1″ : 1,100′

These maps by Reg Duffin encompass the scene of the 1861 gunfight between Wild Bill Hickok, a stock tender with the stage line, and David McCanles, owner of the log building leased to the company. Accounts of the shooting differ. This is the version advanced by Irene D. Paden in her book, *Wake of the Prairie Schooner:* McCanles, allegedly drunk,

attempted to collect past due rentals in a belligerent manner, threatening the wife of the station keeper. Hickok interfered. Two of McCanles' employees went after Wild Bill. When the smoke had cleared, Hickok was unscathed and the other three men were dead.

It is improbable that the Little and Big Sandy stations should be so close together, but that is where the best sources say they were. They may indeed have been there, but at different times. Some of the stage stations moved several times after burnings by Indians. Ask 10 authorities where the Millersville Station was and you will get 11 answers.

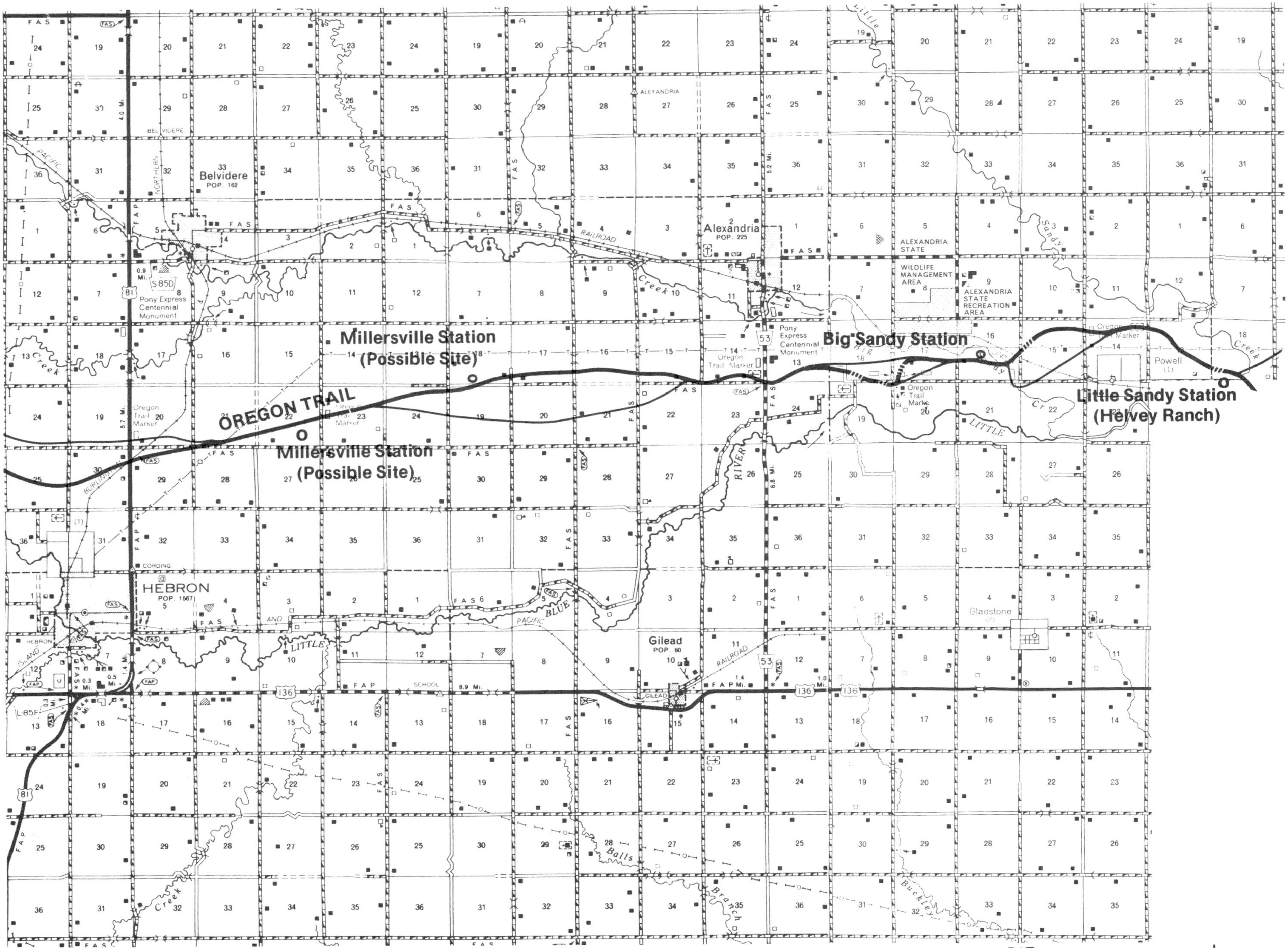

Map 65 — Thayer County, Nebr. · Map 48 — Jefferson County, Nebr.

Little Sandy Station
(Helvey Ranch)

Big Sandy Station

Millersville Station
(Possible Site)

Millersville Station
(Possible Site)

OREGON TRAIL

Alexandria
POP. 225

ALEXANDRIA STATE WILDLIFE MANAGEMENT AREA

ALEXANDRIA STATE RECREATION AREA

Pony Express Centennial Monument

Oregon Trail Marker

Belvidere
POP. 162

Pony Express Centennial Monument

Gilead
POP. 60

HEBRON
POP. 1667

Gladstone

T4N

T3N

T2N

R1W

R1E

R2W

63

64

People have been driving through this area for years thinking it was not especially interesting. That's all changed now, thanks to some beautiful historical cartography by Reg P. Duffin, prepared especially for this book. It appears on page 67. His legend, slightly edited, is on page 66.

Map 65 — Nuckolls County, Nebr. | Map 85 — Thayer County, Nebr.

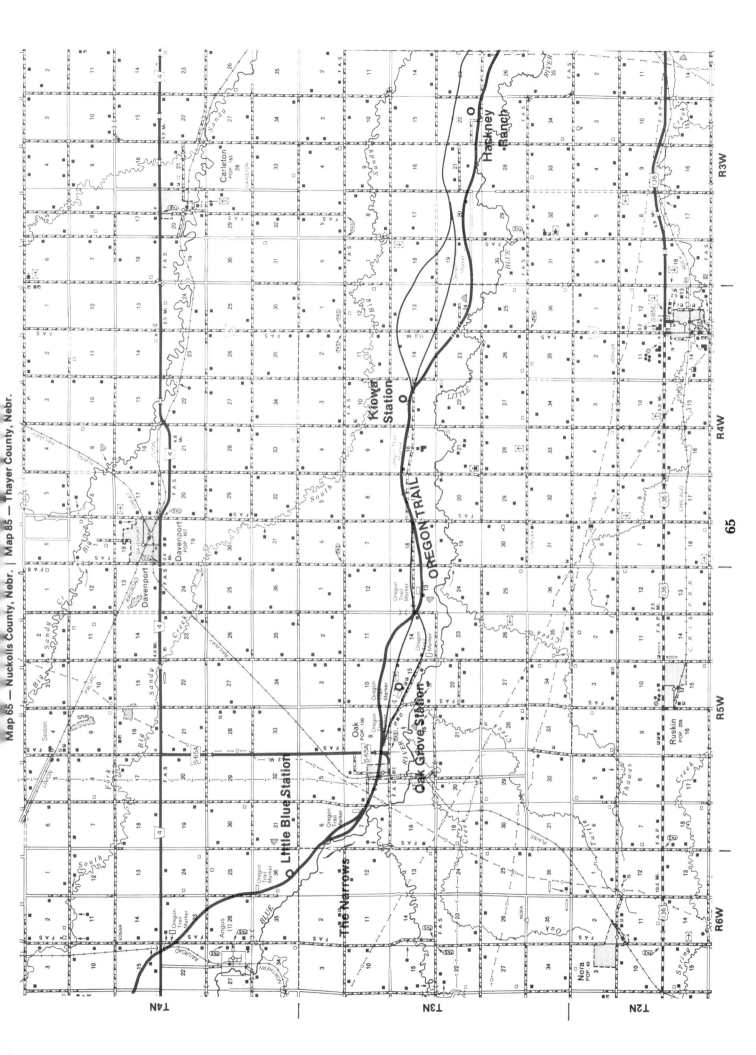

Carleton
POP. 163

Davenport
POP. 427

Hackney Ranch

Kiowa Station

OREGON TRAIL

Oak
POP. 100

Oak Grove Station

Little Blue Station

The Narrows

Ruskin
POP. 229

Nora
POP. 43

Angus
(1) 26

Sedan

Deshler

65

R3W

R4W

R5W

R6W

T4N

T3N

T2N

OREGON TRAIL THROUGH NORTHEAST CORNER OF NUCKOLLS COUNTY, NEBRASKA (Map by Reg Duffin, 1982)

Key: 1 — Kiowa Ranch Oregon Trail marker. The Pony Express station and ranch site are approximately .3 mile east of here. This station survived the Indian raids of 1864. 2 — Oregon Trail marker immediately west of the Nuckolls County line. 3 — Robert Emery Oregon Trail marker. This commemorates the narrow escape of a stagecoach and nine 1864 Robert Emery, stage driver, discovered Indians in ambush on the trail just ahead 22 ft. due south of this point, wheeled his horses under hot fire and raced back to a wagon train three miles east, saving the lives of his nine passengers." 4 — Small wooden marker denoting the site of the Bowie Ranch. William Bowie and his wife were killed and the ranch destroyed in Indian raids on August 9, 1864. 5 — Oregon Trail marker low in the drainage ditch in front of the farm area. 6 — Comstock Ranch monument. Inscription lists those killed and the survivors of the Indian raids of August 7, 1864. The ranch and buildings which stood in the area to the north of the monument were burned on August 8, 1864. 7 — Oregon Trail marker in the center of the grass triangle at the junction of S65A and the county road. 8 — Town of Oak. There is an orientation map of the Little Blue Valley in the northeast corner of the city park. 9 — Oregon Trail marker. In the summer, high roadside brush partially obscures this monument. 10 — This farmhouse is on the east side of the county road approximately 1.3 miles north of Oak. Almost opposite on the west side of the road is a farm gate. A cattle path leads one mile west to The Narrows area. This is private property and it is advisable to check in Oak for permission to enter. In any event, please remember that valuable livestock graze in this area. Be certain to securely close gates when entering and leaving. 11 — The Narrows Oregon Trail marker. This stands atop the bluff overlooking The Narrows. Additional inscription reads: "The Narrows Trail 65 feet west." 12 — A steel post topped with a wooden board is inscribed "Indians Capture Laura Roper." It denotes the site where on the afternoon of August 7, 1864, 16-year-old Laura Roper, Mrs. William Eubanks, her 4-year-old daughter Belle and 6-month-old baby son were captured by the Cheyennes. In 1929 Miss Roper (then an elderly Mrs. Laura Roper Vance of Oklahoma) returned here and identified this site. 13 — Wooden marker, now lying on the ground atop a small knoll to the southeast of the Roper site is inscribed "Grave of 16-year-old boy and Wagonmaster." Circumstances uncertain, this incident is possibly referred to in the booklet "Historical Markers in Nebraska" compiled by the National Society of the Daughters of the American Revolution in Nebraska (1951), as "Hanged Murderer's Grave": "A man of authority in a wagon train killed a young lad whose job it was to prod the oxen. The boy had become weary and sat down to rest, which infuriated the man who wantonly killed him. The man was hanged and his grave marked." 14 — Eubanks Ranch site. A steel post and wooden marker at the section line fence denote the Eubanks Ranch site. Bill Eubanks and his son were killed just north of here on August 7, 1864. The Eubanks ranch home was destroyed. 15 — Probable site of the Little Blue Station. This is believed to be one of only two stage stations along the 200-mile stretch between Kiowa, Nebraska, and Julesburg, Colorado, which survived the 1864 Indian depredations. 16 — Oregon Trail marker. 17 — Camp Kane site. This is the gravesite of Parson Bob (Philip R. Landon), a frontier scout associated with General Custer and Calamity Jane. (Not trail related.) 18 — A reconstructed Nebraska soddy (not trail related) is within the town of Angus. 19 — Oregon Trail marker. 20 — Oregon Trail marker. (The double lines denote the county roads which may be followed to reach the route of the Oregon Trail.)

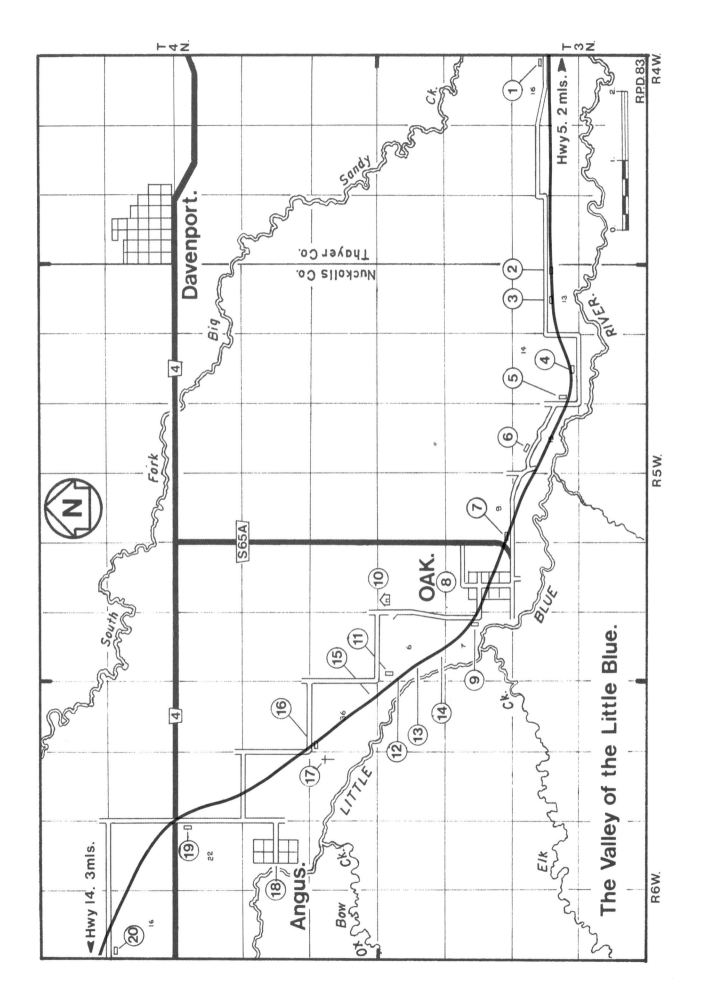

The Valley of the Little Blue.

The emigration now is on the plateau separating the valleys of the Little Blue and the Platte. "Road ranches," or pioneer-day motels, were located alongside the trail to serve stagecoach passengers of the late 1850s and 1860s. Charlie Martin identifies the Elizabeth Taylor grave, significant because she is believed to have been one of only three women of the West to be lynched. Martin found the Fremont campsite, from June 25, 1842, on the first plat map of Adams County. Again, Reg Duffin has prepared a fine map of the Liberty Farm/Spring Ranch area. It appears on page 71, with his legend on page 70. The key has been slightly edited.

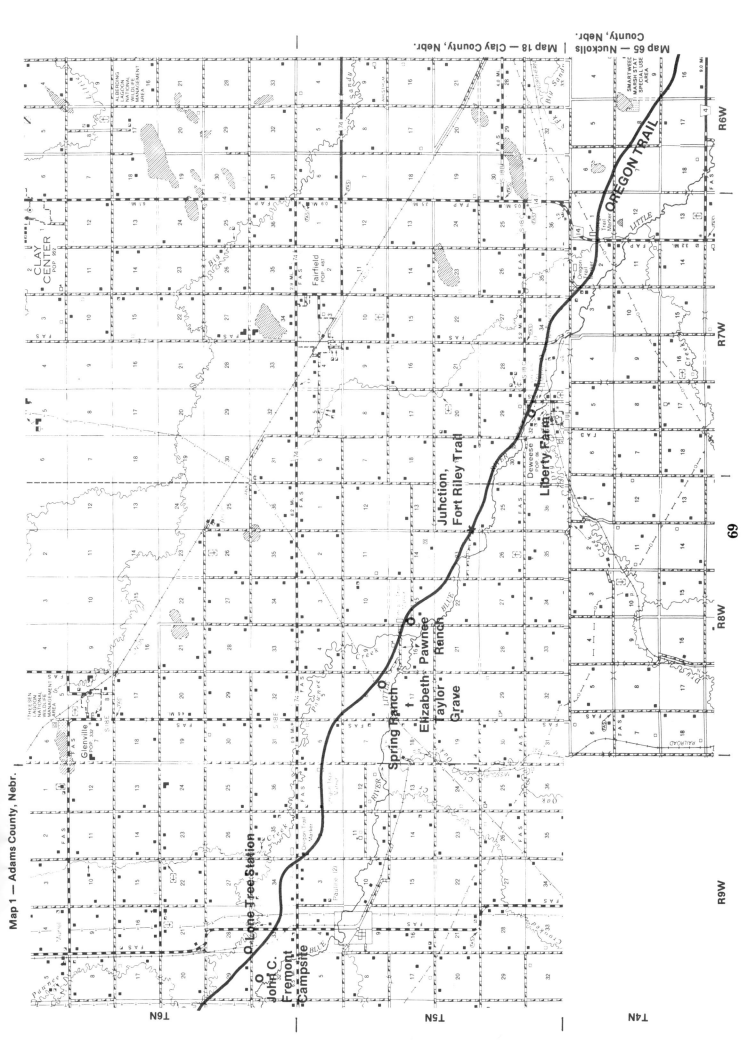

Map 1 — Adams County, Nebr.

Map 65 — Nuckolls County, Nebr.

Map 18 — Clay County, Nebr.

OREGON TRAIL

Juhction, Fort Riley Trail

Liberty Farm

Spring Ranch

Elizabeth Taylor Grave

Pawnee Ranch

O Lone Tree Station

John C. Fremont Campsite

CLAY CENTER POP 952

Fairfield POP. 487

Glenville POP. 332

Dewese POP. 86

Pauline (2)

69

R6W

R7W

R8W

R9W

T6N

T5N

T4N

OREGON TRAIL THROUGH SOUTHWEST CORNER OF CLAY COUNTY, NEBRASKA (Map by Reg Duffin, 1982)

The Oregon Trail through the valley of the Little Blue River has long since been dispersed by farm and plow. However, this trail section is unique, having the greatest concentration of Oregon Trail markers along the entire 2,000-mile route of the old trace.

Key: 1 — An Oregon Trail marker used to be located at the Highway 14 rest area, immediately south of the Little Blue River. It was removed in the summer of 1981, due to highway construction. It ought to be relocated in this proximity. 2 — Oregon Trail marker located within the grass triangle at the T intersection of county roads. 3 — Liberty Ranch Oregon Trail marker. 4 — Probable site of Liberty Farm Ranch and Pony Express Station, destroyed in Indian raids in August 1864. 5 — Fort Riley-Oregon trails junction marker. This small stone is on the east side of the drainage ditch, in front of a grove of scrub fir trees which forms a windbreak for the farm area. 6 — Junction of the trails to Fort Riley, Kansas, and Oregon. 7 — Pawnee Ranch site. This may be the site of a Pony Express station destroyed in an Indian raid in 1864. 8 — Marker for the Oregon Trail and the grave site of Francis Huff. Huff is described as a 25-year-old man who died of appendicitis. He was buried with six soldiers (including a Patrick Burke) plus several Indians in the Pawnee Station cemetery. It is on a slight ridge 100 yards west of this marker. 9 — Oregon Trail crossing at Pawnee Creek. This is just north of where the county road crosses a bridge. 10 — Probable site of the early Weston and Ropers ranch. 11 — Oregon Trail marker in the town of Spring Ranch. A local historical group is starting to mark the sites of early frontier buildings and business establishments along what was probably known as Meston Avenue. 12 — Oregon Trail marker at the site of the Spring Ranch stage station. The marker is on the east side of the county road heading north to Highway 74. It is on private land, centered within a farm compound. This stage station was destroyed in August 1864. 13 — Oregon Trail leaves the Little Blue River to head northwest to the Lone Tree Station and 32-Mile Creek.

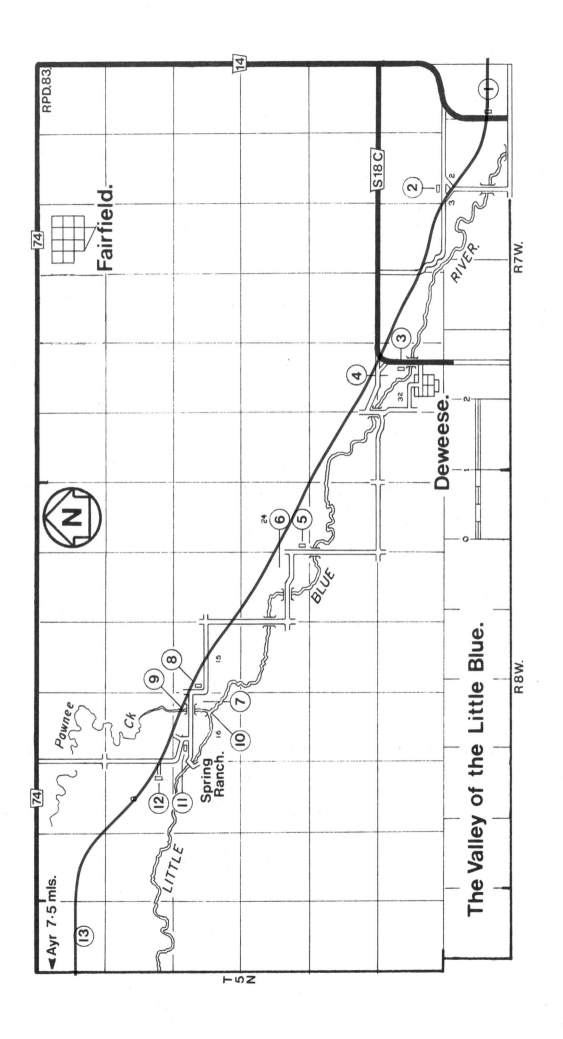

The Valley of the Little Blue.

The travelers left the valley of the Little Blue, which had sheltered them since they departed from Alcove Spring, and struck across the sandy prairie to the Platte. The first glimpse came at about the place where Susan Hail is buried, on a knoll overlooking the wooded islands in the distance. During the 1860s the trail along here was dotted with road ranches. Although they originally provided overnight accommodations for stage travelers, they eventually became bona fide ranches. Two of the better known road ranches, Liberty Farm and Spring Ranch, are shown on the preceding page. The ruts in the lower right corner of this map are southeast of a cattle pond. The Smith-Simonton marker is a horizontal concrete slab inscribed: "8 Men Killed by Indians Aug. 7, 1864."

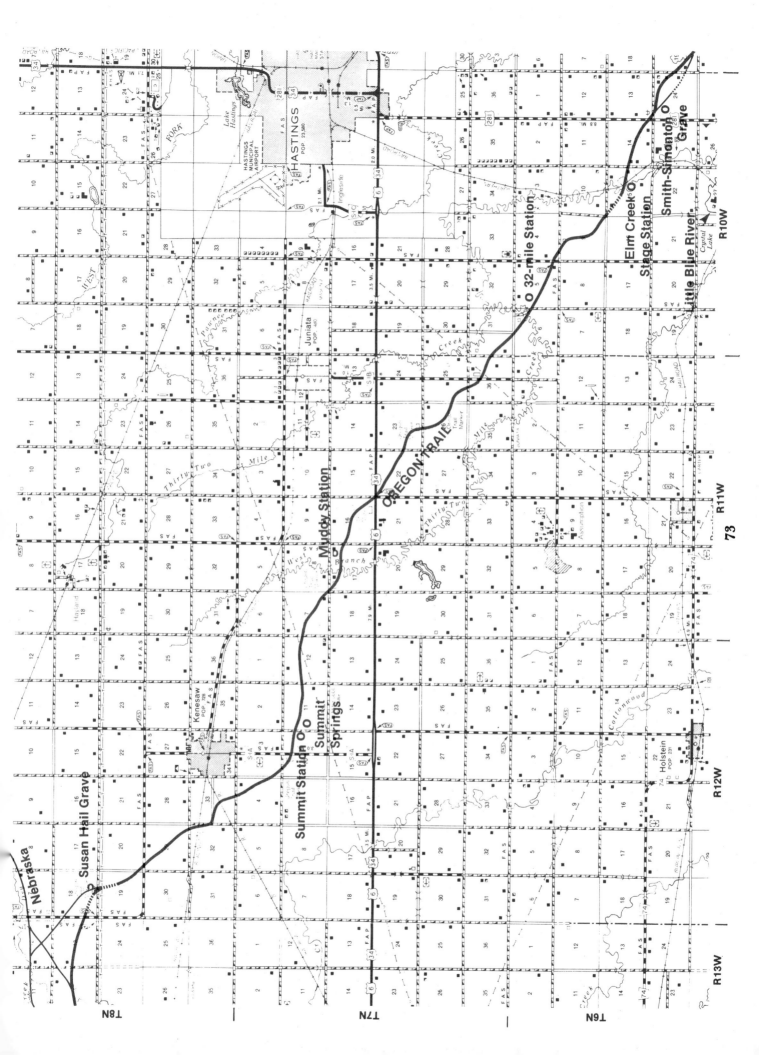

Fort Kearny, built in 1848, was the first of six major forts the emigrants would pass on their way west. Further on, at the edge of the military reservation, was Dobytown, or Kearney City, which catered to the needs of soldiers, freighters and emigrants. Catering of a somewhat different nature transpired at Dirty Woman Ranch. Charlie Martin refers to it as a "sex house." His research discloses that it was on the site of the original town of Central City. Kearney City started somewhat later and nearer the west line of the Fort Kearny Military Reservation. It grew faster and, except for Dirty Woman Ranch, Central City just faded away. Valley Station, known also as Valley City or Hook's Ranch, was located just east of the east line of the military reservation. Martin and Mattes found a number of artifacts on the site, including an ox shoe. Some feel the stage line from Council Bluffs and Omaha crossed the Platte just northeast of Fort Kearny, and others feel the crossing was 15 miles west. Some of the emigrants coming from Kanesville (Council Bluffs) crossed to the south side in this vicinity but most of the north side traffic preferred to stay on the left bank all the way to Fort Laramie before crossing. In 1852 there was also a lot of crossing from the south bank to the north, in a vain effort to flee the cholera epidemic. The majority of north bank traffic, except for the years 1847 and 1848, was not Mormon.

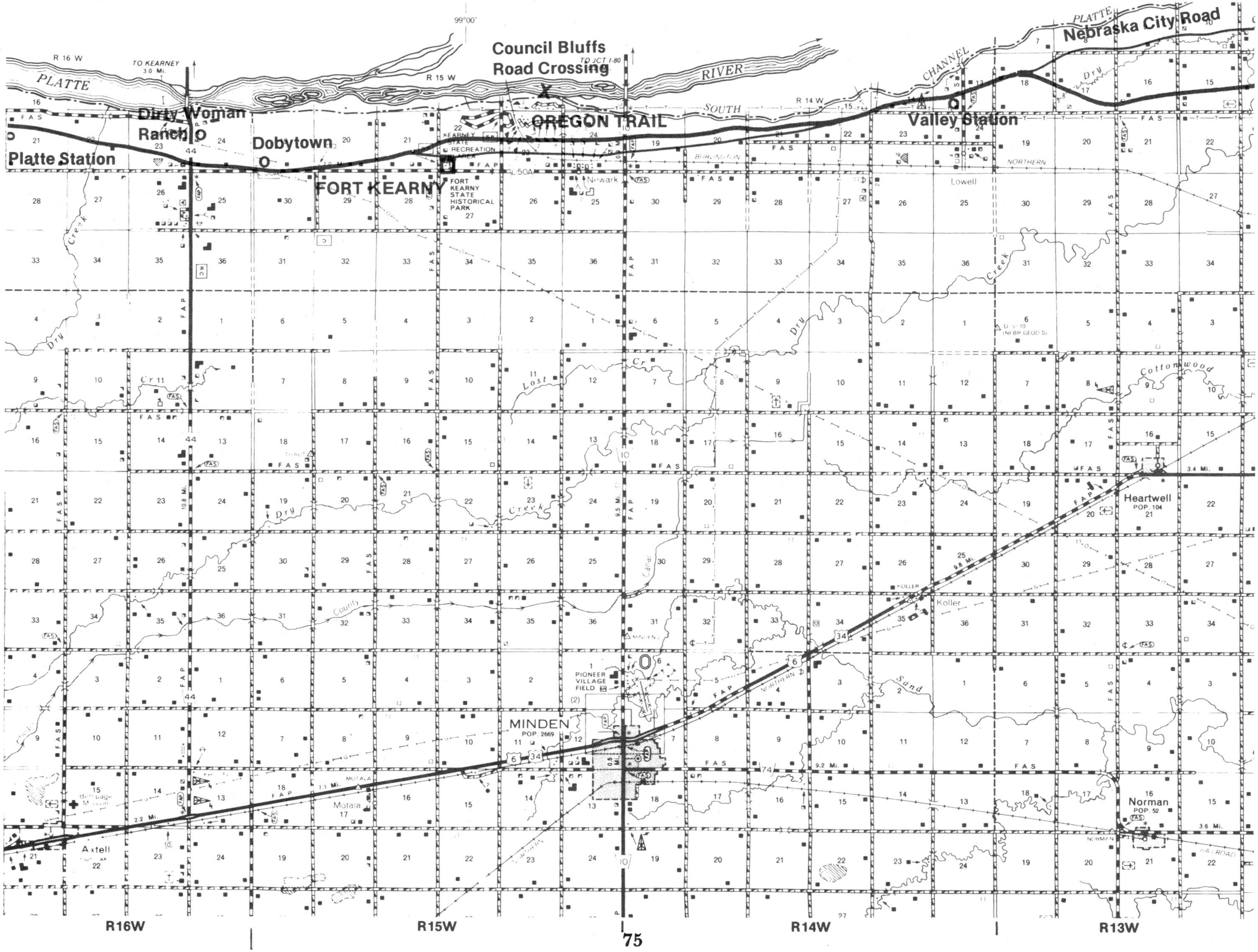

Map 30 — Kearney County, Nebr.

Nebraska City Road

PLATTE

Council Bluffs
Road Crossing
TD JCT I-80

OREGON TRAIL

Valley Station

Lowell

Heartwell
POP. 104

Norman
POP. 92

RIVER

SOUTH

CHANNEL

PLATTE

Dirty Woman Ranch

Dobytown

FORT KEARNY

FORT KEARNY
STATE RECREATION

FORT KEARNY
STATE
HISTORICAL
PARK

Platte Station

TO KEARNEY
3.0 MI.

Newark

Koller

Sand

Newark

PIONEER
VILLAGE
FIELD

MINDEN
POP. 2669

Mirage

Axtell

R 16 W

R 15 W

R 14 W

R13W

R14W

R15W

R16W

75

T8N

T7N

T6N

The 17-mile Station was also known as Platte Station, which means this location could be in conflict with the one shown four miles to the east. Furthermore, the Garden Station could well be the Craig, or ''Shakespear'' Station, meaning there is a five-mile difference there too. Lots of people have studied these problems with mixed results. The subject ought to be a meaty one for a master's thesis.

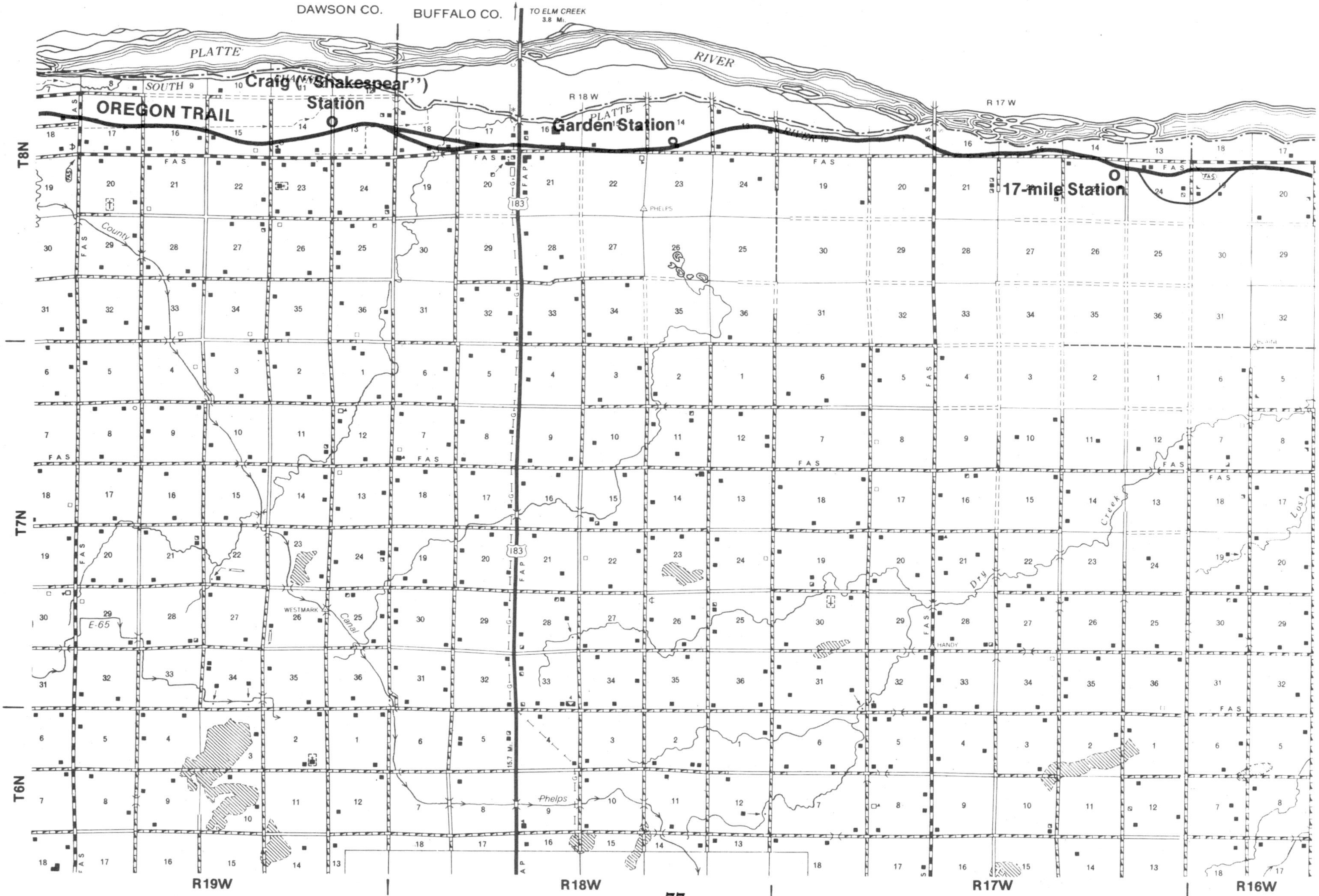

Map 89 — Phelps County, Nebr. | County, Nebr.

OREGON TRAIL

17-mile Station

Garden Station

Craig ("Shakespear") Station

PLATTE RIVER

SOUTH PLATTE

DAWSON CO.

BUFFALO CO.

TO ELM CREEK
3.8 M.

WESTMARK

Canal

OREGON TRAIL

R 19 W
R 18 W
R 17 W
R 16 W

T8N
T7N
T6N

R19W
R18W
R17W
R16W

77

LOST CREEK

HANDY

PHELPS

Phelps

County

E-65

183

183

15.7 M.

FAS

CRAIG

The travelers noticed marked changes in their environment as they traveled along the Platte River. The land was starting to pitch and heave. The prairie wasn't as green anymore, and the nights were cooler even though midsummer was approaching. The prairie thunderstorms still exploded like cannonfire and could thoroughly drench everybody and everything in a matter of a few seconds. Plum Creek was the first important campsite west of Fort Kearny. On August 4, 1864, a small wagon train stopped to camp at a small stream along the east border of this map. They left the next morning, traveled a little over a mile and were attacked by Indians. All 11 men were killed. Nancy Jane Fletcher Cotton was captured by the Indians. Joe Bisonette was doing business up on the Powder River at the time and was able to trade for her. She was brought back to the Platte Bridge and returned to her home in Iowa on March 9, 1865. The victims of the Plum Creek Massacre are commemorated in the cemetery, which is about two miles west of the point where they are believed to have been buried. A cabin, believed to have been the Pony Express Station at Willow Island, now is exhibited in the city park at Cozad, Nebraska.

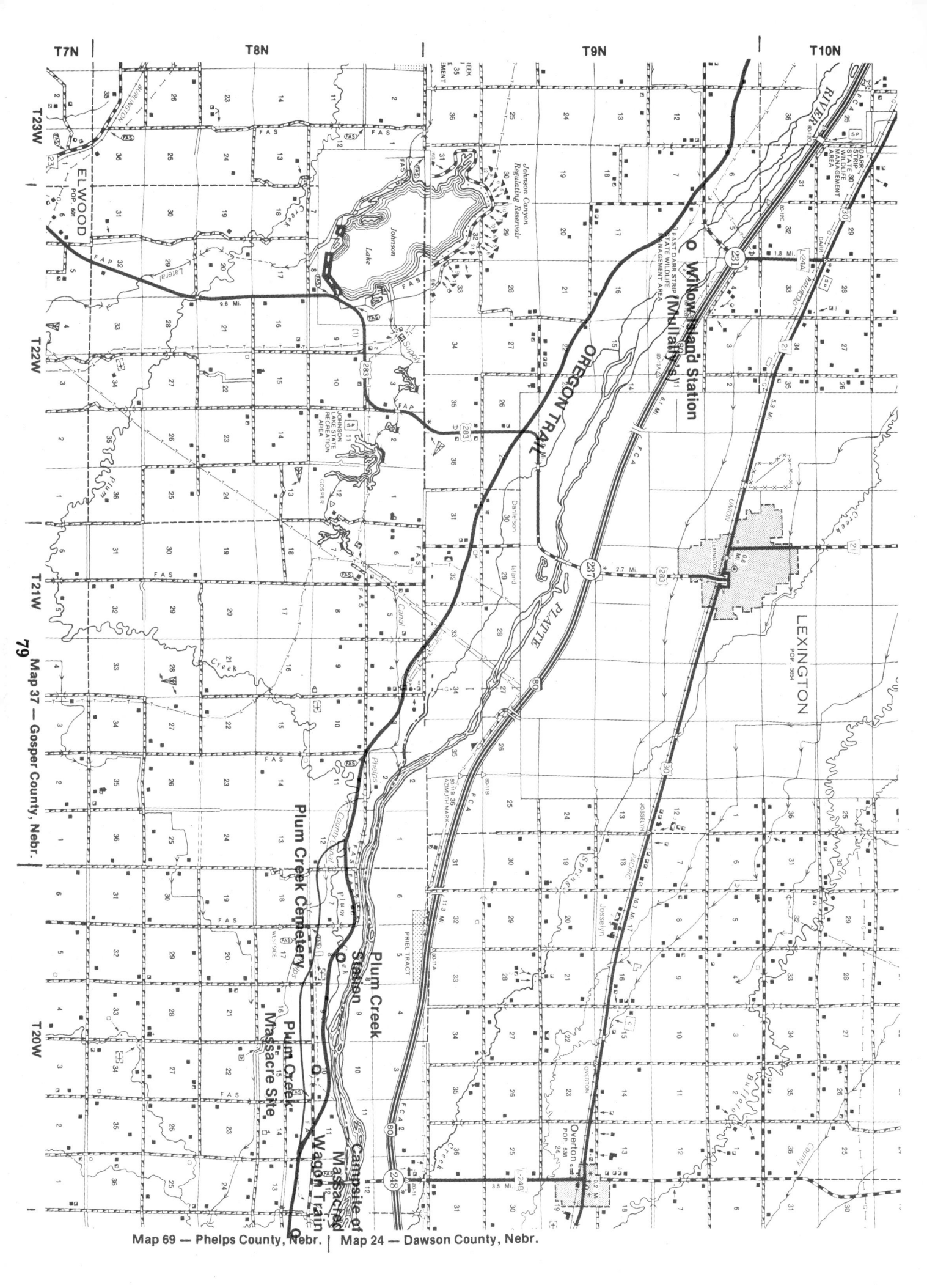

Map 69 — Phelps County, Nebr. | Map 24 — Dawson County, Nebr.

80

This map is reproduced with permission from Musetta Gilman's charming book, *Pump on the Prairie*. This is the story of a purported Pony Express station and known stage station operated by her husband's forebears. It boasted a great luxury on the plains, an iron pump. The paperback is still in print and copies may be obtained from Mrs. Gilman for $5.61 p.p. Her address is 5340 Colby Street, Lincoln, NE 68504. According to the Mattes-Henderson book, the reconstructed and misplaced "Pony Express Station" in the Gothenberg City Park is a remnant of Gilman's stage station. The photo above, taken by the author, is of the building usually identified as the Midway Pony Express Station, two miles southeast of Gothenburg. Research by Merrill Mattes, Mrs. Gilman and Charles W. Martin leaves little doubt that it isn't at all; that it is really the 1864 "Dan Smith West Ranche" building and neither a stage nor a Pony Express station. The real Midway Station, seen burning from an Indian raid in 1866, evidently was five miles east of this structure.

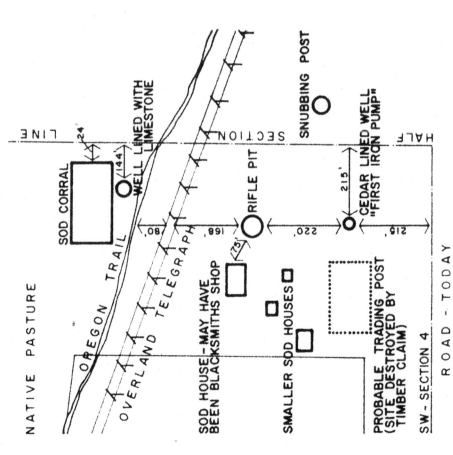

GILMAN'S STATION
IN PECKHAM PRECINCT

NATIVE PASTURE

SOD CORRAL

WELL LINED WITH LIMESTONE

SNUBBING POST

RIFLE PIT

CEDAR LINED WELL "FIRST IRON PUMP"

SOD HOUSE—MAY HAVE BEEN BLACKSMITHS SHOP

SMALLER SOD HOUSES

PROBABLE TRADING POST (SITE DESTROYED BY TIMBER CLAIM)

SW - SECTION 4

ROAD - TODAY

NW - SECTION 9

STAGE STATION—"PEG LEG" FIRST STOP EAST OF FORT McPHERSON

APPROXIMATE MEASUREMENTS BY HENRY H. STRICKLAND, SILVER CREEK, NEBR.

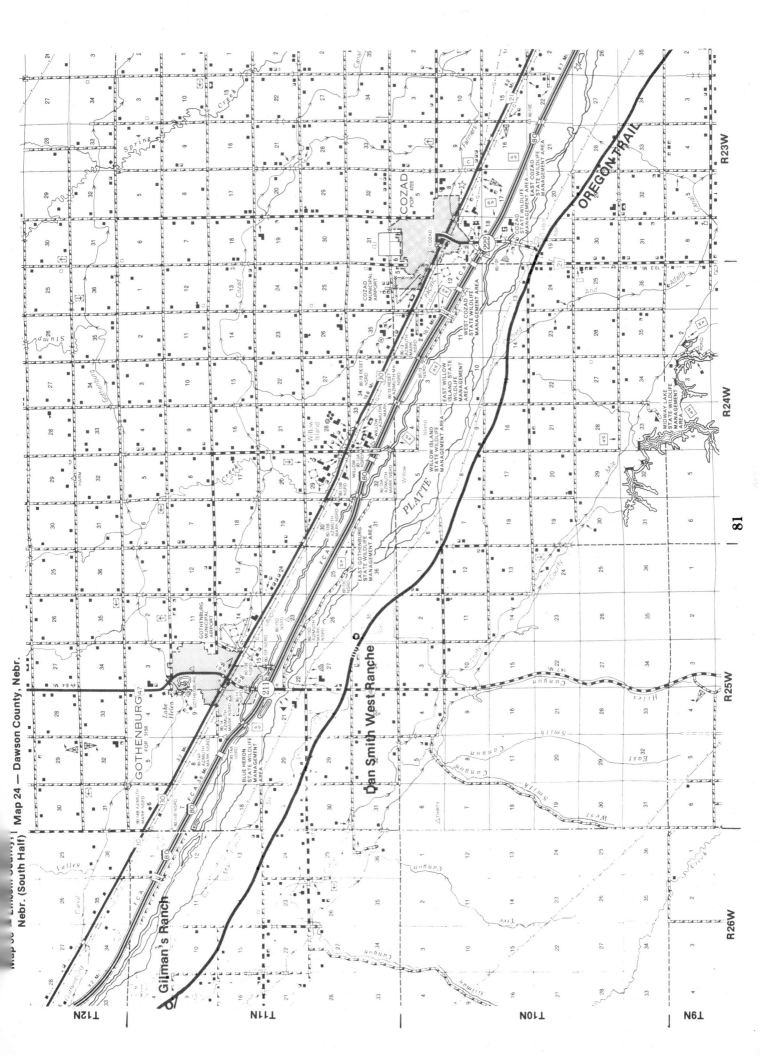

Cottonwood Springs was a major campsite, trading post and Pony Express Station. Cottonwood Canyon, in the hills to the south, was a prime source of timber. Fort Cottonwood is the original name of Fort McPherson. The site is about a mile southeast of the cemetery of that name. The climb to the top of "Sioux Lookout" is a pleasant experience and gives a thrilling view of the countryside.

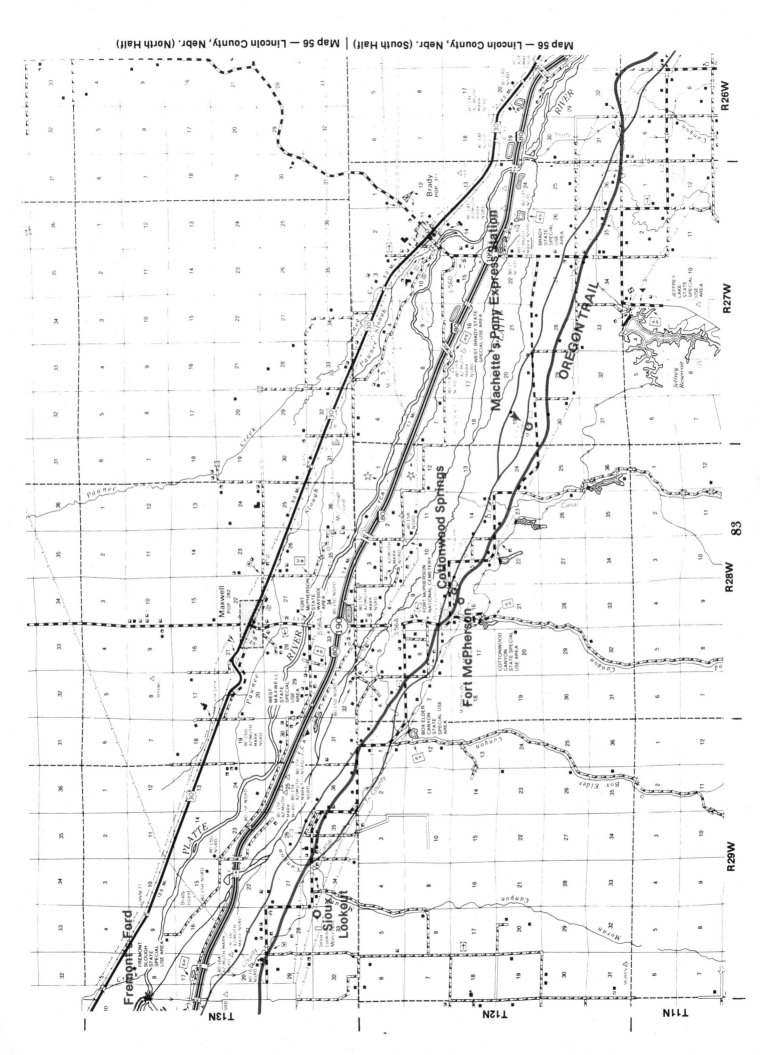

The North and South Platte rivers join on the right edge of this map. The so-called lower ford of the South Platte was in the vicinity of Hershey and was used heavily in the early years, according to research performed by Merrill Mattes. The travelers, in his words, had to "roller coaster up the North Platte and join the trail from the upper ford in Ash Hollow." Note that Interstate Highway 80 closely parallels the route of the old trail. After 150 years of civil engineering experience our society has yet to better the emigrant route for most of the way to the Pacific Northwest.

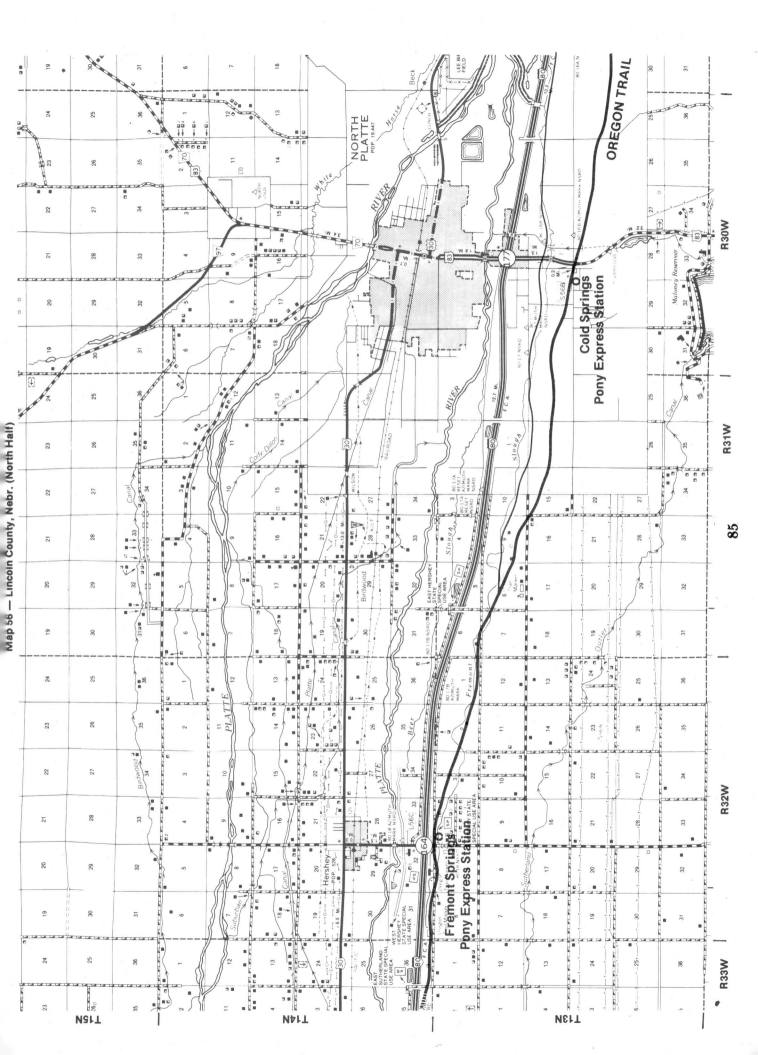

Map 56 — Lincoln County, Nebr. (North Half)

NORTH PLATTE
POP. 19,447

OREGON TRAIL

Cold Springs
Pony Express Station

Fremont Springs
Pony Express Station

Hershey
POP. 526

85

R30W

R31W

R32W

R33W

T15N

T14N

T13N

86

The State of Nebraska has done travelers a wonderful service by building their I-80 rest stops on the flank of O'Fallon's Bluff. The eastbound stop is the better one. From there travelers may walk the gentle rut swale along the big bluff for 1,000 feet. Those headed west should continue on to Sutherland, two miles ahead, and then backtrack east to the rest stop. They will have to continue another five miles to turn around at the Hershey interchange but it would be worth it if it were 50 miles. In his *Great Platte River Road*, Mattes writes that emigrants using the middle ford (Ford No. 2) had the option of crossing over to the north fork or following up the left bank of the South Platte to the upper crossing and California Hill. His research of more than 1,000 emigrant diaries establishes heavy use of both the lower and middle fords in the 1840s and 1850s.

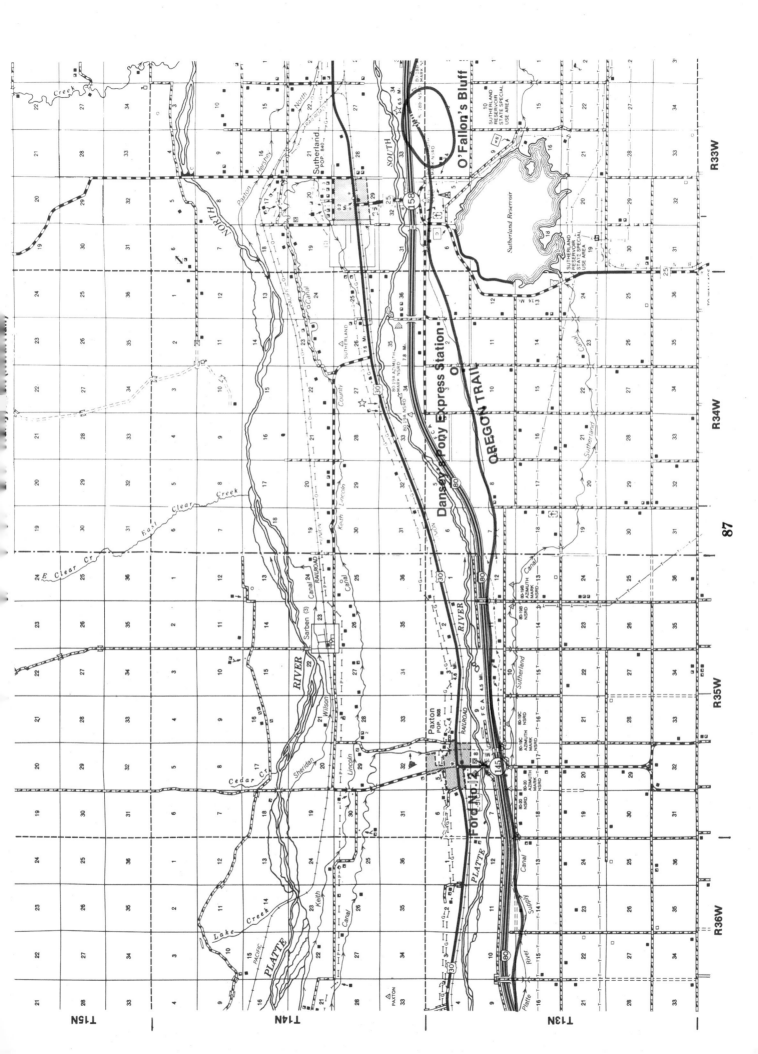

88

The Pony Express sites in red sometimes differ from those on the base maps. Those in red are taken from the Mattes-Henderson study of 1960, and the markers indicated on the base maps either could reflect the results of later study, or could be just plain wrong. Ogallala has done a nice job of rebuilding their historic Front Street, with several gift shops, a nice restaurant and entertainment places.

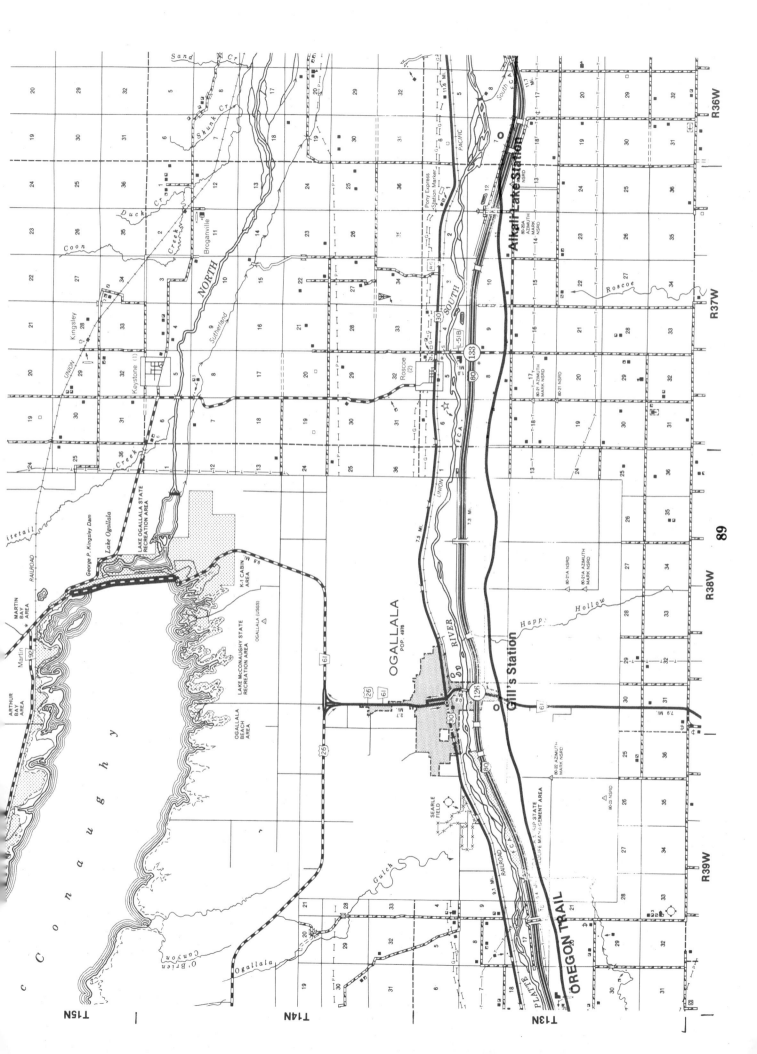

89

In 1860 the so-called upper ford became known as the Lower California Crossing. (The Upper California Crossing, used largely by freighters and the Pony Express after that date, is near Julesburg, Colorado.) Before the North Platte was harnessed by irrigation it was a rushing torrent at this point; now it is more like a backwater. There is a tremendous swale up California Hill (see photo), started by the wagons and continued by erosion. It is on private land, occupied by a bull who is second in meanness only to the owner, should you be caught trespassing without permission. The Oregon Trail marker at the base of California Hill is in front of a farmhouse on the north side of Highway 30. The trail goes by the marker and through a feedlot before climbing the hill. Troy Gray has counted six individual rut swales starting up the hill, all of which merge up the slope. The ruts leading to the steep descent now known as Windlass Hill are still visible, as are the erosion effects on the hill itself, caused by the trail scars. The hill is now part of Ash Hollow State Park. (Photo by the author.)

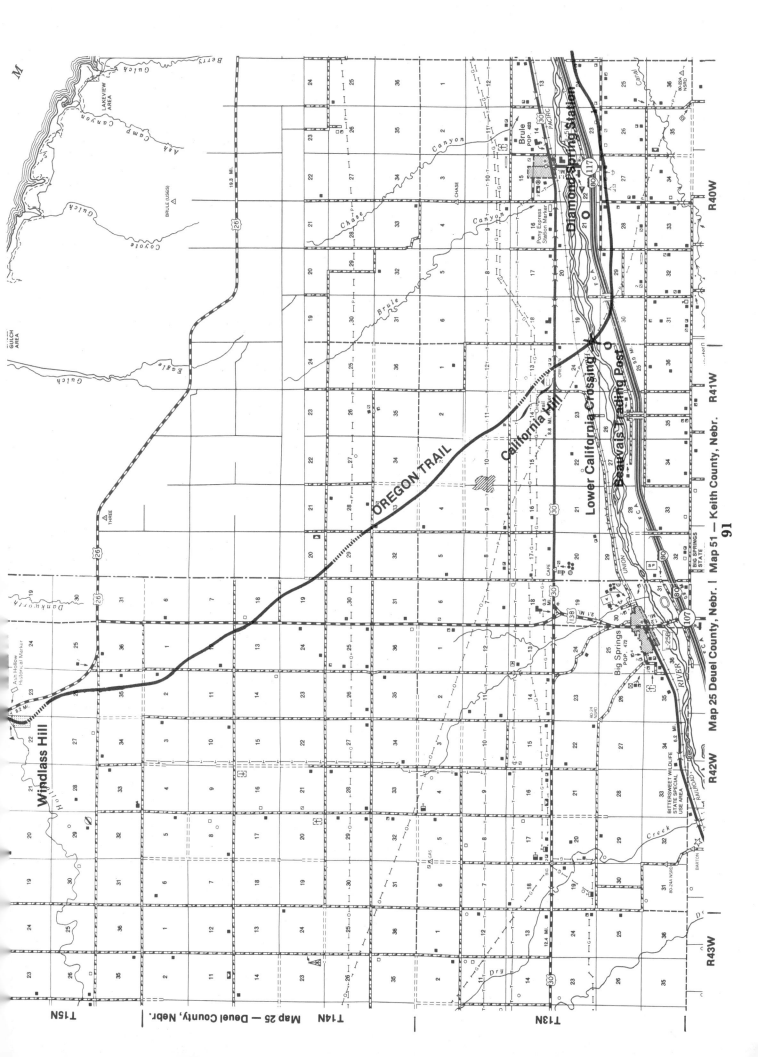

Windlass Hill

OREGON TRAIL

California Hill

Lower California Crossing

Beauvais Trading Post

Diamond Spring Station

Brule
POP. 423

Big Springs
POP. 472

Map 25 — Deuel County, Nebr.   Map 25 Deuel County, Nebr. | Map 51 — Keith County, Nebr.   R41W

91

R40W

R42W

R43W

T15N

T14N

T13N

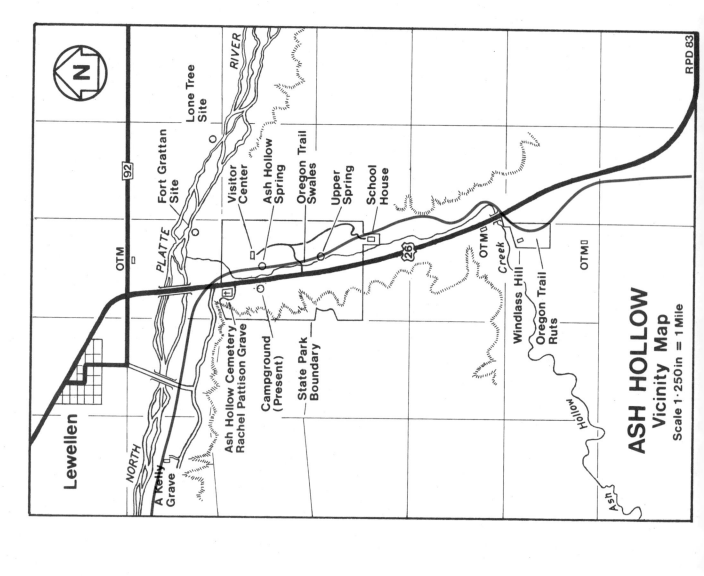

ASH HOLLOW
Vicinity Map
Scale 1·250in = 1Mile

RPD 83

In 1849 young Rachel Pattison had the distinction of being the first burial in the Ash Hollow Cemetery, although she probably wasn't all that pleased about it. It has been estimated that one out of 17 of those who started on the Oregon Trail died enroute. If so, there would be a grave every 193 yards. Only a small percentage of the graves alongside the trail — those which were particularly well marked — may be found today. Some of the bodies were interred right in the trail. In 1855 Gen. William S. Harney led an overwhelming Army force in massive retaliation against Little Thunder's Sioux at the Battle of Blue Water. The one-sided engagement was fought to avenge the so-called Grattan Massacre. The map at right was prepared especially for this book by Reg P. Duffin, of La Grange Park, Illinois.

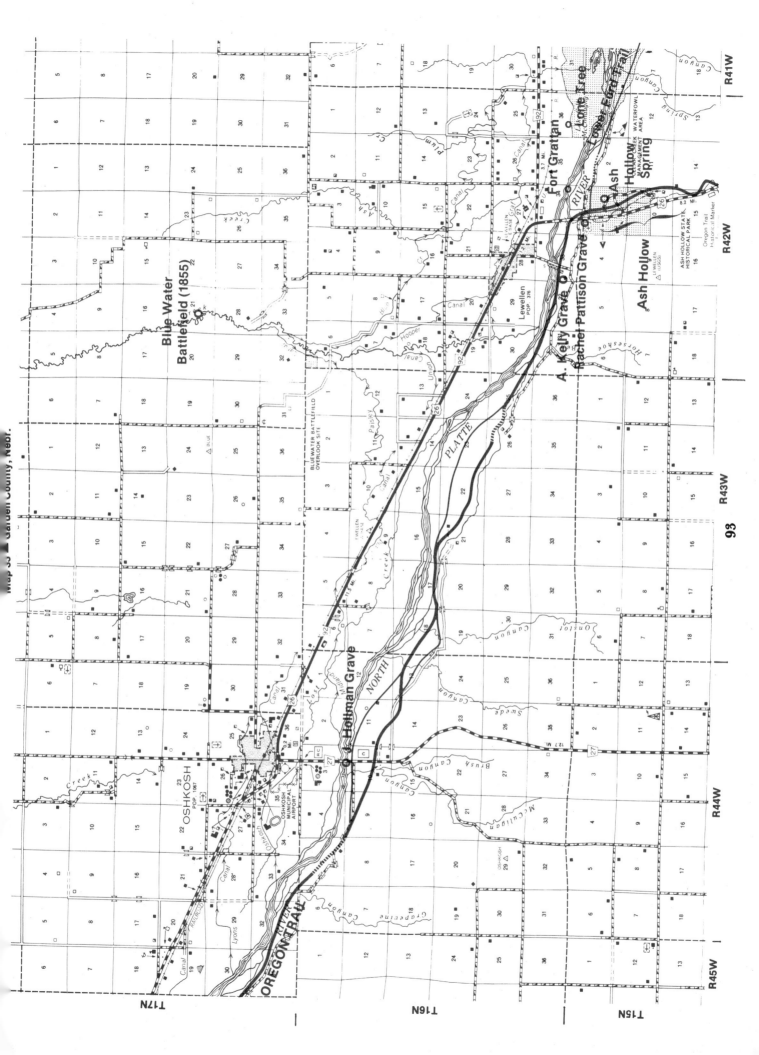

Map 33 — Garden County, Nebr.

94

William Clayton, official journalist of the 1847 Mormon pioneer trek, noted the Ancient Bluff Ruins in his guidebook. Dozens of others traveling on both sides of the river mentioned this phenomenon in their diaries. Reg Duffin recalls seeing some good deep ruts in the eastern portion of the trail on this map, but help is needed in pinpointing them.

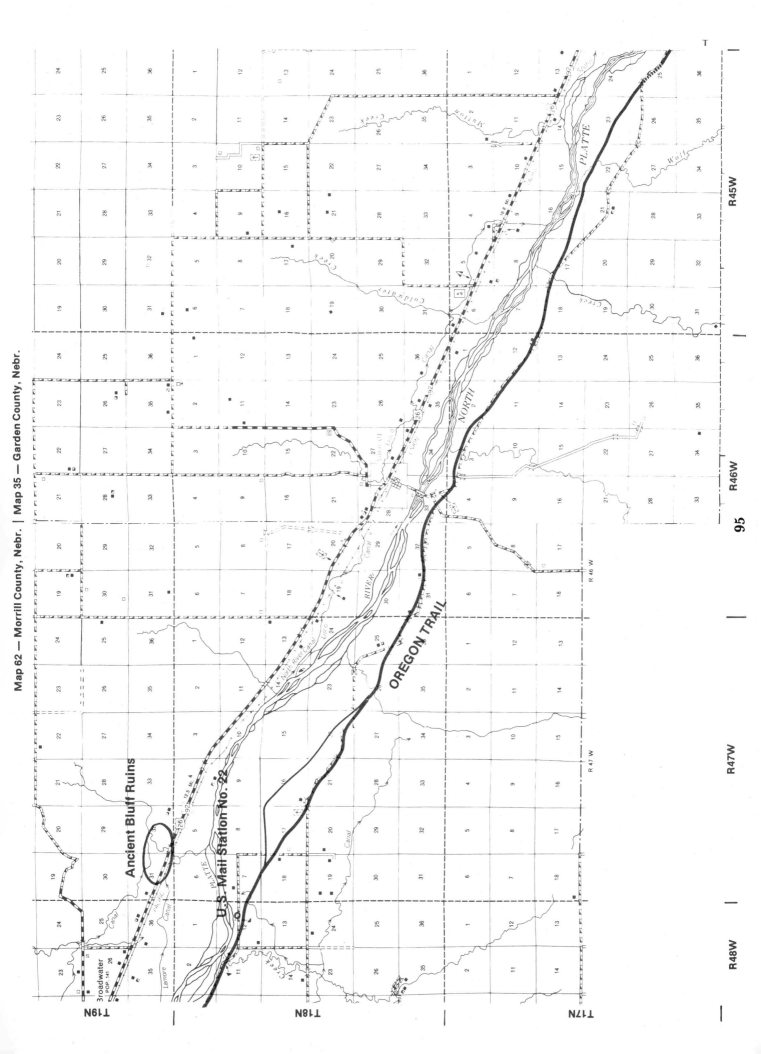

Map 62 — Morrill County, Nebr. | Map 35 — Garden County, Nebr.

Ancient Bluff Ruins

U.S. Mail Station No. 22

OREGON TRAIL

Broadwater
POP. 141

95

R48W · R47W · R46W · R45W

T19N · T18N · T17N

NORTH PLATTE RIVER

The Pony Express route headed north from the Upper California Crossing, passed west of Courthouse Rock and joined the Oregon Trail west of present Bridgeport. In sheltered niches of Courthouse Rock, many names are still visible which date from the 1850s. There are still some intermittent ripple-like ruts both east and west of the grave of Amanda Lamin, but the land in the immediate vicinity of the marker was plowed for the first time in the spring of 1981. So those ruts, now are gone forever. There are ruts on either side of the cemetery west of Bridgeport. In that cemetery lies Paul Henderson, the greatest of the Oregon Trail scholars. He had researched the old trail for 52 years, and it is altogether fitting that he should rest next to the old trace that played such an important role in his life.

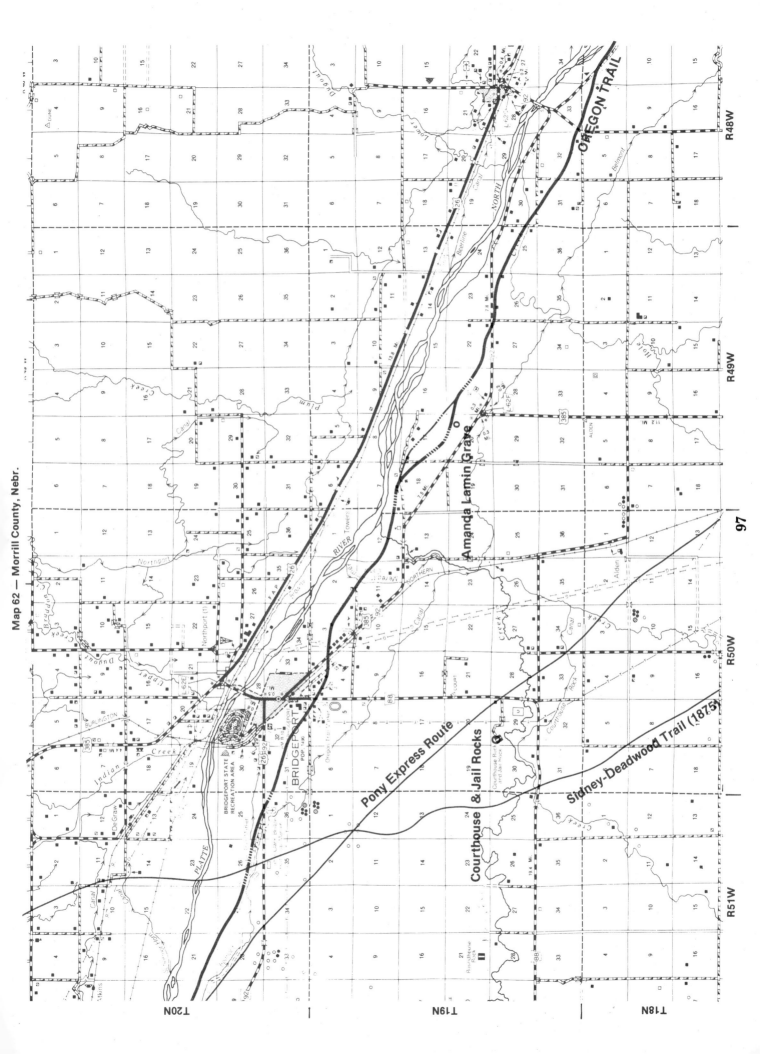

Map 62 — Morrill County, Nebr.

OREGON TRAIL

Amanda Lamin Grave

Pony Express Route

Courthouse & Jail Rocks

Sidney-Deadwood Trail (1875)

BRIDGEPORT
POP. 1490

BRIDGEPORT STATE
RECREATION AREA

97

William H. Jackson is believed to have been standing at the "Jackson Panorama" site in 1866 when he originally sketched the scene before him in his trail days. He painted it in watercolors in 1931. Famous Chimney Rock is in the background. (Both the original sketch and the painting are in the Jackson wing of the Oregon Trail Museum at Scotts Bluff National Monument.) Jackson's perspective is greatly exaggerated.

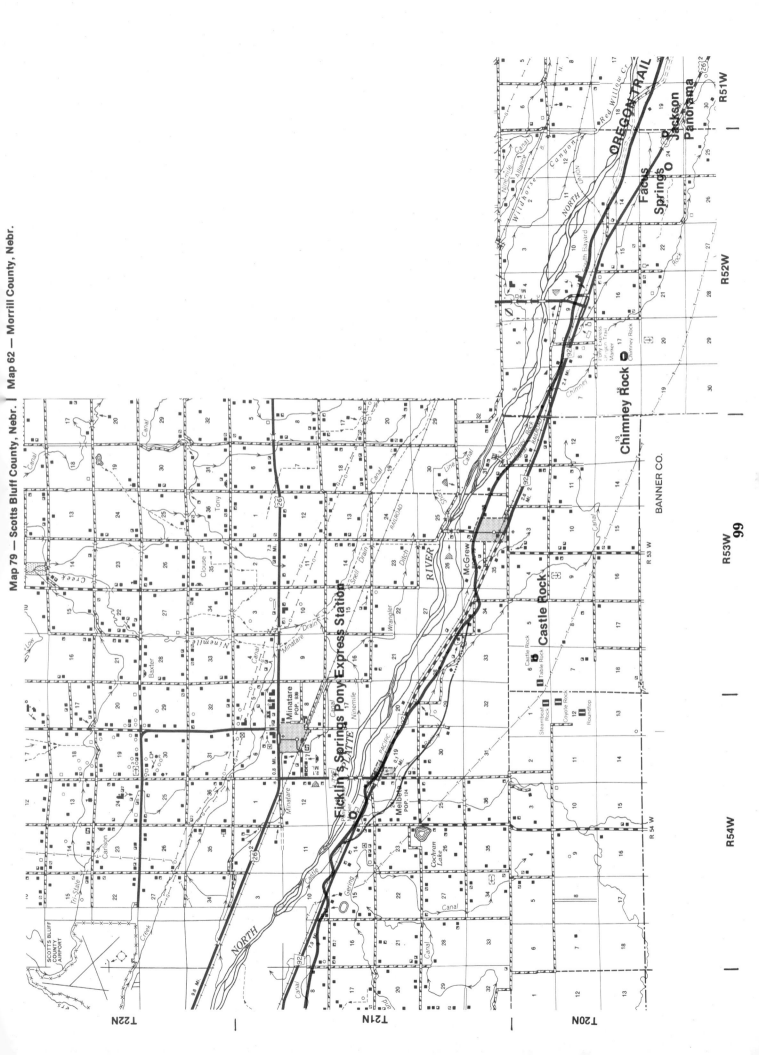

Visitors who want to do it right should plan to spend at least a full day in this area. The nature trail to the top of Scotts Bluff is thrilling. The Oregon Trail through Mitchell Pass must be hiked. The Robidoux Pass area, with its springs, emigrant graves, blacksmith shop site and trail remains, must be explored. So must the sites of the second Fort John and the second Robidoux Post. The Oregon Trail Museum at Scotts Bluff National Monument is one of the best in the West and deserves several hours.

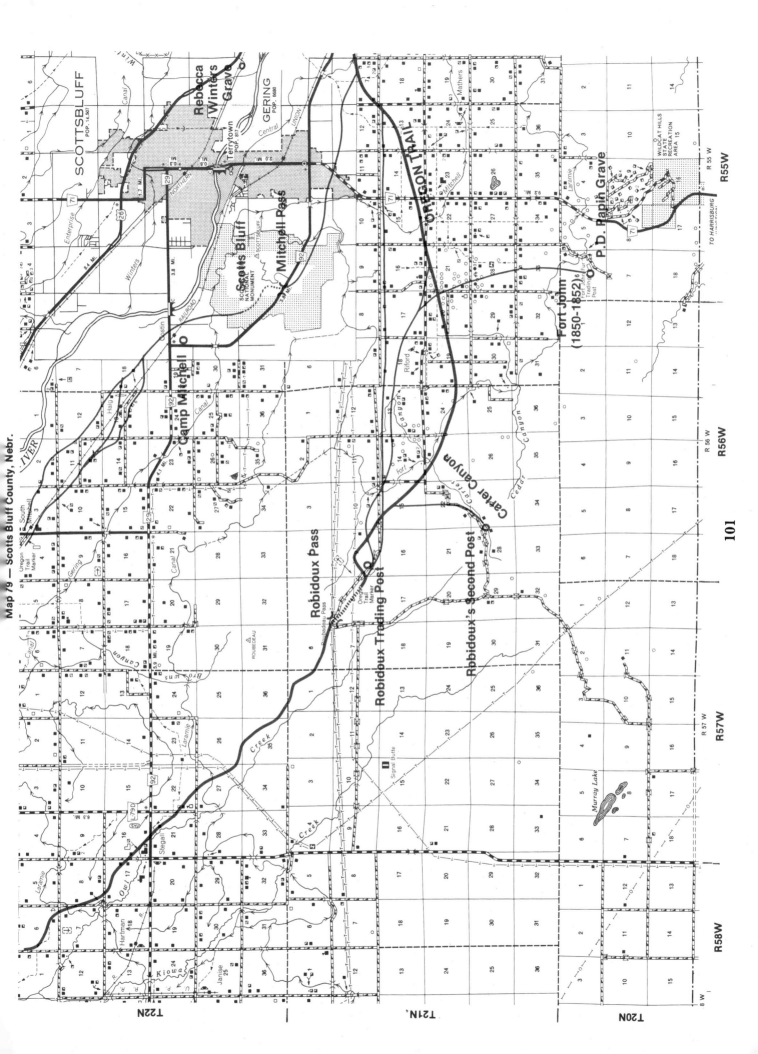

Map 79 — Scotts Bluff County, Nebr.

101

102

The photo of the re-erected stump was taken by Page.

In June 1949 the Nebraska State Historical Society published the article, "Robidoux's Trading Post at 'Scott's Bluffs,'" and the California Gold Rush," by Merrill J. Mattes. By then both Mattes and Paul Henderson were already well-known as thorough researchers. Here is Henderson's map, which illustrated that article. The map is reproduced here with permission of the Society.

Sleuthing on the Oregon Trail never stops. Since the location of the Papin grave evidently had been lost, three men decided to try to find it. Mert Davis and Lanny Page, longtime seasonal employees of Scotts Bluff National Monument, joined area resident Archie Snocker in the quest.

The following is from a letter by Page, dated September 29, 1983:

"We learned that the Papin site was discovered by T.L. Green of Scottsbluff in the 1930s. A cedar post marking the grave was still standing then and still bore the name, "Papin." A three-foot-high stump was all that remained of the original grave marker of 1853, which had been a large cross. The earliest picture of the site that I can find was taken in 1938.

'Davis, Snocker and I found that downed cedar post in August 1983. Next to it was a pipe pounded into the ground. Comparing the present-day background to the 1930s photos, we felt sure this was the grave. It is the only known grave in Helvas Canyon and is some 400 yards northeast of the site of the second Fort John.

"After speaking to local landowners, I realized why historians have long been baffled in their search for the grave, guided as they were by the 1930s photos. According to Mac McClenahan, who is intimately acquainted with the land, the gravel road seen in the far background in many of those pictures was moved in the 1950s. The county road now passes within 50 yards of the grave, and runs in a direction different from the old road.

"Our most important verification comes from Joe McClenahan. He moved into the farmhouse near the grave in 1923 at the age of 5. The land is now owned by his sister, Marjorie Schleicher. McClenahan explored his surroundings often as a youth and recalls the site well. He can remember the cedar post standing as late as 1940 and the carving in it could be read as 'Papi,' the 'n' having faded away. He was not then aware of the Papin name and read this as 'Papa,' thinking part of the 'a' was missing. In time the base of the post rotted and he drove a piece of pipe beside it for support.

"About 40 feet from the marker there is a mound of stone, sometimes suspected to be the Papin grave but actually that of a family dog."

The location of the second Fort John trading post, as marked by the D.A.R. in 1947, is inconsistent with the Henderson cartography of 1949, as shown on page 103.

Detail of Robidoux Pass Area at "Scott's Bluffs"

MITCHELL PASS

R 55 W

R 56 W

T 21 N

BIG SPRING AND RAVINE

NAMELESS GRAVES

JOHN DUNN GRAVE

AMERICAN FUR CO'S FIRST POST

SMALL SPRING AT TRANSVERSE DRAW

ROBIDOUX PASS

TRAIL TO CALIFORNIA 1849

ROBIDOUX'S FIRST POST

ROBIDOUX'S SECOND POST

AMERICAN FUR CO'S SECOND POST

36

31

DETAIL OF ROBIDOUX PASS AREA AT "SCOTT'S BLUFFS"

HENRY

MORRILL

MITCHELL

SCOTTSBLUFF

GERING

MINATARE

MELBETA

MORMON TRAIL

NORTH PLATTE

OREGON-CALIFORNIA TRAIL

SOUTH MITCHELL

MITCHELL TRAIL

MORMON TRAIL

LYMAN

Horse Creek Crossing

FORT LARAMIE — 50 MILES

VIEW TOWARDS LARAMIE PEAK OR THE BLACK HILLS

SCOTTS BLUFF NATIONAL MONUMENT

ROBIDOUX PASS

ROBIDOUX TRADING POST 1849-1850

(GERING VALLEY SURROUNDED BY HISTORIC "SCOTT'S BLUFFS")

CARTER CANYON

ROBIDOUX TRADING POST 1850-1851

WILD CAT HILLS

FORT JOHN (AMERICAN FUR CO. TRADING POST) 1850-1852

HELVAS CANYON

CALIFORNIA

OREGON

MC GREW

CASTLE ROCK

CHIMNEY ROCK

RIVER

TRAIL

103

ROBIDOUX & MITCHELL-PASS-ROUTES

The great Fort Laramie Treaty of 1851, which attracted the largest assemblage of Plains Indians of all time, was held in the valley of Horse Creek and promised a peaceful solution to the Indian unrest. The peace, negotiated with the greatest skill, lasted just three years and was broken by a trigger-happy second lieutenant, John L. Grattan. He fired on Indians assembled to receive annuities. They retaliated with a wipeout of Grattan and his force of 30. A lame Mormon cow was the cause of the dispute. Beautiful ruts near the Henry Hill grave were found by Troy Gray, who advises that permission must be gained before going into the area. The land is sandy and the roads should not be attempted unless they are dry.

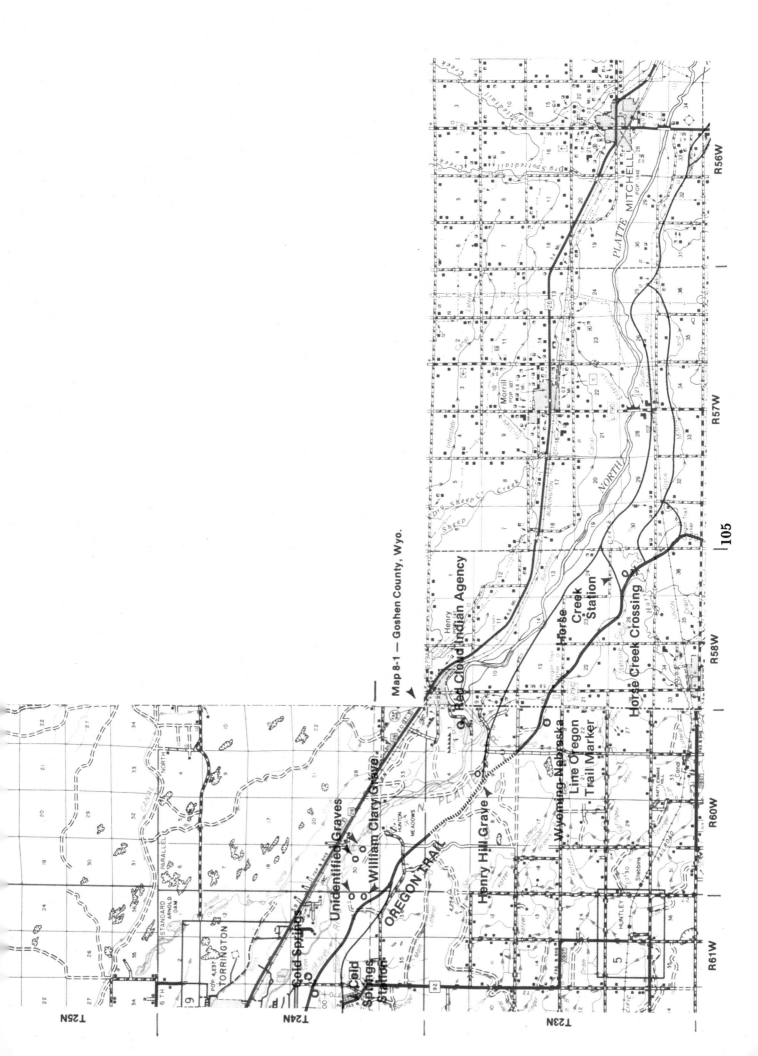

Map 8-1 — Goshen County, Wyo.

105

Researching the Oregon Trail continues to this day. The one most knowledgeable person about Fort Laramie is its official historian, Merrill J. Mattes. He, working with Paul Henderson and others, originally posited the probable location of Fort William (pictured here as sketched by Alfred J. Miller in 1836) as about 1½ miles east of the site of present Fort Laramie. This was based upon vague notations contained in dozens of diaries, interviews with old timers, studies of old maps, and just plain hearsay. It was not only the best guess, but virtually the only one. Yet, Mattes was never comfortable with it, his unease being fed by the fact that, down through the years, occupational debris at the supposed site simply failed to surface. Here is a remarkable quote from a letter by Mattes to the author, dated February 13, 1982:

Regarding the first Fort Laramie (Fort William, 1834), I am now convinced, despite my previous line of thinking, that it was located within the 1849-1890 military parade ground area. In 1963 a sizable fragment of a rotting wooden structure (several feet long) was found at the rear of Old Bedlam [the beautifully restored Bachelor Officers' Quarters]; in fact, it was underneath the rear or west side veranda and staircases at that time being reconstructed. The information was suppressed by the project architect to avoid awkward delays; I did not learn about it until 1977 in the process of researching my *Fort Laramie Park History* when I interviewed the retired project foreman. There has never been **formal** archaeological confirmation of this; however, Fort William seems the probable explanation because prior to 1849, when Old Bedlam was started, **the only building on the premises** was the adobe Fort John, built in 1841 at the south end of the present parade ground. The Fort William evidence is sufficiently removed from the adobe Fort John to allow for the reasonable hypothesis that it (Fort John) was built **before** Fort William was altogether dismantled or abandoned. In other words, they did **not** first tear down Fort William and build Fort John in its **exact** place. The two stockades probably coexisted briefly in 1841, one going up while the other was coming down. The 1834 wooden structure rapidly disappeared as its timber was used for Fort John firewood, or maybe even unrotted portions were used as part of the Fort John framework!

All visible preserved and restored structures at Fort Laramie today are of the military post, 1849-1890. Troy Gray reports good ruts on two routes east of Fort Laramie.

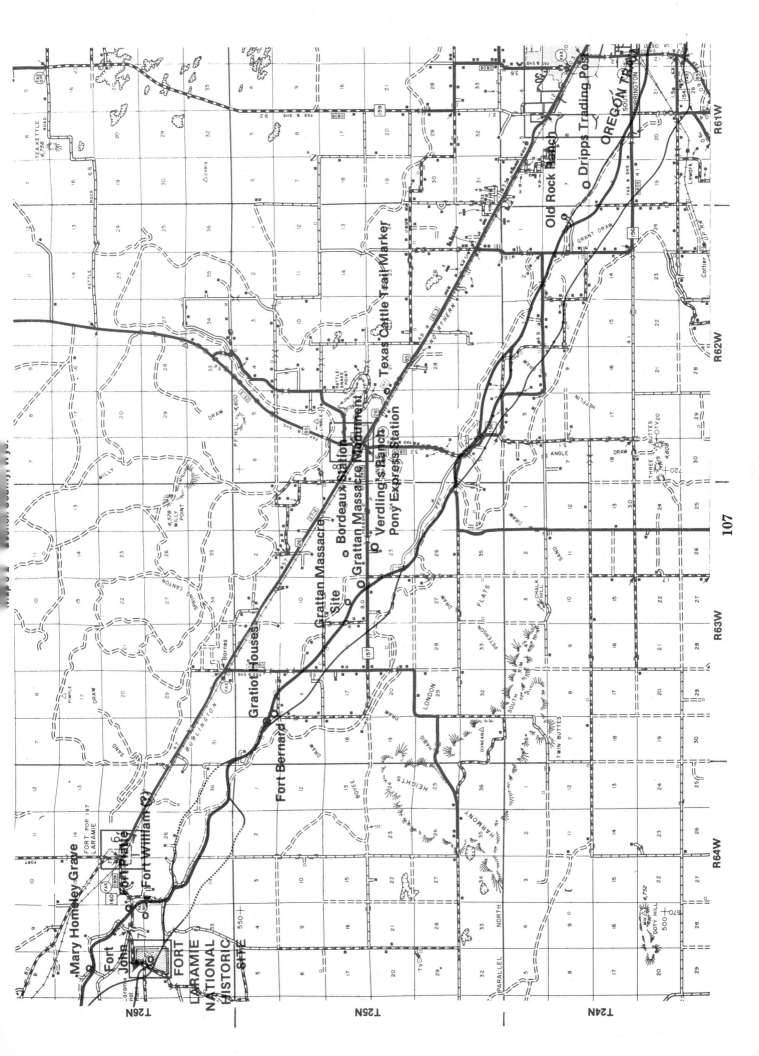

Mattes has devoted several years to a concentrated study of every known diary or reminiscence left by a 19th century traveler over the Oregon or California trails, and has yet to find a single one which describes the act of an emigrant placing his name on Register Cliff. Of course they did — the names there now attest to that. In emigrant days the cliff had no fame comparable to such other registers as Courthouse, Chimney or Independence rocks. Beginning in 1850 most travelers who had started on the north bank of the Platte stayed there, although they usually made a side trip to Fort Laramie for mail. The way along the so-called Chiles's Route (often called the Mormon Trail) was no more difficult, and it eliminated two dangerous crossings of stock and wagons over the North Platte River. On page 111 is a map prepared especially for this book by Reg Duffin. His text, on page 110, briefly covers the multiplicity of sites in the area, and has been slightly edited. For more detail, see Haines' *Historic Sites Along the Oregon Trail.*

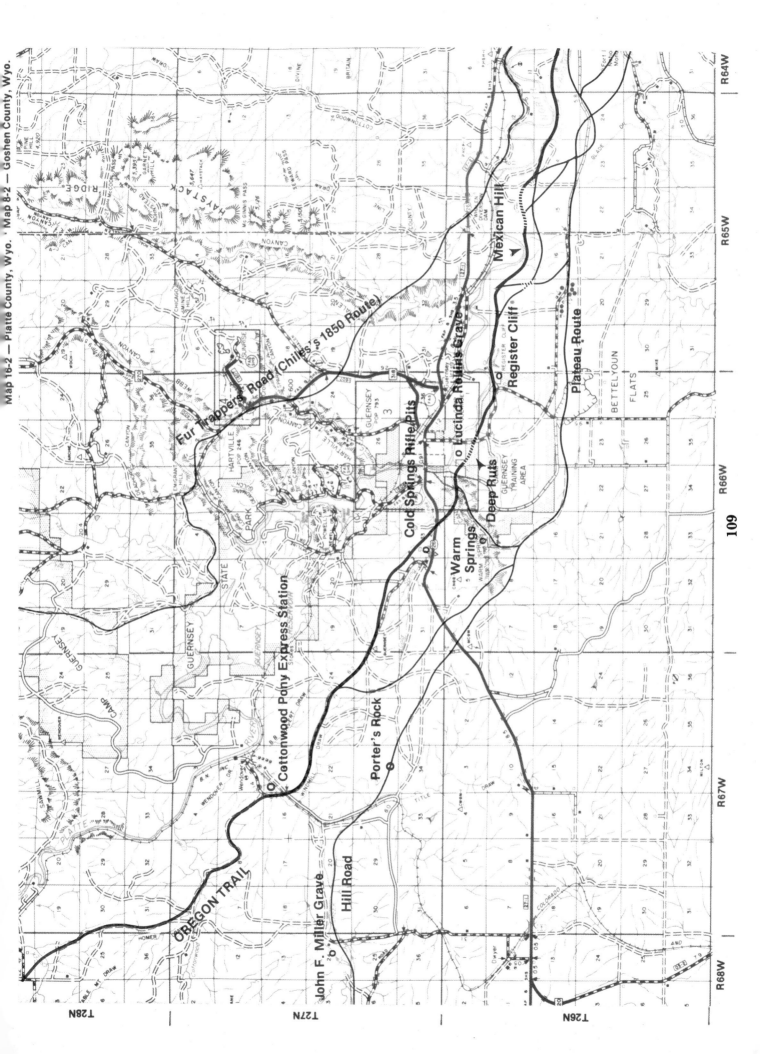

Map 16-2 — Platte County, Wyo. · Map 8-2 — Goshen County, Wyo.

Fur Trappers Road (Chiles's 1850 Route)

Mexican Hill

Lucinda Rollins Grave

Register Cliff

Cold Springs Rifle Pits

Plateau Route

Deep Ruts

Warm
Springs

Cottonwood Pony Express Station

Porter's Rock

OREGON TRAIL

John F. Miller Grave

Hill Road

T28N

T27N

T26N

R68W

R67W

R66W

R65W

R64W

OREGON TRAIL AND RELATED SITES IN VICINITY OF GUERNSEY, WYOMING (Map by Reg P. Duffin, 1982)

Key: 1 — Highway 26 Rest Area. Wooden posts with eye alignment holes locate Oregon Trail landmarks southeast of Guernsey. The Mexican Hill alignment was incorrect as of 1981. 2 — Register Cliff and unknown graves. The site is well marked from Guernsey. 3 — Sand Point Stage and Pony Express Marker. The old Sand Point Trading Post here was operated by Ward and Guerrier in the 1840s. The stage station was operated by Jules E. Coffee in the 1850s. 4 — Deep Wagon Ruts in Sandstone. This is a National Historic Landmark. The site is well-marked from Guernsey. A small parking area and access pathway is provided. 5 — Monument and gravesite of Lucinda Rollins, from Ohio, who died June 11, 1849 at the age of 24. The original headstone has been removed from the niche and destroyed by vandals. 6 — Lower wagon road from Fort Laramie. 7 — Warm Springs. Often described as Emigrants Wash or Laundry Tub, the spring gushes in a constant volume from a limestone rock. Southwest from the spring across the extent of the draw, on a small level mesa at the foot of the bluffs, is an unidentified pioneer grave marked by an elongated stone pattern with metal stakes both head and foot. Paul Henderson observed six old graves here in 1927, all but one of which have since washed away. 8 — Cluster of probable early emigrant graves is visible on the sandstone bluffs. 10 — Two steel stakes mark the grave of Solomon Dill of St. Joseph, Missouri, who died here on June 20, 1850. [It was Duffin himself who identified this one.] 11 — Cold Springs and Rifle Pit Hill. A Highway 26 marker locates this site. 12 — An Oregon Trail marker which was placed by Ezra Meeker. 13 — Graves of Hauphoff children. This was an early area pioneer family. The site is atop the hill east of the road as it descends to the railroad crossing. (Not trail related.) 14 — Oregon Trail Marker. This is immediately south of the railroad tracks. The marker was donated and placed by the Rice family and the Colorado and Southern Railway. The Oregon Trail may be seen descending the hill from the south. 15 — Approximate site of the Old Bitter Cottonwood Stage Station. 16 — Porter's Rock. The Oregon Trail passes both sides of this outcrop of exposed, eroded sandstone. 17 — The John F. Miller grave on the Jerry Cundal Ranch is to the west of Cottonwood Creek crossing. Permission should be obtained prior to a visitation. 18 — Andrew Chiles's 1850 cutoff route proceeds along the north side of the Platte past the upper crossing at Casper. 19 — Emigrant or Mormon Hill. There is an unidentified emigrant grave as a sharp right turn is made at the top of the hill. 20 — Unidentified emigrant grave. 21 — Grave of Elva Ingram. She died June 23, 1852, aged 4 years 6 months (?), from Salem, Iowa. This is the original headstone.

OREGON TRAIL HISTORIC SITES
GUERNSEY WYOMING

To Fort Laramie

To Fort Laramie

Hartville

Sunrise

T 27 N

318

18

Guernsey

RIVER

19

20

21

GUERNSEY STATE PARK

PLATTE

1

2

3

4

5

6

7

8

9

10

11

33

12

NORTH

Wendover

13

14

15

16

17

Creek

Cottonwood

Dwyer

26

R 66 W

R 67 W

N

To I-25 ▼ 5·5 MIs

R.P.D. 83.

111

112

There are some fine ruts on Chiles's Route east of the Glendo Reservoir but they are on private land. Get permission first. Troy and Billie Gray found another nice stretch of ruts leading toward the Elkhorn Station.

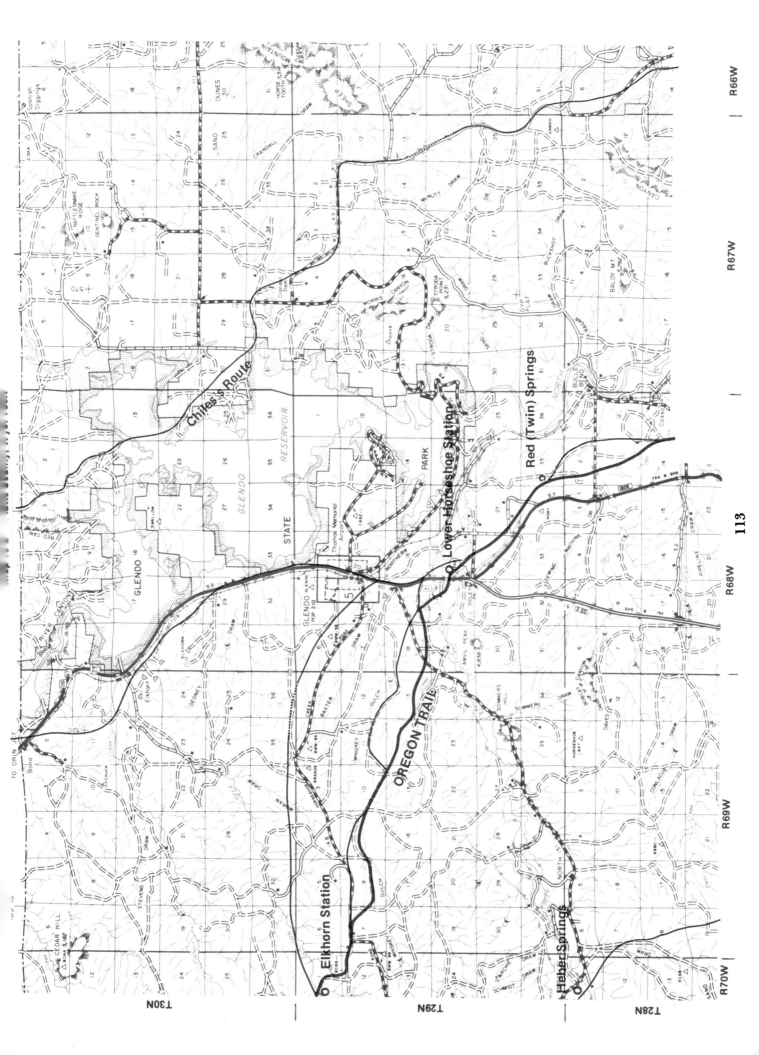

Paul Henderson searched with all his literary and field skills but failed to find proof of the site of the LaBonte Cabin. It is believed to be within 100 feet or so of this site but to date no surface evidence has been found. Few diarists failed to note their arrival in the "red earth country," characteristic of Wyoming's "Black Hills," as they were known in the 1840s and 1850s.

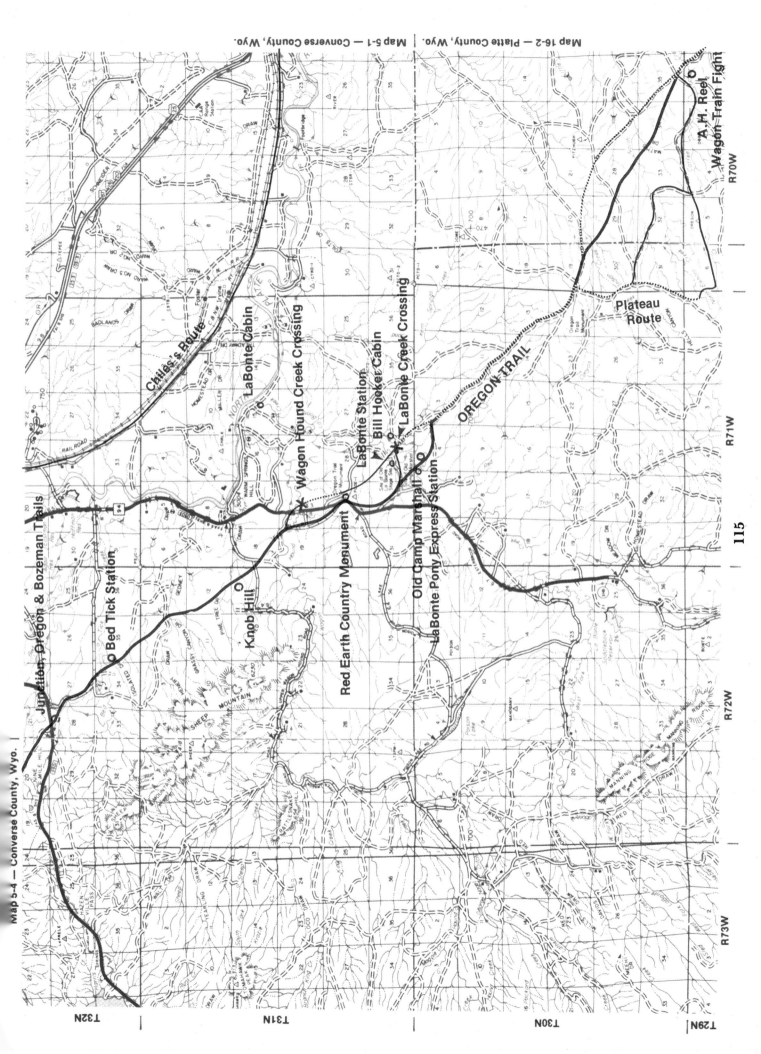

Map 16-2 — Platte County, Wyo. | Map 5-1 — Converse County, Wyo.

Map 5-4 — Converse County, Wyo.

Junction, Oregon & Bozeman Trails

Bed Tick Station

Knob Hill

Red Earth Country Monument

Old Camp Marshall

LaBonte Pony Express Station

Callas's Route

LaBonte Cabin

Wagon Hound Creek Crossing

LaBonte Station

Bill Hooker Cabin

LaBonte Creek Crossing

OREGON TRAIL

Plateau Route

A.H. Reel

Wagon Train Fight

T32N

T31N

T30N

T29N

R73W

R72W

R71W

R70W

115

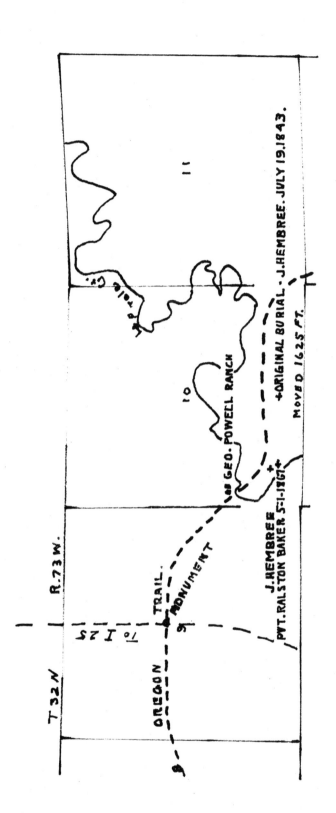

Henderson sketched this little map in three colors for the author in 1971. Each square is one mile. He directed the party which exhumed the skeleton of little Joel Hembree from its bureau-drawer coffin and moved the grave to higher ground, safe from later impoundment of the original site. A.H. Unthank, who had scratched his name in Register Cliff about a week earlier, met his demise here. His gravemarkers are in good condition, but the center letters of his autograph on Register Cliff have washed away. At this point there began a proliferation of bridges and ferries designed to carry the vast south bank emigration over and away from the North Platte. Reg Duffin says the so-called "Mary Kelly Grave," also holds the bodies of Messrs. Sharp, Taylor and Franklin, all of whom died July 12, 1864, as well as Mary Kelly, who died the following day. Duffin believes the graves have been moved, due to the inundation of the site a mile to the northwest, where these emigrants were killed by Sioux Indians.

Map 5-4 — Converse County, Wyo.

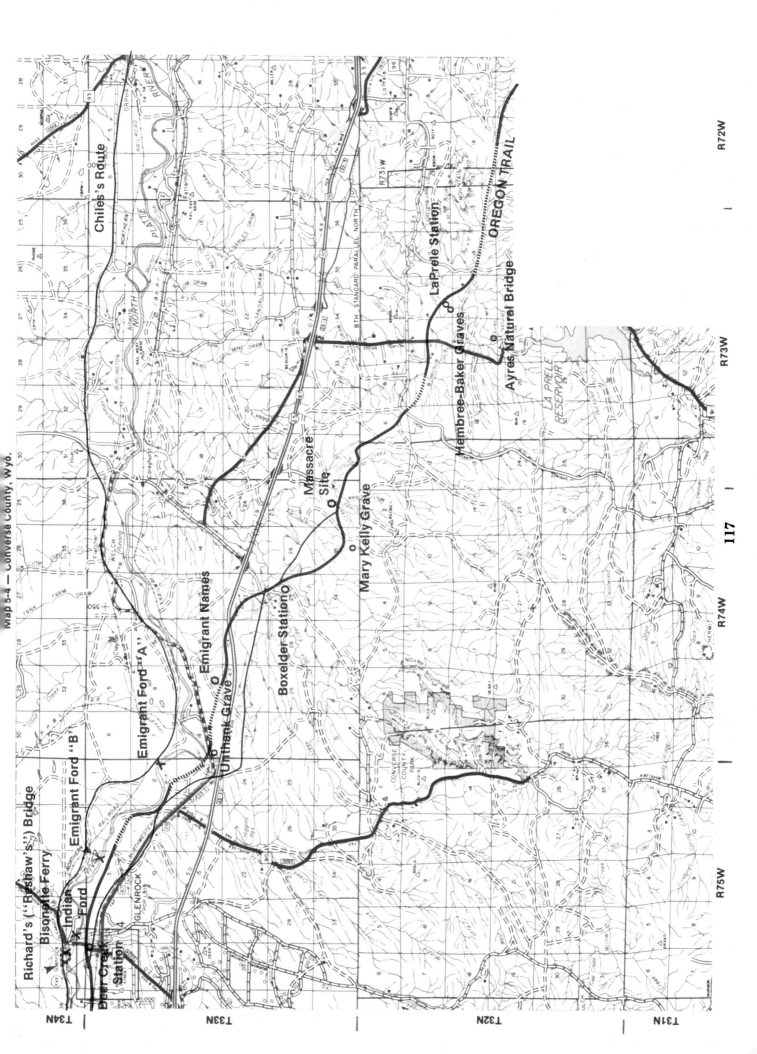

Chiles's Route

OREGON TRAIL

LaPrele Station

Hembree-Baker Graves

Ayres Natural Bridge

LA PRELE RESERVOIR

Massacre Site

Mary Kelly Grave

Emigrant Names

Boxelder Station

Emigrant Ford "A"

Emigrant Ford "B"

Unthank Grave

Richard's ("Reshaw's") Bridge

Bisonette Ferry

Indian Ford

Deer Creek Station

GLENROCK

R72W

R73W

R74W

R75W

117

T34N

T33N

T32N

T31N

118

The caravans traveled side by side on this stretch nearing present-day Casper, separated only by the North Platte River. Some of the south bank travelers had forded by this time; most had not.

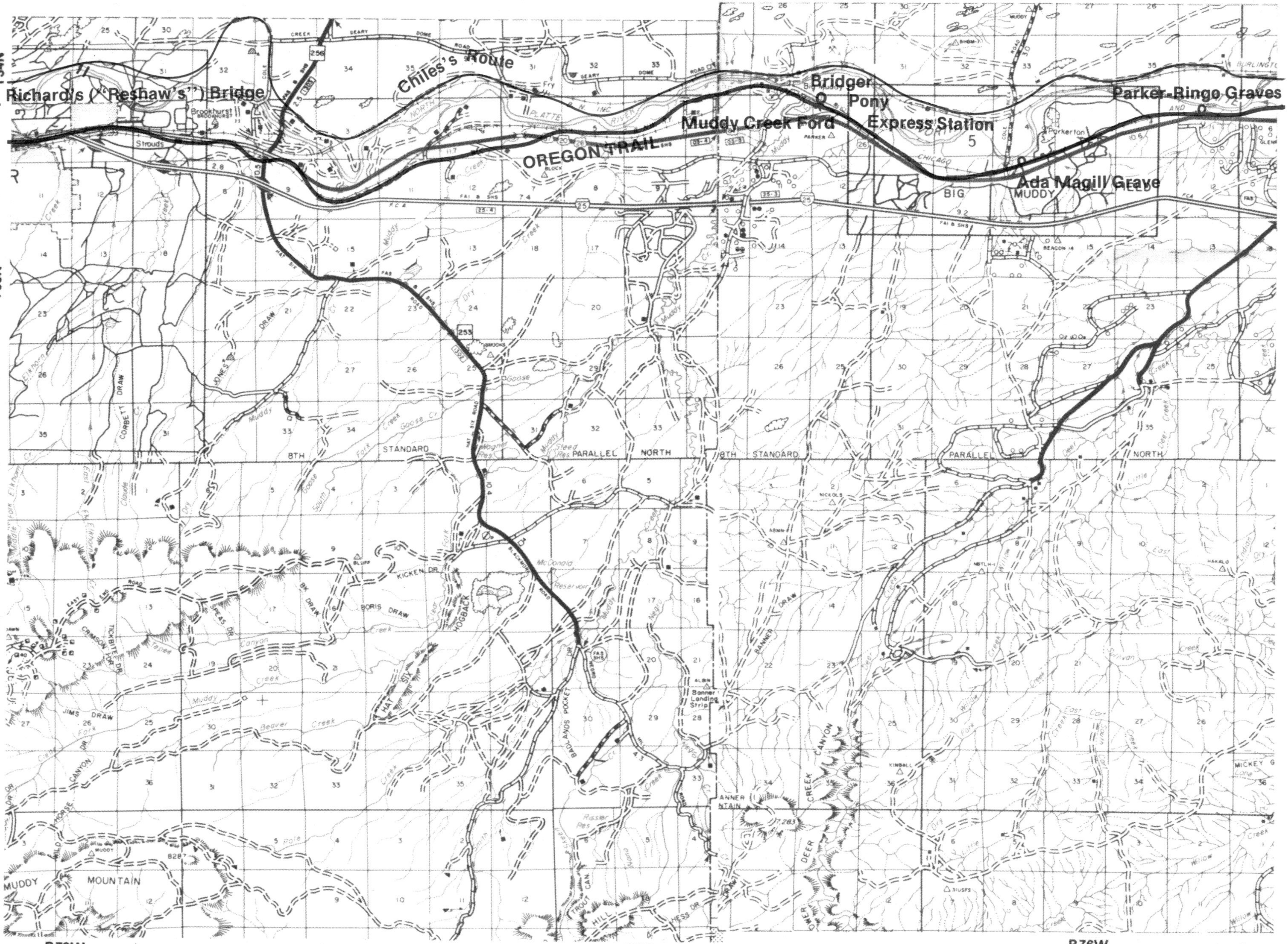

Map 13-5 — Natrona County, Wyo. • Wyo. • Map 5-4 — Converse County, Wyo.

Parker-Ringo Graves

Ada Magill Grave

Bridger Pony Express Station

Muddy Creek Ford

OREGON TRAIL

Chiles's Route

Richards' (Reshaw's) Bridge

R76W

R77W

R78W

R79W

T34N

T33N

T32N

T31N

119

Using his leather boat, *Revenue Cutter*, Brigham Young established a ferry in this area during his pioneer trek to found Salt Lake City in 1847. The ferry site probably is within the city limits of Casper but the exact location has yet to be found and probably never will be. The Mormons continued ferry service at different locations in later years. Most of the emigrants crossed somewhere in the Casper area and headed down the Poison Spider Route via Emigrant Gap. In the 1970s, Rock Avenue was almost totally destroyed, including miles of pristine ruts, by pipeline builders.

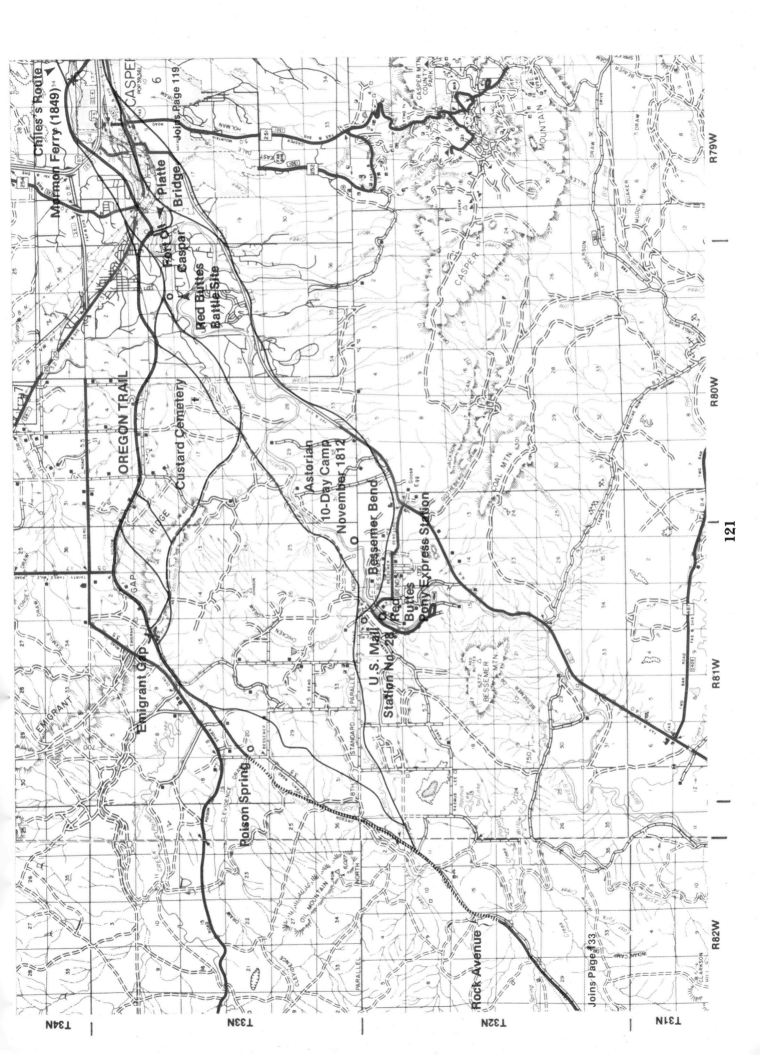

Chiles's Route (1849)

Mormon Ferry

CASPER

Platte
Bridge

Fort Caspar

Red Buttes
Battle Site

OREGON TRAIL

Custard Cemetery

RIDGE

Astorian
10-Day Camp
November 1812

GAP

Bessemer Bend

Pony Express Station

U.S. Mail
Station No. 28

Red Buttes

Emigrant Gap

Poison Spring

Rock Avenue

CASPER MTN.
COUNTY
PARK

CASPER

MOUNTAIN

R79W

R80W

R81W

R82W

T34N

T33N

T32N

T31N

121

The route of the trail through Casper has been extrapolated from small scale maps and may be off in places by as much as two or three city blocks. The site of Richard's ("Reshaw's") Bridge, however, is right on the money.

Chiles's Route

Richard's (Reshaw's) Bridge 1853-1865

RIVER

VANSVILLE
Population 832

Texas Oil Company

White Eagle Oil Company

OREGON TRAIL

TO DOUGLAS

Johns Page 125

123

The Mormon Ferry shown here is the 1849 version and probably had more use than all others combined. The location has been verified by scholars with abundant surface evidence.

Chiles's Route

Mormon Ferry

NORTH

OREGON TRAIL

(Poison Spider Route)

Bessemer Bend Route

Sewage Treatment Plant

125

City of Casper, Wyo.

Poison Spider Route

Bessemer Bend Route

Standard Oil Company Refinery

127

128

Equally spaced mounds are positioned in a line between Fort Caspar and the North Platte River. In the mounds is the rock formerly enclosed by the cribs which held the approaches to the Platte Bridge. The bridge and its cribwork burned in 1867, after serving the post and the emigrants for eight years. Fort Caspar did not figure significantly in the emigration, but the reconstruction is a good one and lots of fun to visit.

City of Casper, Wyo.

130

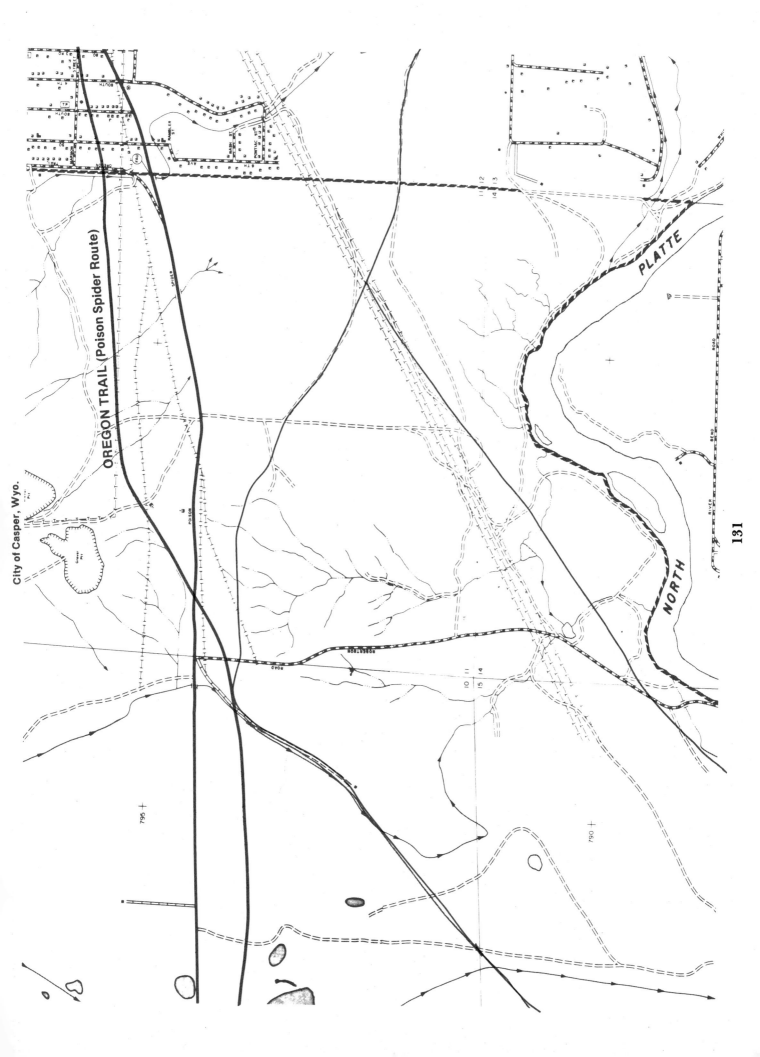

City of Casper, Wyo.

OREGON TRAIL (Poison Spider Route)

PLATTE

NORTH

131

132

The alkali pools in this bitter desert were terrible things, and the emigrants had to club their cattle to keep them away from the tantalizing waters. Willow Spring, the first pure water after a long day's march, was a welcome sight. It still flows. There followed a tough pull up Prospect Hill and a superb view of the desolation on all sides. About 1½ miles north of the point where the trail crosses Highway 220, the Martin Handcart Company was marooned by an early snowstorm, in November 1856. They were able to move ahead to the place known now as Martin's Cove, west of Devil's Gate, and faced even greater hardship there.

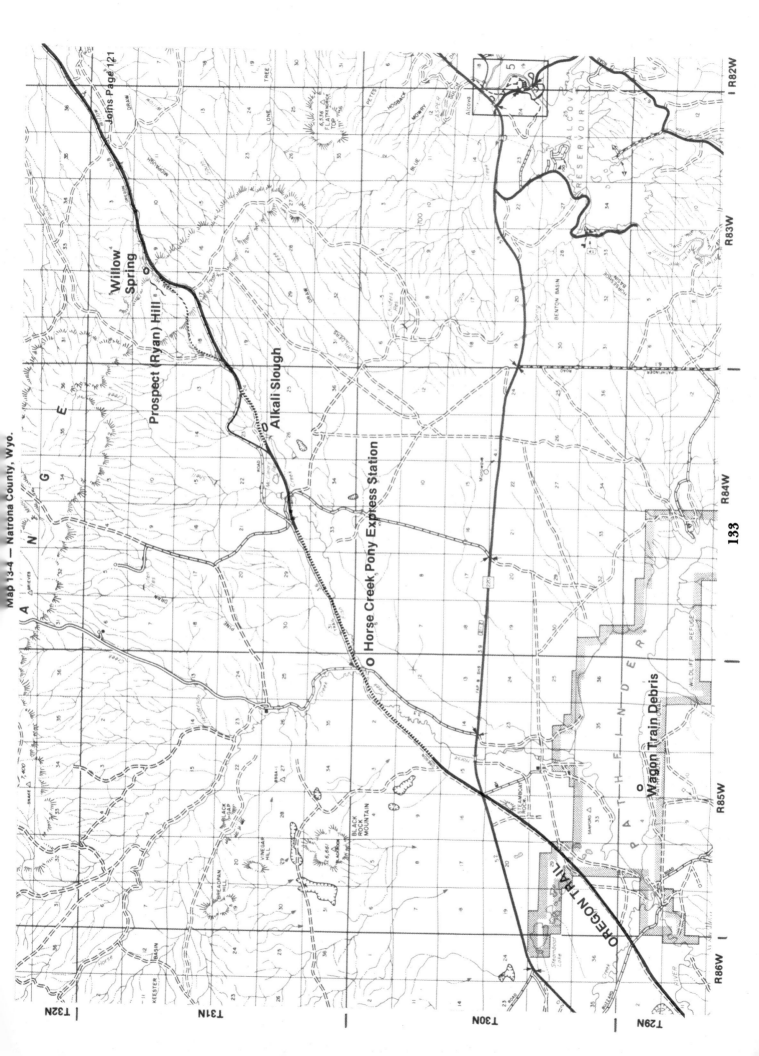

Map 13-4 — Natrona County, Wyo.

Joins Page 121

Willow Spring

Prospect (Ryan) Hill

Alkali Slough

O Horse Creek Pony Express Station

Wagon Train Debris

OREGON TRAIL

133

R82W

R83W

R84W

R85W

R86W

T32N

T31N

T30N

T29N

Emigrants figured that if they came to Independence Rock by the Fourth of July they would get the rest of the way without being trapped in snow. That was true. They also thought they were halfway to Oregon here, but they still were well short of that mark. Aubrey Haines makes a good case for locating Martin's Cove a mile west of where the mapmakers think it is, but Reg Duffin, Troy and Billie Gray are convinced that it bears 030 degrees from the marker. Split Rock (see map on next page) was in view as soon as the trail rounded Devil's Gate. On this page the South Pass Hiking Segment begins. It should be emphasized that, although many individuals have hiked portions of this 125-mile segment and a few have gone all the way, it does cross private land in many places. There is practically no habitation along the way. Permission should be asked in advance when crossing private property. The ruts for most of the way are absolutely pristine, but Merle Wells notes that some of the route in the vicinity of Soda Lake has been improved. Hiking or driving in the ruts will help keep vegetation down. The Oregon Trail crosses the Sweetwater nine times, so a pair of waders would come in handy for any hiker.

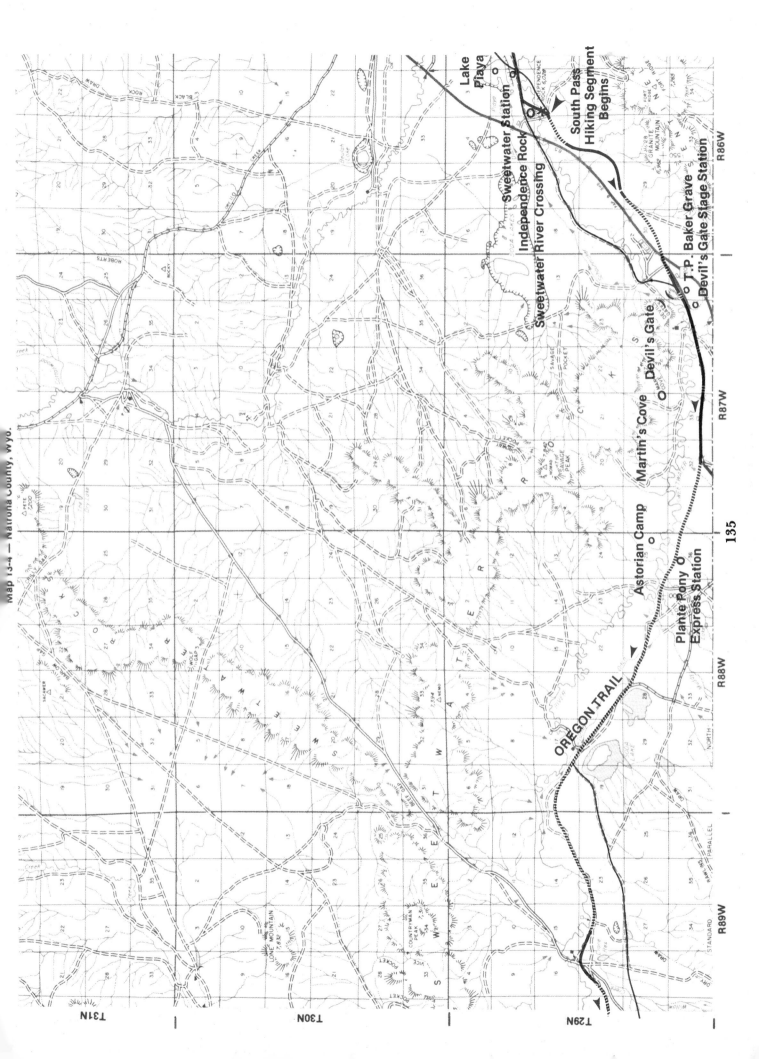

Map 13-4 — Natrona County, Wyo.

Lake
Playa

Sweetwater Station

Independence Rock

Sweetwater River Crossing

South Pass
Hiking Segment
Begins

J.P. Baker Grave

Devil's Gate Stage Station

Devil's Gate

Martin's Cove

Astorian Camp

 OREGON TRAIL

Plante Pony
Express Station

135

R86W

R87W

R88W

R89W

T31N

T30N

T29N

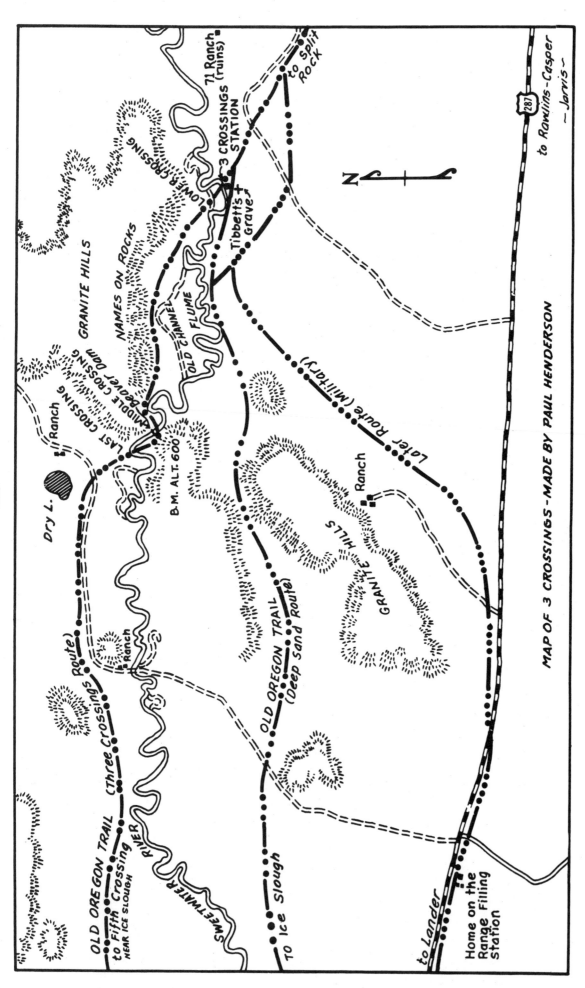

MAP OF 3 CROSSINGS – MADE BY PAUL HENDERSON

Paul Henderson made this map in the 1930s, a generation before the uranium company set up in Jeffrey City, which is now at the site of the "Home on the Range Filling Station." Western Nuclear Company and the Bureau of Land Management own all the land around here. A hike through the area must start with permission from Western Nuclear. Tailings from the firm's plant, two miles west of the last of the Three Crossings, already block portions of the Deep Sand Route. Reg Duffin notes that the BLM has installed an interpretive Split Rock overlook on Highway 220, just west of the Fremont County line. He also notes that the grave of Bennett Tribbetts (also spelled Triplett, Tribbett), a soldier who was killed in April 1862, is across the ruts south from the site of the Three Crossings Stage Station. There are a number of names remaining on Names Cliff.

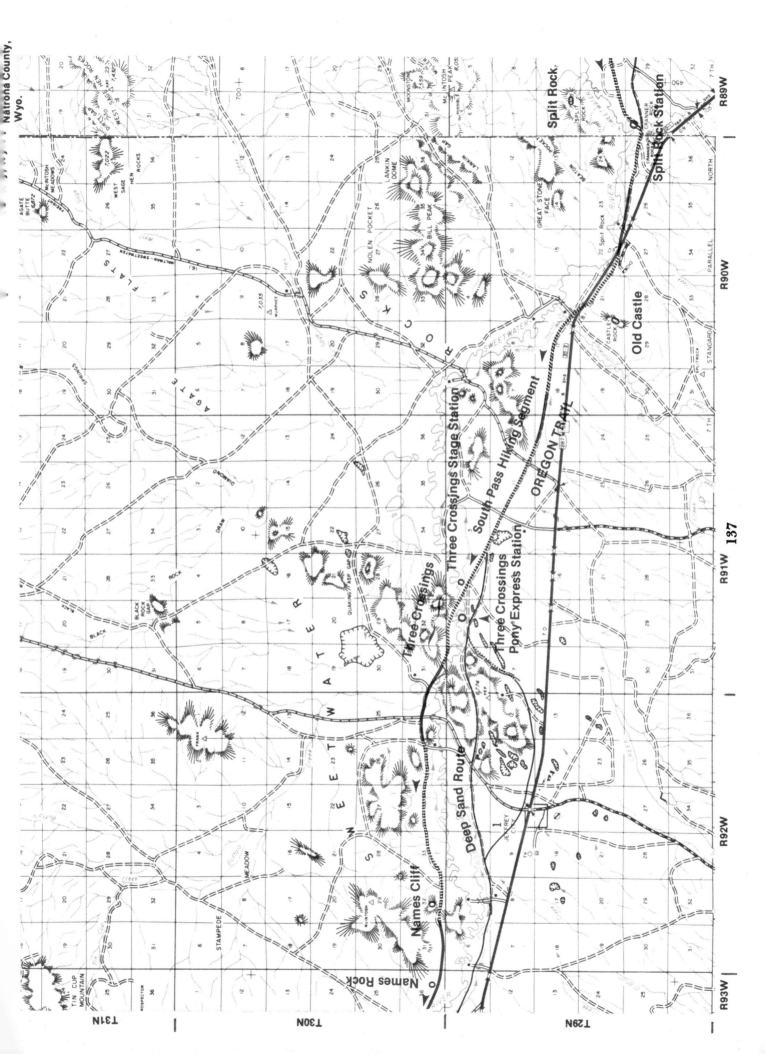

Split Rock,

Split Rock Station

Old Castle

OREGON TRAIL

South Pass Hiking Segment

Three Crossings Stage Station

Three Crossings

Three Crossings
Pony Express Station

Deep Sand Route

Names Cliff

Names Rock

R89W

R90W

R91W

R92W

R93W

T31N

T30N

T29N

A piece of private land must be crossed to reach Ice Spring, but the Ice Slough is right on the public road. In the slough, ice still may be found in the springtime, but not in the summer. Most of the way west from here is BLM property, and as such the hiking segment may be negotiated without obtaining permission.

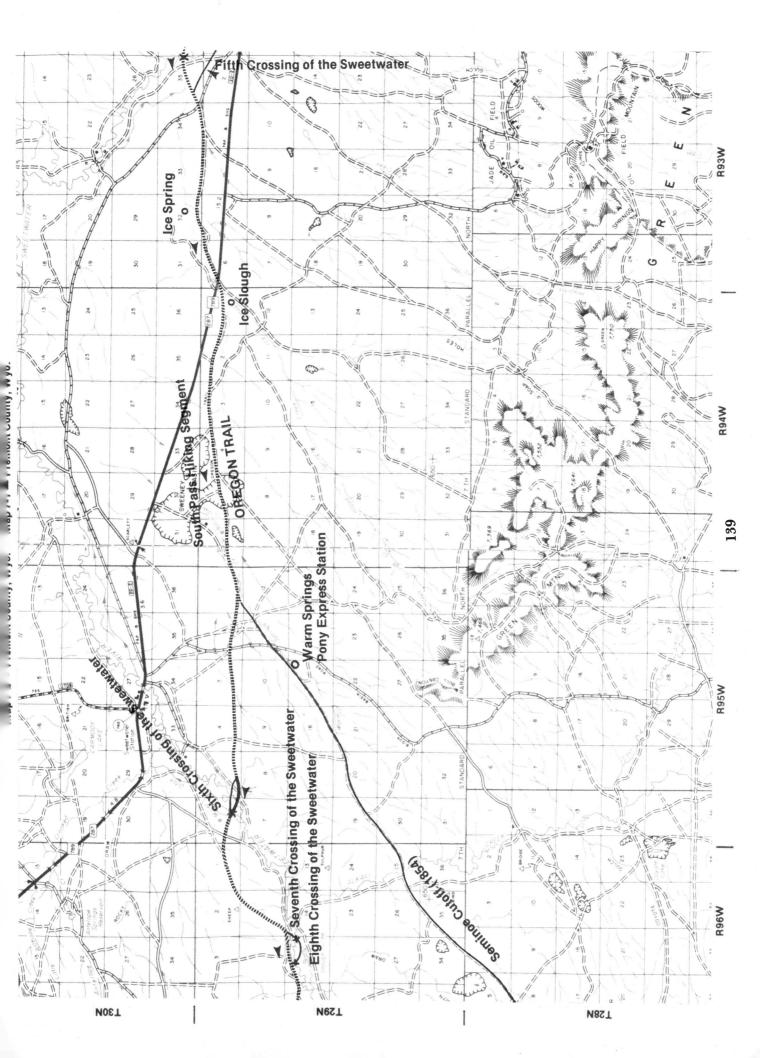

Fifth Crossing of the Sweetwater

Ice Spring

Ice Slough

South Pass Hiking Segment

OREGON TRAIL

Warm Springs
Pony Express Station

Fifth Crossing of the Sweetwater

Sixth Crossing of the Sweetwater

Seventh Crossing of the Sweetwater

Eighth Crossing of the Sweetwater

Seminoe Cutoff (1854)

GREEN

139

R93W
R94W
R95W
R96W

T30N
T29N
T28N

There is a magnificent view of the trail to the east and to the west from the summit of the desolate Rocky Ridge. It is a godawful place to reach and should not be attempted except on foot. Most 4x4 drivers won't touch it. "The Meadows," the area from Rocky Ridge to Strawberry Creek, is private land. A number of spring creeks flow over the trail and ranchers should be consulted before penetrating the region, even with a 4x4. The Willie's monument, on the bank of Rock Creek, is often mistaken for a cemetery. Members of the ill-fated handcart company who perished here were simply buried in the deep snow. The survivors had no choice. Some of the route in the vicinity of St. Mary's Station is on private land.

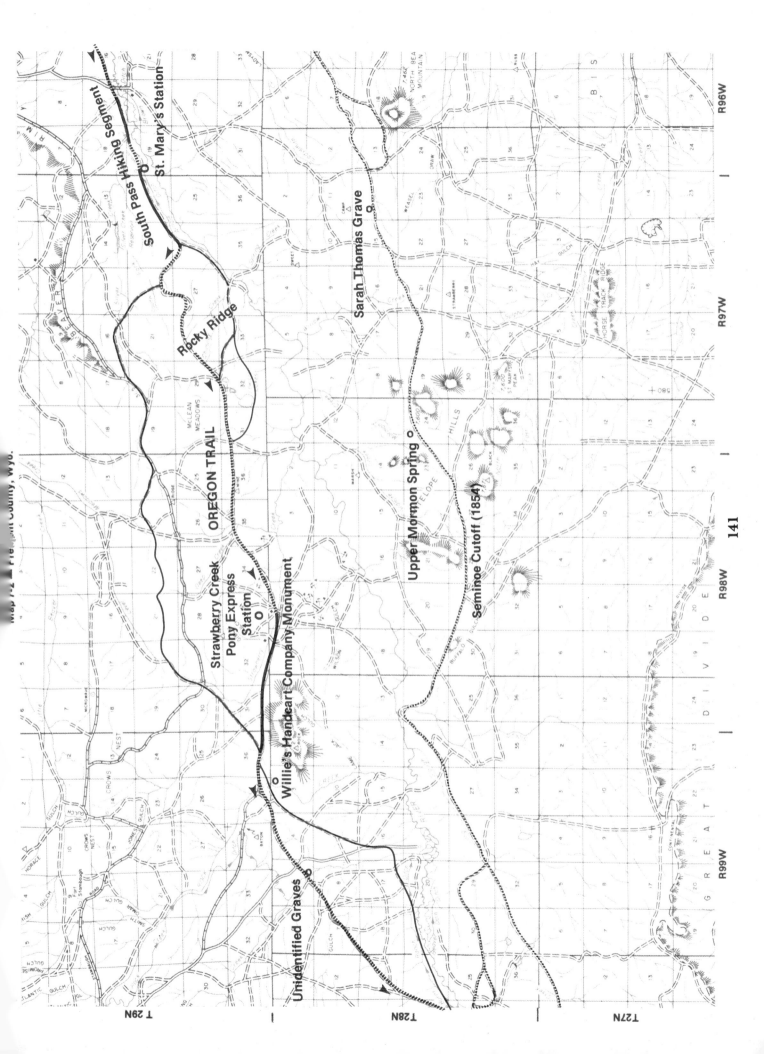

Map 112 ▲ Fremont County, Wyo.

South Pass Hiking Segment

St. Mary's Station

Rocky Ridge

OREGON TRAIL

Sarah Thomas Grave

Strawberry Creek
Pony Express Station

Willie's Handcart Company Monument

Upper Mormon Spring

Seminoe Cutoff (1854)

Unidentified Graves

141

R96W

R97W

R98W

R99W

T29N

T28N

T27N

142

The Burnt Ranch is on private land. The primitive buildings on the site are in deplorable shape, but they are watched by the owner, who is trying to keep vandalism down. Trespassing could be a problem. The BLM has marked the trail where it crosses public land. Troy Gray feels the Lander Road of 1857 was the best of all, but far too late to do much good. It is incorrectly marked on the highway map. Reg Duffin has driven from Highway 28 to the Oregon Trail marker (not shown) at the west end of the dotted line, but is unsure of other ruts east or west of that segment. There is a Lander Road marker on the southeast corner of its intersection with Highway 28. Although this highway map is much superior to earlier versions, it is still best to follow the directions to South Pass exactly as they appear in *The Oregon Trail Revisited*. Visitors may drive to Pacific Springs in a few minutes, but as it is only two miles away, it's lots more fun to walk. A tour of restored South Pass City is good entertainment for the entire family.

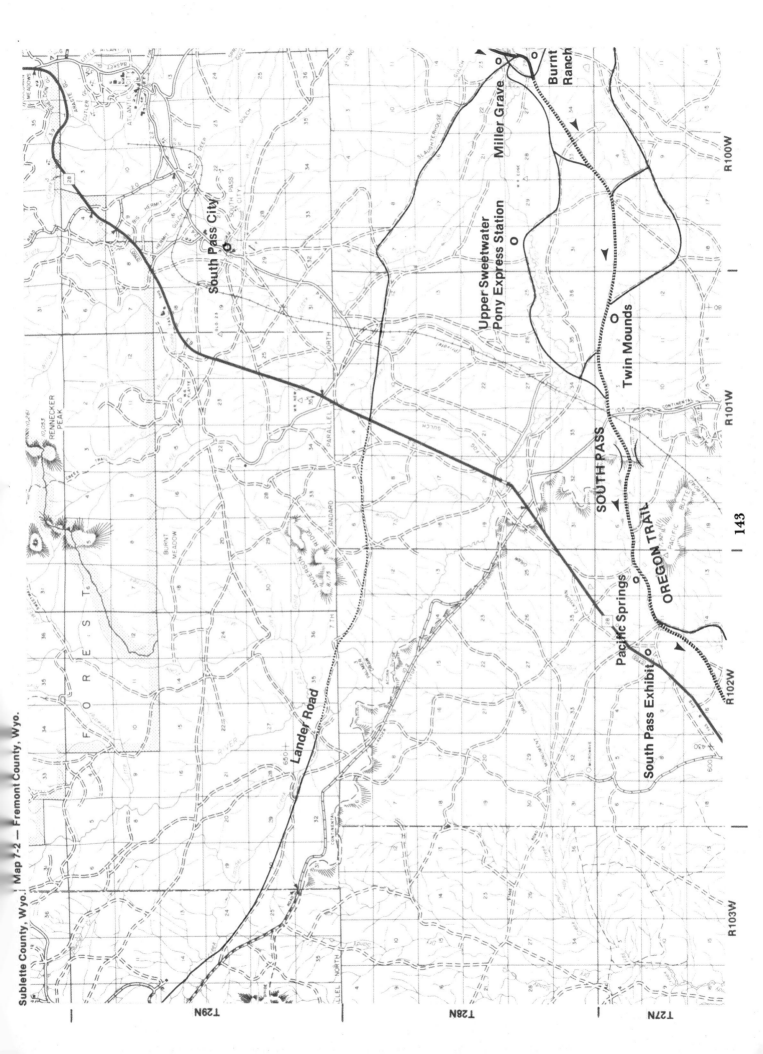

Sublette County, Wyo. | Map 7-2 — Fremont County, Wyo.

143

The False Parting of the Ways still announces that it is the real thing, but the dramatic real parting is still several miles down the line. A short hike (don't try to drive this) from the False Parting turnout will bring the visitor to the Dry Sandy Crossing, where the "wells" dug to provide subsurface water for the 19th century livestock may still be seen. Continue west on Highway 28 for 2.2 miles past the False Parting. Turn right and drive to a good view of the Plume Rocks. They weren't kidding when they named it the "Sandy" — hikers can sink in eight inches or more. It is only another five miles to the true parting, over some badly beat up ruts. They were magnificent just five years ago, but have since been badly damaged by oil company construction equipment. This is an utterly flat sage plain, and at the parting both trails stretch away as far as the eye can see. The rocks placed there by Henderson and Clark Bishop so many years ago are no longer there. The land around the Little Sandy Crossing of the main trail is in private hands, so permission should be gained before crossing it.

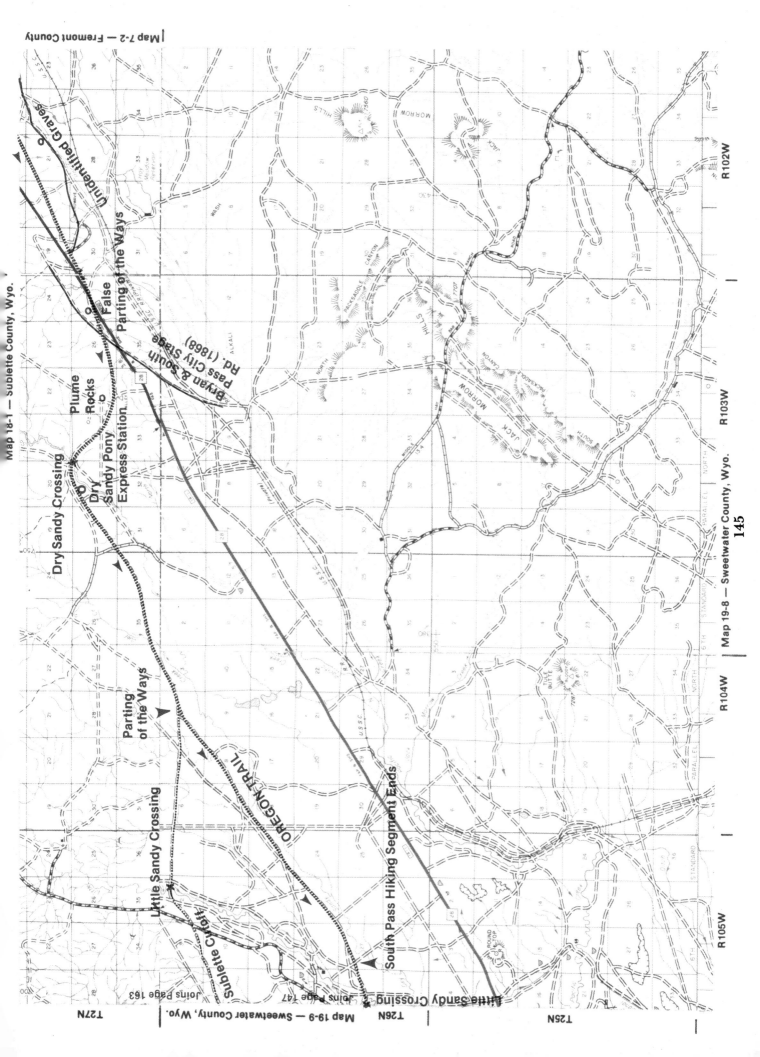

Map 18-1 — Sublette County, Wyo.

Map 7-2 — Fremont County

Undentified Graves

False
Parting of the Ways

Plume
Rocks

Bryan & South
Pass City Stage
Rd. (1868)

Dry Sandy Crossing

Dry
Sandy Pony
Express Station

Parting of the Ways

OREGON TRAIL

Little Sandy Crossing

Sublette Cutoff

South Pass Hiking Segment Ends

Little Sandy Crossing

MORROW

JACK

PACKSADDLE CANYON

NORTH

HILLS

MORROW

JACK

PACKSADDLE CANYON

SOUTH

TULE
BUTTE

ROUND
TOP

Map 19-9 — Sweetwater County, Wyo. | Joins Page 147

Joins Page 163

T27N

T26N

T25N

R105W

R104W

R103W

R102W

Map 19-8 — Sweetwater County, Wyo.

Few stretches of the trail are as bitter as the desert lands southwest of Farson, through which the Fort Bridger trail passed. For much of the way the road, known as the Lower Farson Cutoff, is directly over the route of the Oregon Trail. The Wyoming Department of Transportation has the paving of that road among its priorities. A second Parting of the Ways is at the Little Sandy Crossing and afforded what some travelers believed to be a better route to the Sublette Cutoff.

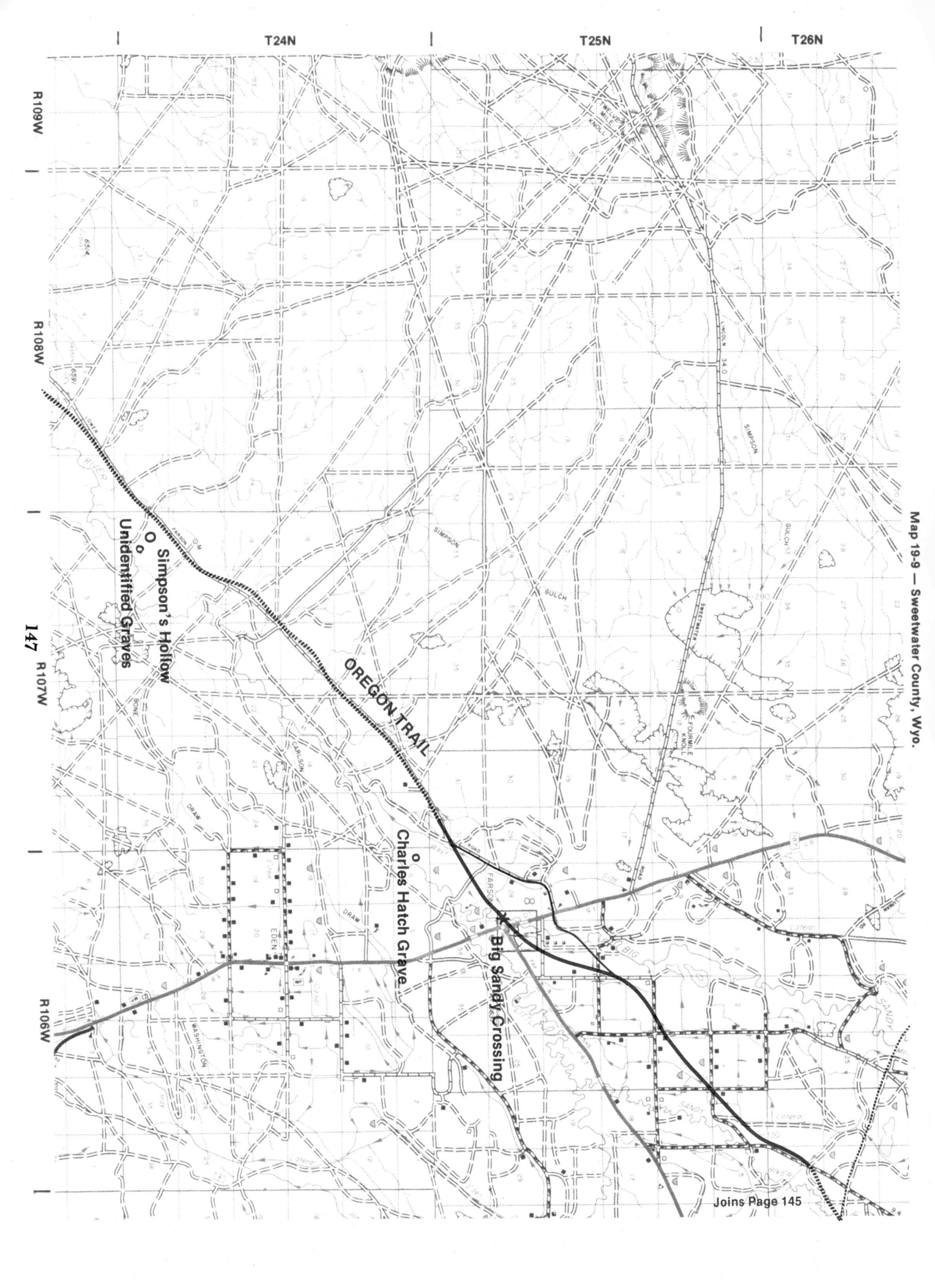

Map 19-9 — Sweetwater County, Wyo.

T24N

T25N

T26N

R109W

R108W

147 R107W

R106W

Simpson's Hollow

Unidentified Graves

OREGON TRAIL

Charles Hatch Grave

Big Sandy Crossing

Joins Page 145

The starting points of the Slate Creek and Kenney cutoffs are often confused. The maps of Paul Henderson and L. Clark Bishop, another veteran trail sleuth, show them this way. The Slate Creek route loops to the north to arrive at the Green River at the site of the old Case Ferry. The Kenney generally follows what is now the Farson Cutoff Road. The last miles of the route to the Lombard Ferry are through the Little Colorado Desert. The first train west, the Bidwell-Bartleson party of 1841, is believed to have crossed at the Lombard site, on July 23. The "Great Migration" of 1843 forded here August 9-11. The troubles of the Sager family began here, when Henry Sager died and was buried on the west bank. Two of his sons were murdered by the Cayuse during the Whitman Massacre in 1847. Brigham Young ferried here with the Mormon Pioneers July 1-4, 1847. The first Mormon handcart company forded here on September 17, 1856. The Willie Handcart Company, which met with disaster during a blizzard east of South Pass, crossed here with their rescuers on November 1 of that year. William Lombard located here in the 1870s to operate the ferry in the declining years of the emigration. The Lombard Buttes are named for him. During the peak migration years there may have been as many as 50 ferries in operation in this area simultaneously. Reg Duffin researched the ferry locations and drew the map on this page. The trail routings are based upon the work of the late Paul Henderson.

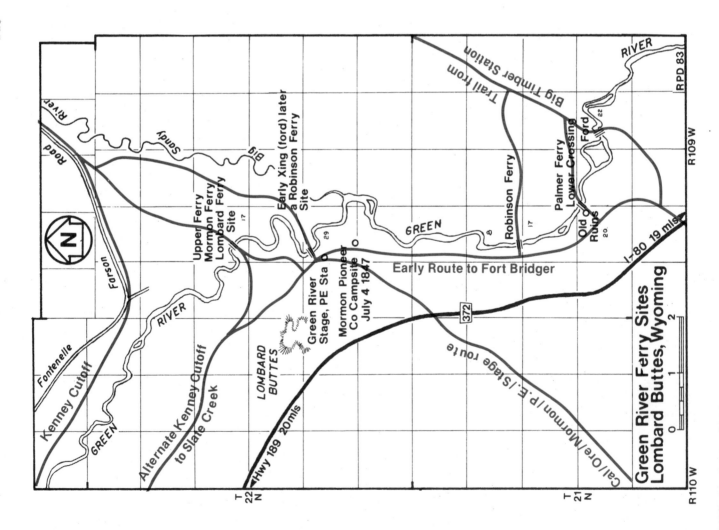

R 110 W

Green River Ferry Sites
Lombard Buttes, Wyoming

Map 19-4 — Sweetwater County, Wyo. | Map 19-9 — Sweetwater County, Wyo.

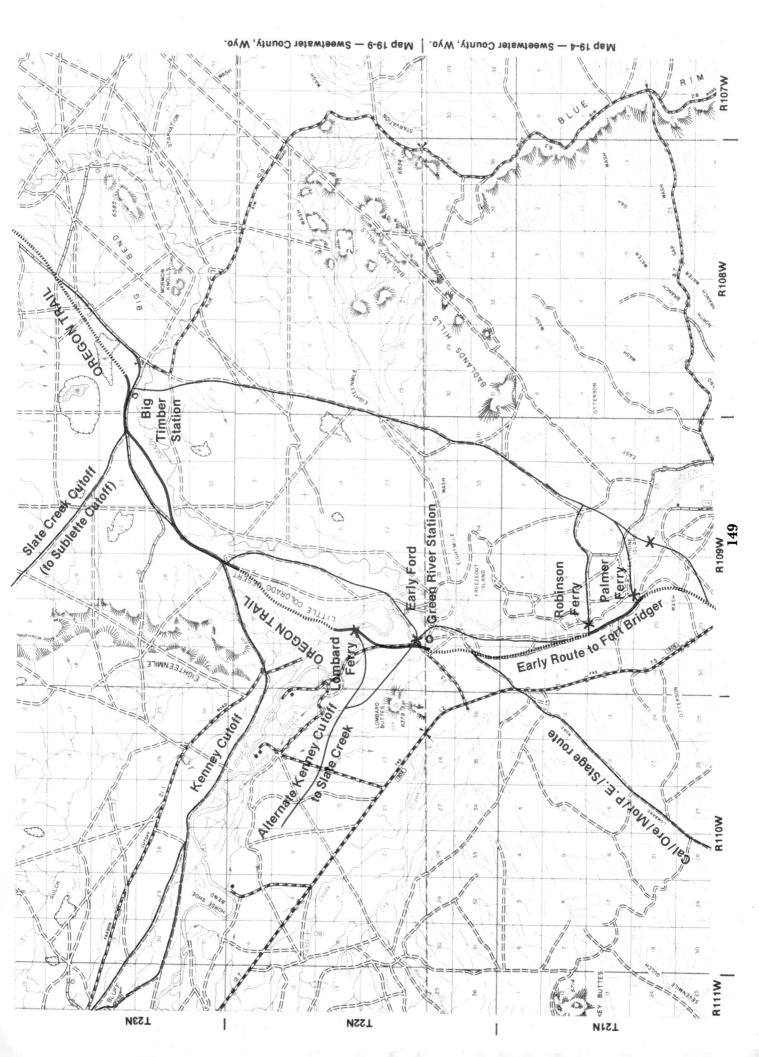

There were frequent creek crossings after leaving the Green, but most of those creeks were dry. That left all the disadvantages, such as steep banks, and none of the advantages. The Blacks Fork (of the Green) was crossed several times enroute to Fort Bridger, and was always aflow with cool, clear water and surrounded by lush grass. There are two Lone Tree Stage Stations shown, the northern site from the maps of Clark Bishop, the other from Paul Henderson. The station may have been destroyed and rebuilt elsewhere, so both could be correct. The Henderson location also includes a trailside cemetery. The Green River Stage Road runs south of Highway 28 from South Pass, then turns due south at a point just south of Farson.

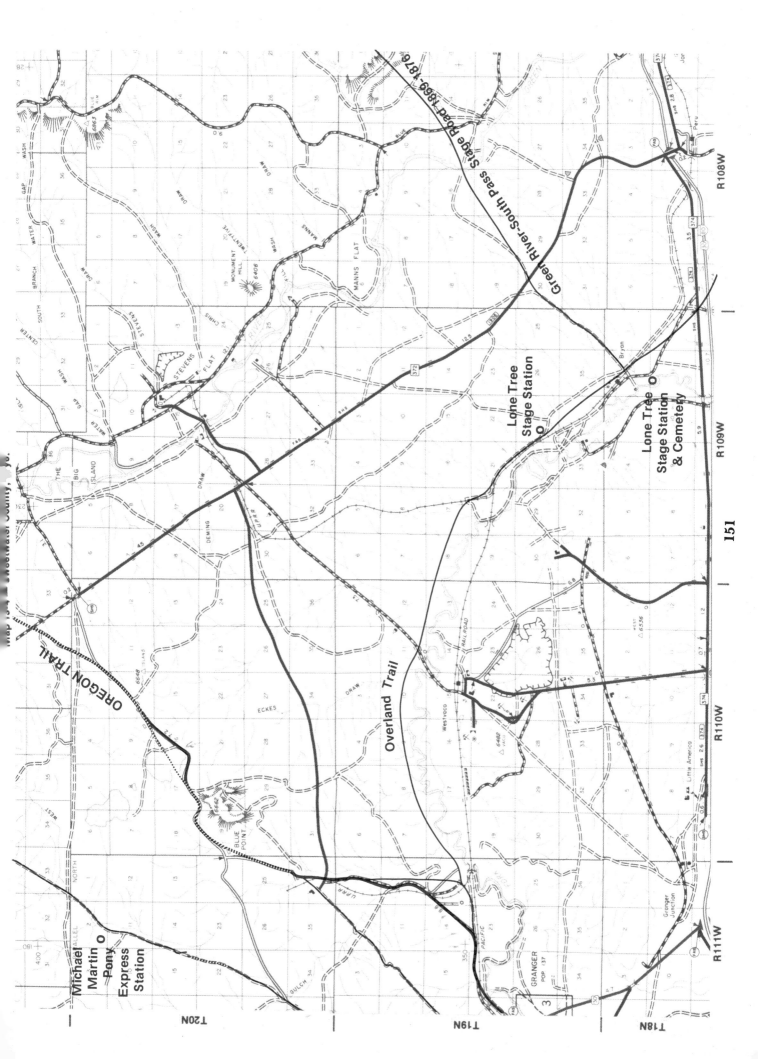

152

Aubrey Haines, in *Historic Sites Along the Oregon Trail*, makes a strong case to the effect that the so-called South Bend Stage Station in Granger is not a stage station at all, but "an incongruous ruin" of a later era. Youngsters on an Oregon Trail vacation will have a wonderful time at Church Butte. It is climbable, but caution is advised. Remnants of what may have been burned wagons have been found right in the trail at the indicated spot. Reg Duffin searched the area in 1981 and was unable to find any evidence.

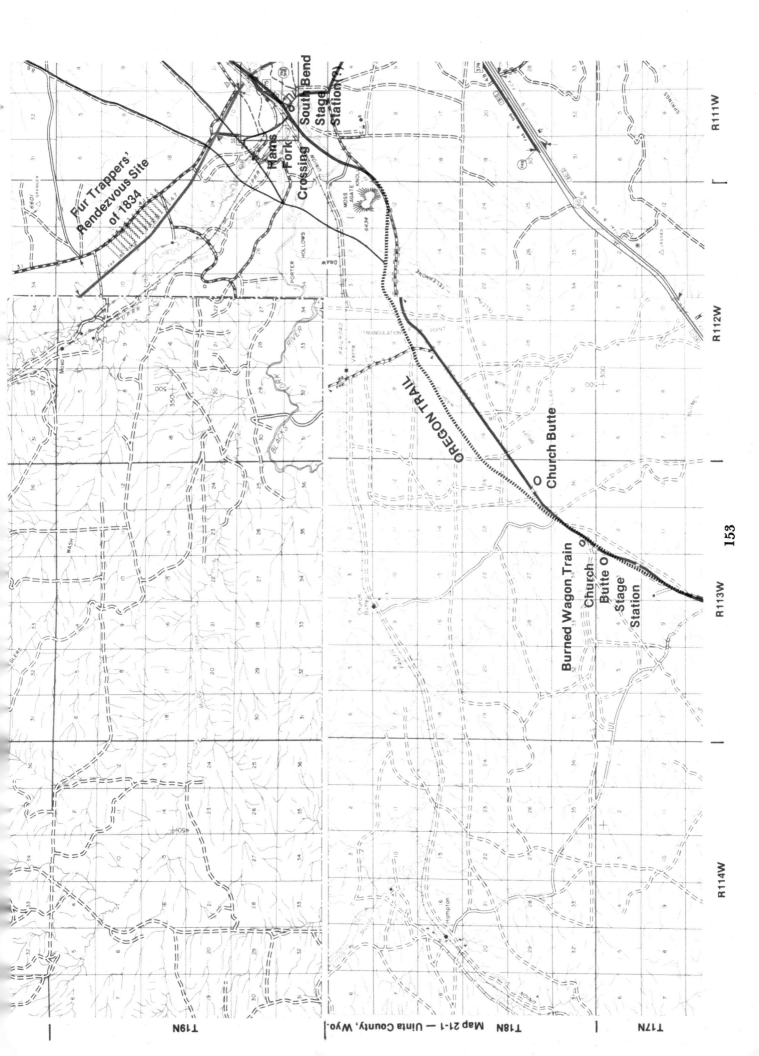

Fur Trappers'
Rendezvous Site
of 1834

Hams
Fork
Crossing

South Bend
Stage
Station

Church Butte

OREGON TRAIL

Burned Wagon Train

Church
Butte
Stage
Station

153

Map 21-1 — Uinta County, Wyo.

R111W
R112W
R113W
R114W

T19N
T18N
T17N

Fort Bridger, built in 1843 as a trading post with a log stockade, was one of the most important points along the Oregon Trail, not only to those bound for Oregon but to Mormons going to the Great Salt Lake. The interpretation on the site is military in nature. The post Bridger knew was burned in 1857 during the "Mormon War", and later was replaced with a military installation, the remains of which are preserved today as a Wyoming Historic Site. Bridger's old ramshackle buildings probably stood in the area behind the present museum, but the site has not yet been confirmed archaeologically.

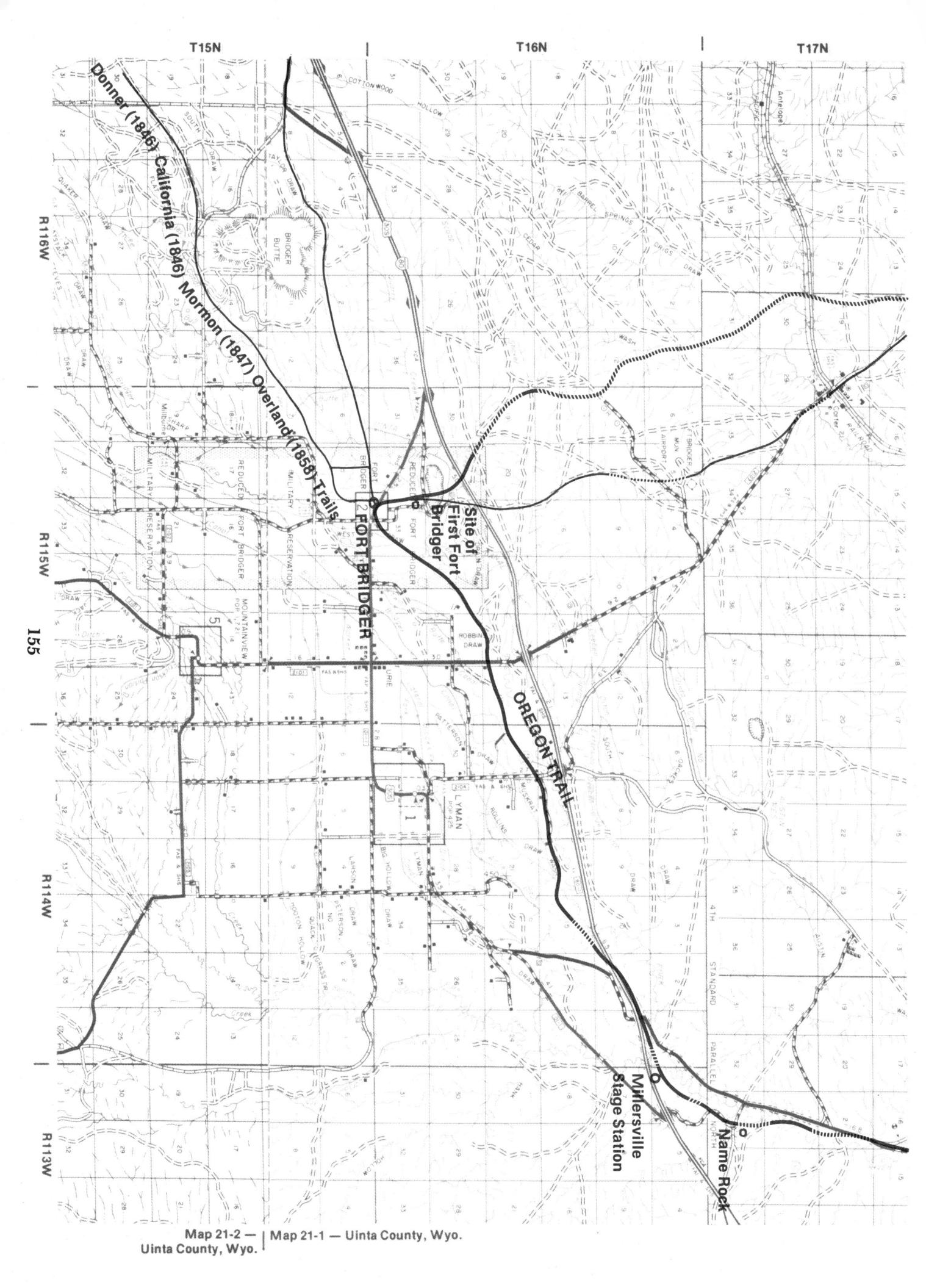

T15N   T16N   T17N

R116W

R115W

155

R114W

R113W

Donner (1846) California (1846) Mormon (1847) Overland (1858) Trails

FORT BRIDGER

Site of First Fort Bridger

OREGON TRAIL

Millersville Stage Station

Name Rock

Map 21-2 — Uinta County, Wyo. | Map 21-1 — Uinta County, Wyo.

156

The Bear River Divide Hiking Segment is 31 miles long and is either on BLM land or on land grant property owned by the Union Pacific Railroad. Some of the stream crossings are too deep even for high-sprung 4x4's. Therefore, the segment should be undertaken only by experienced backpackers, and never alone. About half the distance is in pristine ruts, the balance in ranch roads.

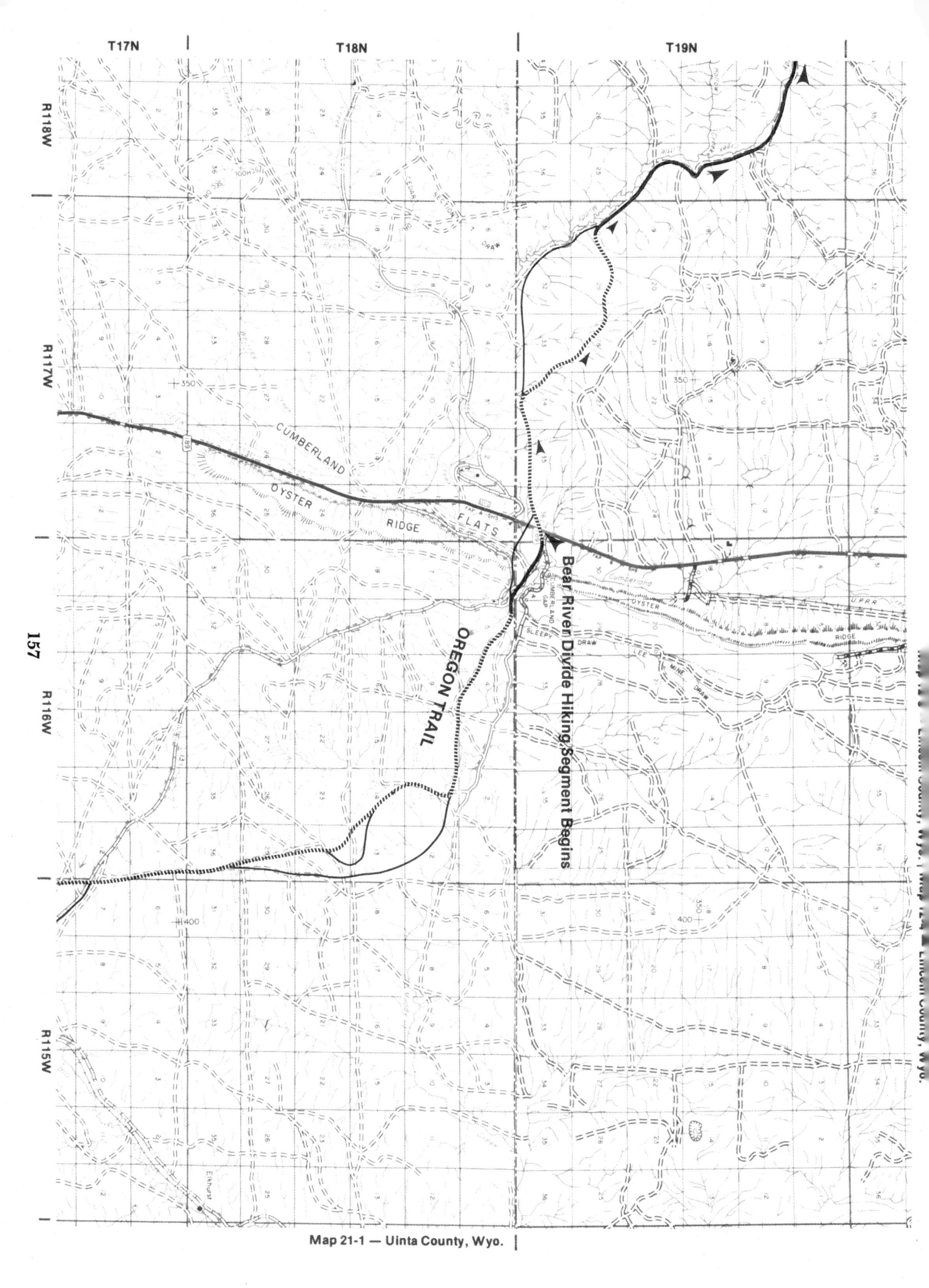

T17N   T18N   T19N

R118W

R117W

157

R116W

R115W

CUMBERLAND

OYSTER

RIDGE   FLATS

OREGON TRAIL

Bear River Divide Hiking Segment Begins

Map 21-1 — Uinta County, Wyo.

Paul Henderson's speculation of the Bear River Divide route is labeled. The "main" route was defined after on-site investigation in 1981. That certainly doesn't mean that Henderson was wrong — both routes could have been traveled heavily.

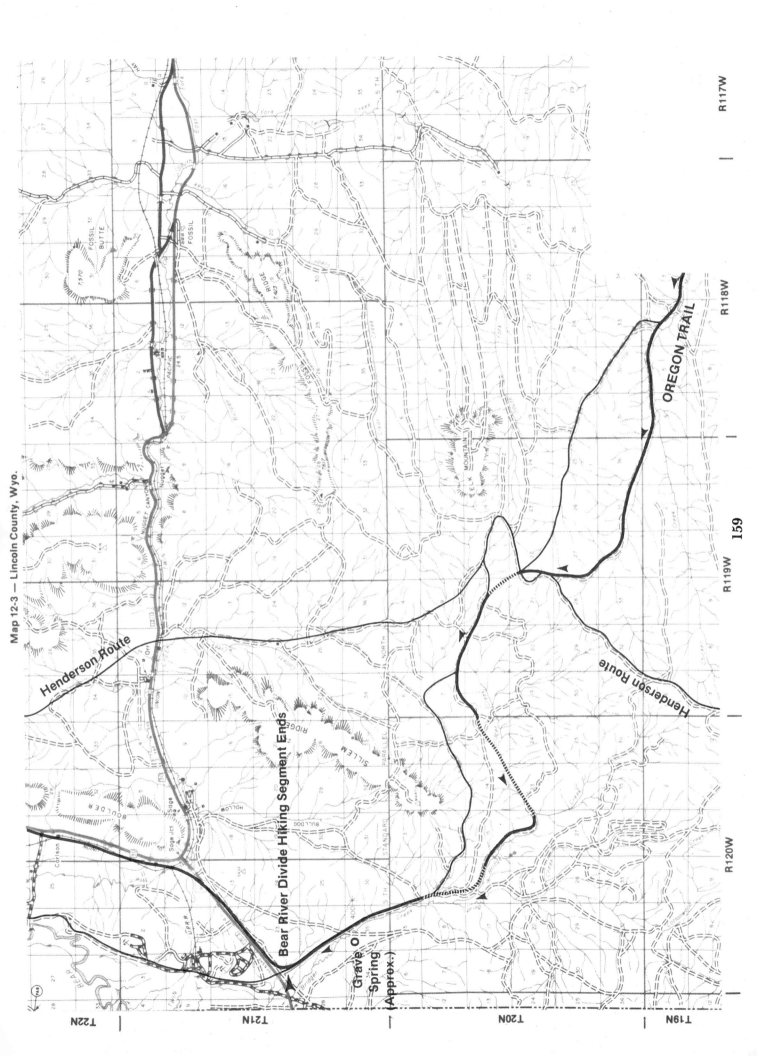

Map 12-3 — Lincoln County, Wyo.

Henderson Route

Henderson Route

OREGON TRAIL

Bear River Divide Hiking Segment Ends

Grave Spring (Approx.)

R120W

R119W

R118W

R117W

159

T22N

T21N

T20N

T19N

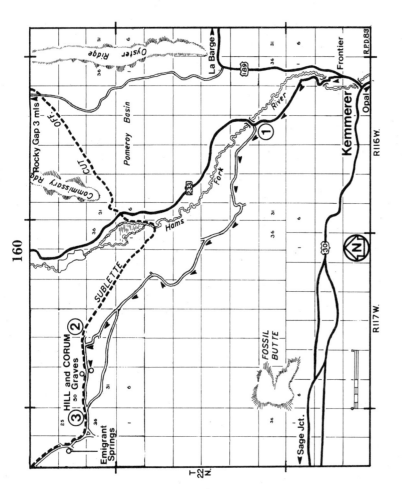

160

Reg Duffin, who drew the access map above, used the first issue of *Overland Journal* to establish that Nancy Hill and Alfred Corum probably do not occupy the graves assigned to them, but in fact are buried two miles to the west, near the western Emigrant Spring. His driving directions: "From Kemmerer drive north on Highway 189 to Frontier. Veer left on Highway 233 and proceed north 3.5 miles. Just before the bridge over the Hamsfork turn hard left at (1). Drive about 11 miles northwest on the county gravel road to (2). Here a concrete post with a bronze medallion marks the Sublette Cutoff. Deep swales are evident here and to the southeast the route can be seen climbing the plateau from Hamsfork crossing. Drive west to the Alfred Corum grave and then another 350 yards to the grave marked for Nancy J. Hill. The map shows these locations as now marked. At (3) is the probable area of the actual Hill and Corum graves. This route is suitable for heavy passenger cars but 4x4's or pickups would be more at home." Since Duffin wrote those lines, a drill pad has been built in the SE¼ of the SE¼, Section 29, about a mile east of the grave sites, and a new all weather road constructed in to it. The new road will take the visitor to the Sublette Cutoff more easily. In the summer of 1983 a bulldozer operator mistakenly ripped out a half mile of the old trail between the new road and the graves. Visitors are

asked to grit their teeth (so the fillings won't jar out) and drive over the ripped-up trace to speed the restoration. Troy and Billie Gray cite the deep ruts ascending the very steep hill at the Hamsfork crossing. There also is an awful hill bringing the Sublette Cutoff down from Dempsey Ridge, where five ruts merge into one. The Grays do their explorations in a ¾-ton pickup truck with high clearance. The Duffins drove the Sublette from the Hill marker to Cokeville in a pickup camper — "Never again!" is their comment. Alice Antilla, a Sublette Cutoff sleuth from Kemmerer, started researching the old trails in the early 1930s. She says the branch leading to the Dempsey from Emigrant Spring went on the east side of the ridge, with a row of trees along the west side of the trail. The present road is about where those trees were. Travelers using this book sometimes will be disappointed in not seeing rut swales where they are supposed to be. They are encouraged to look back from time to time. For example, both the Sublette Cutoff and the trail from Fort Bridger have disappeared at the point of convergence, due largely to the construction of Highway 30. Travelers who look east from that point, however, will be treated to a dramatic view of the wagon road coursing down from the ridgetop.

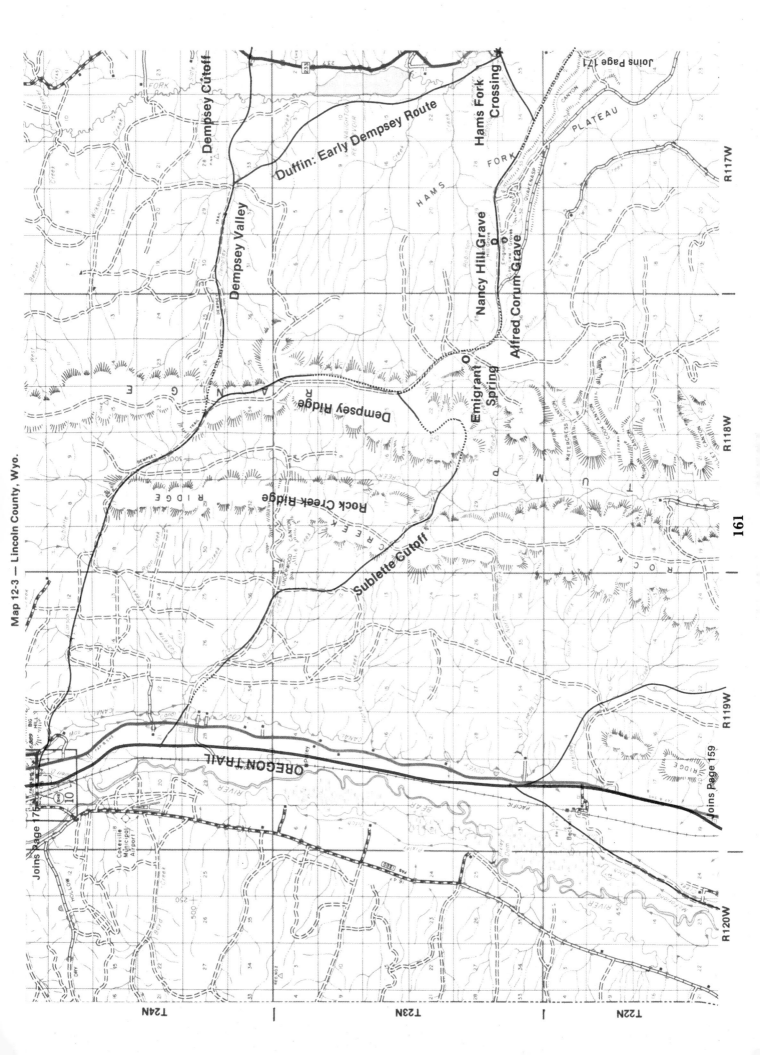

Map 12-3 — Lincoln County, Wyo.

Dempsey Cutoff

Duffin: Early Dempsey Route

Hams Fork Crossing

Dempsey Valley

Nancy Hill Grave

Alfred Corum Grave

Emigrant Spring

Dempsey Ridge

Rock Creek Ridge

Sublette Cutoff

OREGON TRAIL

PLATEAU

HAMS FORK

Joins Page 171
Joins Page 159
Joins Page 175

161

R117W

R118W

R119W

R120W

T24N

T23N

T22N

162

This is the second page of cartography of the Sublette Cutoff. The ruts from Haystack Butte across Sublettes Flat are sometimes a dozen abreast. It is perfectly flat, and there was no reason to eat the dust from wagons in front, so the emigration spread out and traveled in comfort. Troy Gray advises travelers to have a second means of transportation before entering Sublettes Flat, where a breakdown could be fatal. It is more than 20 miles to the nearest water. All vehicles should be high slung, as there is high, tough sage in the crown of the road. The trail is treacherous after a rain. Of course, it doesn't rain here in the summer very often. Usually there is the same choking dust that exasperated the emigrants. The road from the "Second Parting" joined the Sublette Cutoff west of Haystack Butte. Many miles of the pristine ruts west of there have been bladed — utterly destroyed as a convenience to the heavy equipment of the oilfield operators — within the past few years.

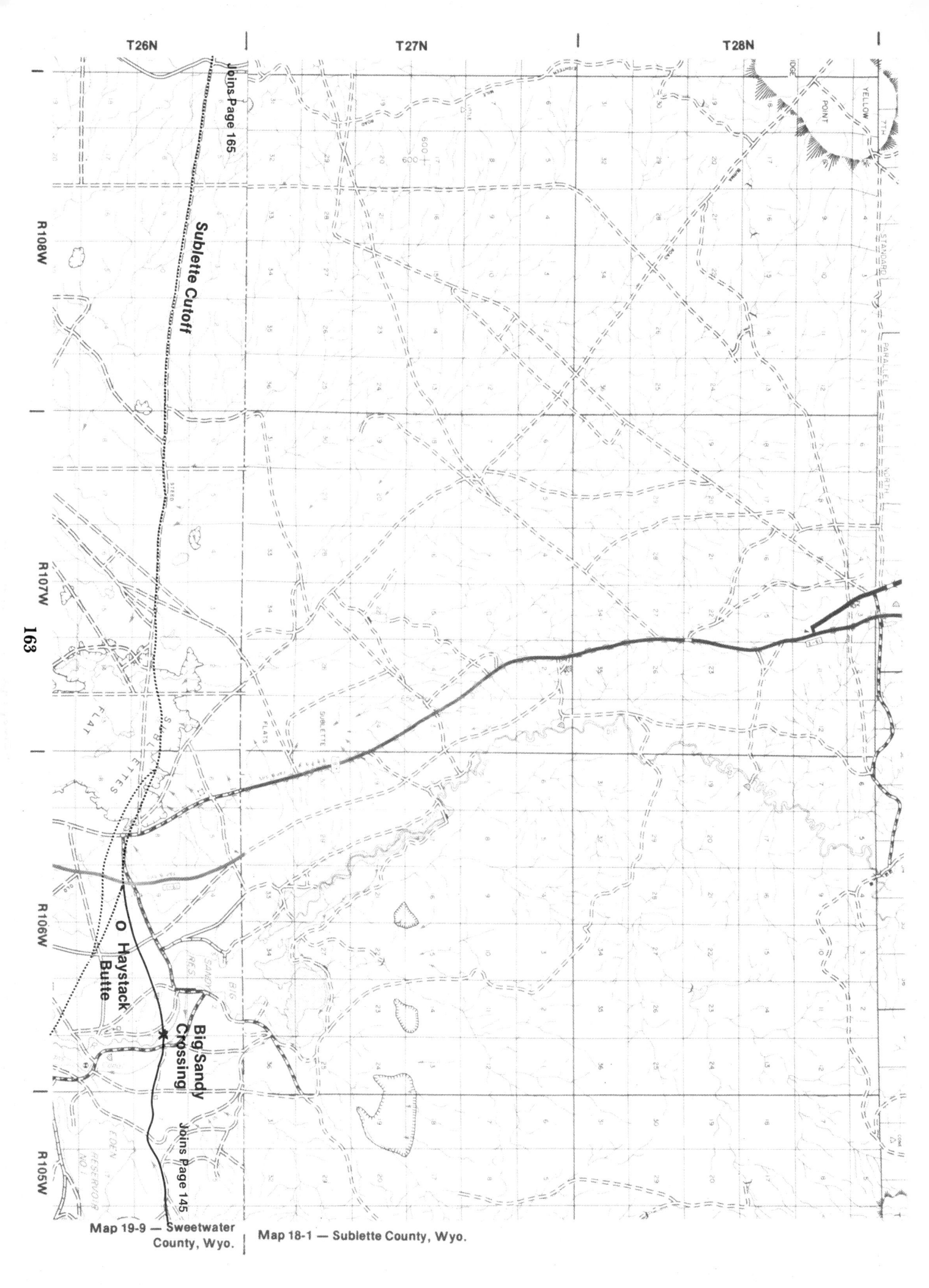

T26N

T27N

T28N

R108W

R107W

R106W

R105W

163

Joins Page 165

Sublette Cutoff

O Haystack Butte

Big Sandy Crossing

Joins Page 145

Map 19-9 — Sweetwater County, Wyo.

Map 18-1 — Sublette County, Wyo.

The race through this land was always telling on man and beast, as the emigration neared the end of the long dry pull to the Green River. Troy Gray advises that the ruts between the Buckhorn and West Fork canyons are intermittent. Duffin says the road from the right edge of this map to a point abreast of Monument Butte is a well-defined jeep road. Gray says the ruts through Buckhorn Canyon are very deep and to the right of the jeep road. They went off the face of the canyon — down in a precise straight line. The swale is very evident today. Ruts are scattered west of that canyon. At the left edge of the map the wagons were lowered to the Green River Canyon with ropes. Karen and Chester Buck, who own ranches in the area, feel the route a mile to the south was a much easier descent with wagons.

Joins Page 163

Sublette Cutoff

Grave of
Lucinda B. Wright
1855

165

R109W   R110W   R111W   R112W

T26N   T25N   T24N

Joins Page 167

FONTENELLE RESERVOIR

166

Good old Big Oil has thrown a fine new bridge over the Green, meaning that a traveler may backtrack a considerable distance east from U.S. Highway 189. This is the site of the old mountain men's ferry, thrown up in gold rush years by competitors to the Mormon ferrymen. The Haines book features a detail map of the several sites around the Green River crossing, and recounts a description of the debris from smashed wagons which littered both sides of the trail leading down the steep hill to the Green River ford. The Sublette Cutoff is most confusing. The Bucks have it going one way, the Henderson-Bishop-Duffin research another, the Grays still another, and the USGS and BLM each have routes entirely different at several places. Probably none are wrong. The trail in this country is more a network than a single road, and covered wagons surely rolled along all of the indicated routes.

Map 12-4 — Lincoln County, Wyo.

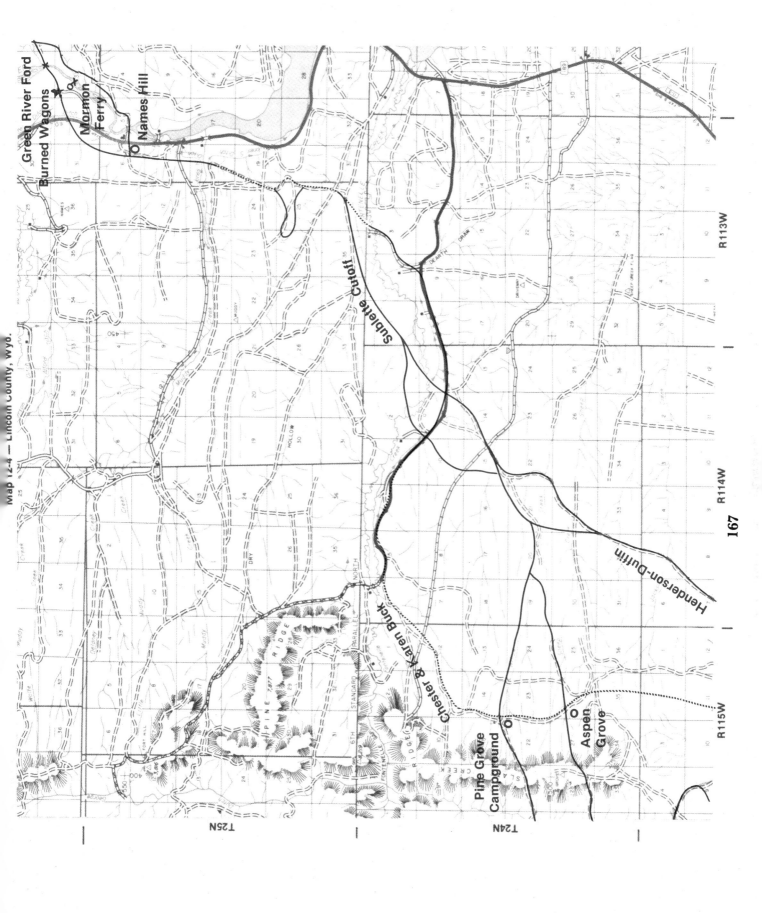

Green River Ford
Burned Wagons
Mormon Ferry
Names Hill

Sublette Cutoff

Chester & Karen Buck

Pine Grove Campground

Aspen Grove

Henderson-Duffin

R113W

R114W

R115W

167

T25N

T24N

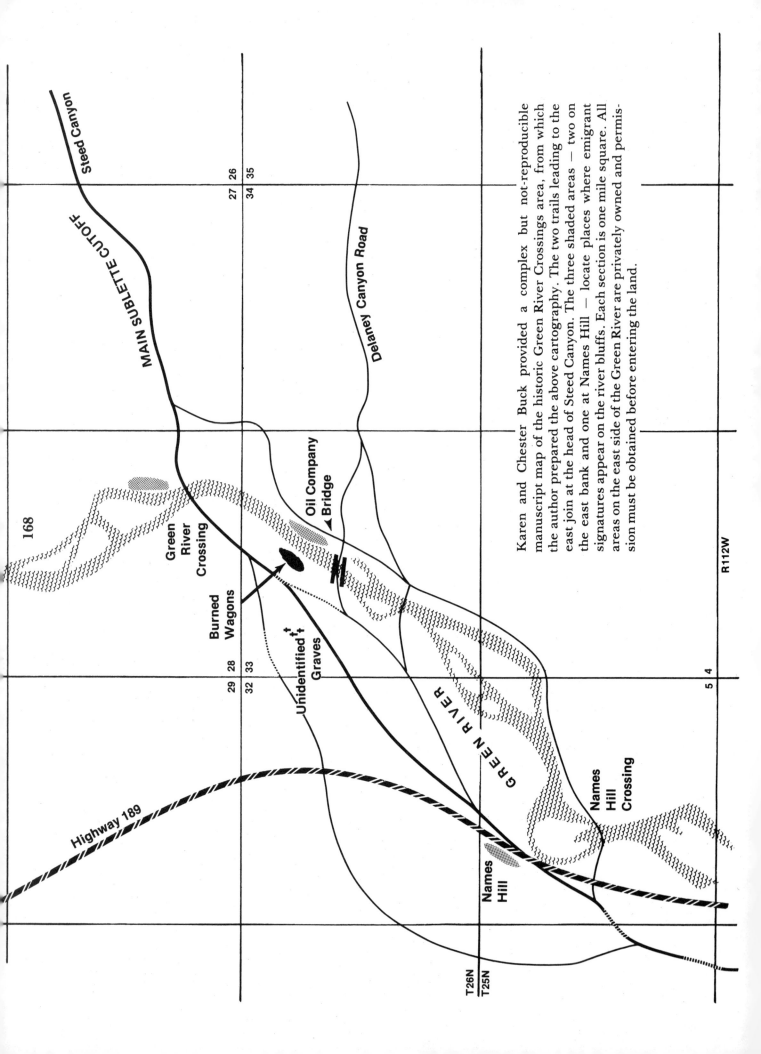

168

Steed Canyon

MAIN SUBLETTE CUTOFF

27 26
34 35

Delaney Canyon Road

Oil Company
▲ Bridge

Green River
Crossing

Burned
Wagons

29 28
32 33

Unidentified † †
Graves †

GREEN RIVER

Highway 189

Names
Hill

Names
Hill
Crossing

T26N
T25N

5 4

R112W

Karen and Chester Buck provided a complex but not-reproducible manuscript map of the historic Green River Crossings area, from which the author prepared the above cartography. The two trails leading to the east join at the head of Steed Canyon. The three shaded areas — two on the east bank and one at Names Hill — locate places where emigrant signatures appear on the river bluffs. Each section is one mile square. All areas on the east side of the Green River are privately owned and permission must be obtained before entering the land.

SLATE CREEK / KENNEY CUTOFF, HIGHWAY 189 TO EMIGRANT SPRINGS (Map by Reg Duffin, 1982)

Key: 1 — The reference points are the junctions of Highway 189 with Highway 240 to Opal, or the Fontenelle Road. From these points the traveler may locate the starting point of the westbound county roads. (This location is about 20 miles northeast of Kemmerer.) 2 — This is a rough, high-centered trail suitable for 4x4's. A standard pickup with high clearance could make it, but definitely not passenger cars or station wagons. 3 — The descent to Emigrant Spring is steep and eroded. Park above, hike down. There are early names on rocks surrounding the pioneer campsite. Certainly there is one grave located among the enormous sagebrush; possibly two. Each square on this map equals one mile. Troy Gray advises that there are no less than three "Emigrant Springs" along the trail in this area.

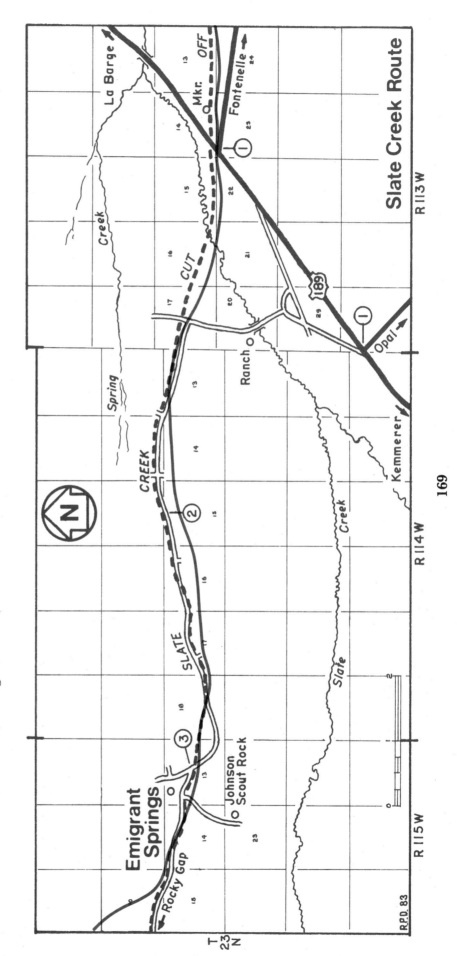

Slate Creek Route

169

Many of the experts seem to be in disagreement as to where the various routes are on this map, so most of their routes have been included. Probably all were heavily used by the emigrants. An example of the sort of confusion which can prevail is contained in a letter from Charlie Martin to the author, dated March 18, 1982: "I realize that Bishop and Henderson show the Slate Creek Route as you do, so know it must be right. However I have copies of several diaries that seem to indicate some of them more or less stayed along Slate Creek instead of being up on the higher ground to the north. Also this results in Johnston Scout Rock being a mile or so off the route and to the south of it. While at the "Scout Rock" last summer, I photographed the name of Orange Gaylord on it, and the date. It corresponds completely with the diary and date of Orange Gaylord on his 2nd trip to the Pacific Coast. At that time Gaylord was traveling in a wagon train with his own wagon and with his wife. Why would he go a mile and a half south of the trail to sign his name?" Karen Buck, daughter of the legendary Alice Antilla, summed it up nicely when she wrote, "Everyone has a different idea of where the trail actually goes. Even those living in this area don't agree. But each in his own way is right, because by the time the emigrants got this far, feed was getting short from previous wagon trains and they would have to find grass as well as a route in the right direction! Then too, crossing from the Sandy to the Green in the dark isn't the easiest thing to do. You can get lost out there in the daylight!" There are intermittent ruts throughout the length of all the routes shown on this map. Troy Gray finds them deep on the very steep hill coming up from the Lower Hams Fork Crossing. He advises that the Sublette is directly beneath a high tension line going over Commissary Ridge, with fine ruts most of the way. The map on page 173 was prepared for this book by Reg Duffin and helps clear up the confusion surrounding the maze of routes in the Green River area. In this case, each square is a township, six miles on a side. His legend, on the facing page, has been slightly edited.

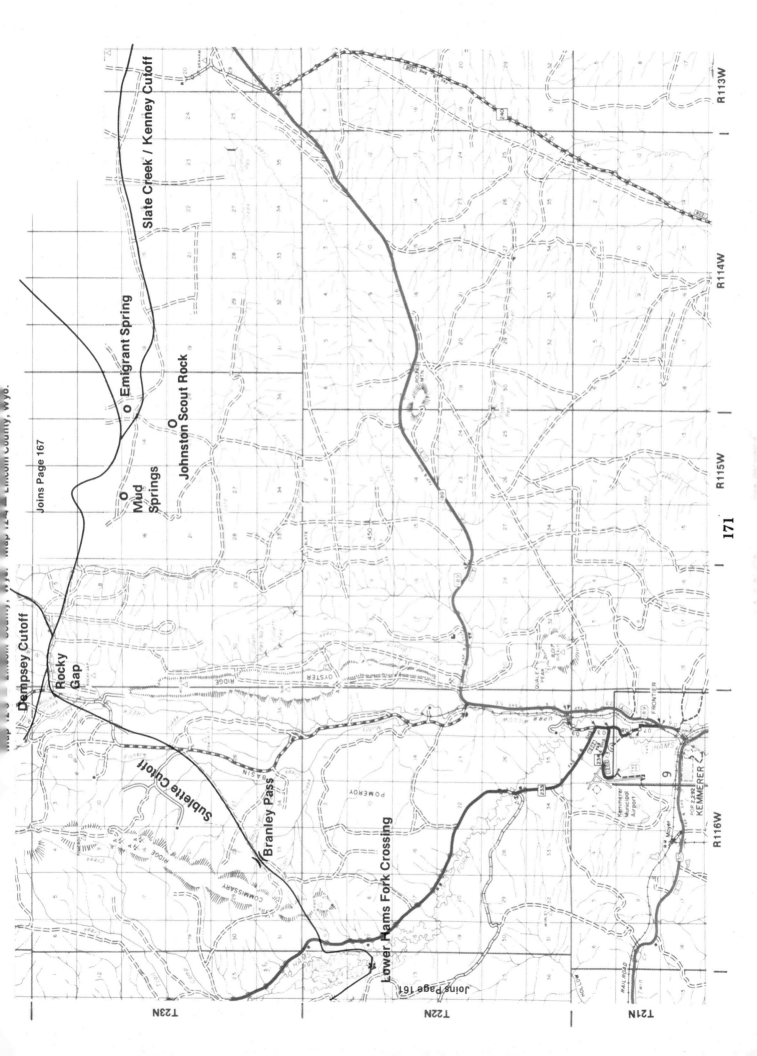

OREGON TRAIL CUTOFF ROUTES ACROSS SOUTHERN LINCOLN COUNTY, WYOMING (Map by Reg Duffin, 1982)

This map has been prepared by Reg Duffin to help the reader understand the complex of east-west cutoff routes across southern Lincoln County. Rocky Gap should be considered as the central merge point.

From the east, the main Sublette Cutoff has left the Fort Bridger road at the Parting of the Ways (page 145) to run almost due west to the Green River crossings south of La Barge. It then runs south, crossing Muddy Creek and veering to the southwest, crossing Fontenelle Creek and continuing southwest to Willow Creek. Here the Sublette divides, with one variant running westerly along Willow Creek to climb over Slate Creek Ridge, then running south, then west to Rocky Gap. From the Willow Creek junction another Sublette variant runs southwest to Emigrant Springs, to join the Slate Creek route. Together they run west-northwest to link with the Willow Creek-Sublette variant just east of Rocky Gap.

The emigrants who used the Slate Creek route followed the road to Fort Bridger as far as the future site of the Big Timber Station. Here the Slate Creek route, also known as the Baker-Davis Road, begins. It loops north, then inscribes an arc southwest to cross the Green River northeast of present Fontenelle at the site of the Case Ferry. Then it continues almost due west to Emigrant Springs, where it joins the Sublette Cutoff.

The Kenney Cutoff starts approximately five miles west of the origin of the Slate Creek Cutoff, in the southeast quarter of Section 33. This was a direct route and ran west-northwest, following the north side of the present Farson-Fontenelle Highway, just to the south. The Kenney route reached the Green River east of Fontenelle at Case Ferry, where it joins the Slate Creek route. This may be considered the original Kenney route, but there was still another alternate taken by the emigrants, who crossed the Green River at what was later known as the Lombard Ferry, then continuing west-northwest along the south side of the Green River to join again with the Slate Creek road; then continuing due west to Emigrant Springs.

To the west of Rocky Gap the main Sublette Cutoff runs southwest through the Pomeroy Basin to cross Commissary Ridge at Branley Pass. Along this route there appear to have been variants heading due west to cross the Commissary Ridge at points north of the Branley Pass. From Branley Pass the Sublette goes over the lower crossing of Hamsfork to climb the Hamsfork plateau, crossing Dempsey and Rock Creek ridges to wind down in a northwesterly direction along Trail Creek. It linked with the earlier Oregon Trail from Fort Bridger in the Bear River Valley, below Cokeville.

The Dempsey-Hockaday Cutoff was first used in 1854. It starts two miles west of Rocky Gap and runs northwest along the Absaroka Creek to climb a most formidable section of Commissary Ridge. Then it drops down to the southwest to the Hamsfork Valley and crosses the Hamsfork approximately eight miles above the lower Sublette crossing. Hockaday is reported to have erected a bridge here in 1854. The Dempsey route continues in an almost direct westerly route to climb the plateau crossing Dempsey Ridge, skirting the northern extent of Rock Creek Ridge and descending to the Bear Valley. There it links up with the earlier Oregon Trail route from Fort Bridger at Cokeville.

For purposes of clarity, the aforementioned north-south ridges, some formidable, are not shown. They appear on the regular maps elsewhere in this book.

The Hamsfork Cutoff, an early trapper route, runs north and west from the Blacks Fork crossing west of Granger. The cutoff proceeds along the Hamsfork River to link with the Sublette at the lower Hamsfork crossing.

This map is based on cartography by the late Paul C. Henderson of Nebraska and the late L. Clark Bishop of Wyoming.

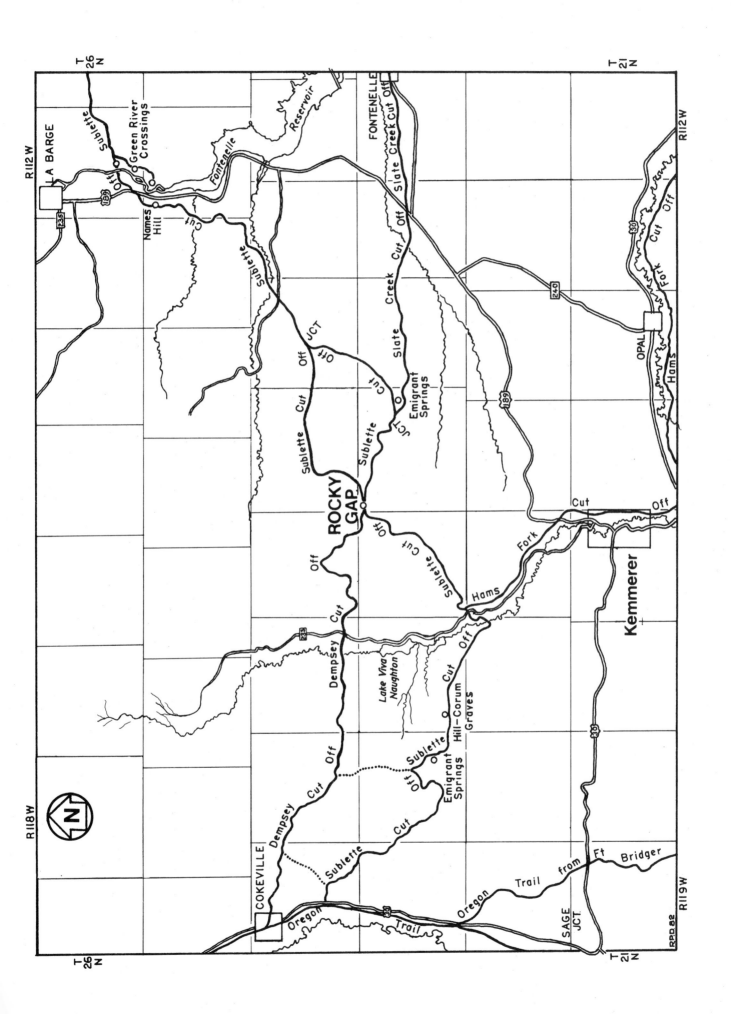

174

The ride up Highway 30 to Border Summit is delightful, with the Bear River to the left and the trail to the right. The ruts may be seen going up the ridge. Gray says the swale leading northwest from the Thomas Fork crossing goes up a ravine behind the hill. The site indicated for Peg Leg Smith's trading post is educated conjecture — it could be anywhere within a mile of where it is shown. Duffin advises that one must look back from the highway to see the ruts south of Montpelier.

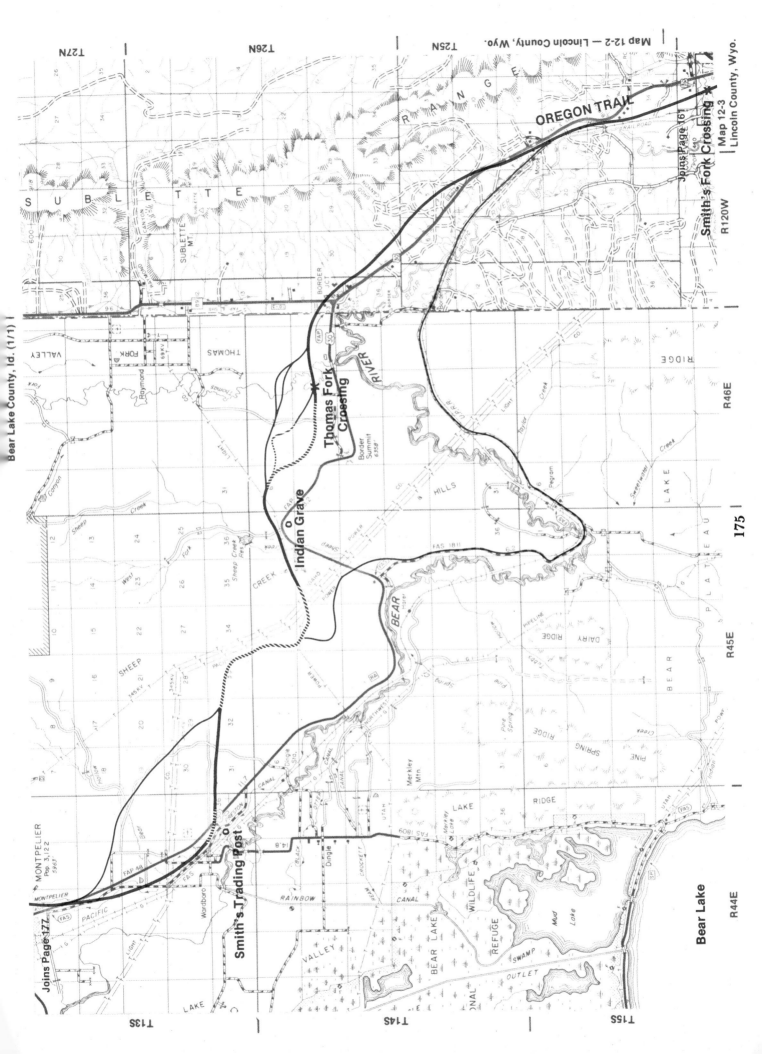

176

The reader may test his own sleuthing skills on this map page. The author recalls seeing rut swales between the Montpelier crossing and Georgetown, but the field notes are missing, and he is getting so old that he can't recall where the ruts are. Please mark the exact locations and send a photocopy of the marked map to Box 42, Gerald, MO 63037.

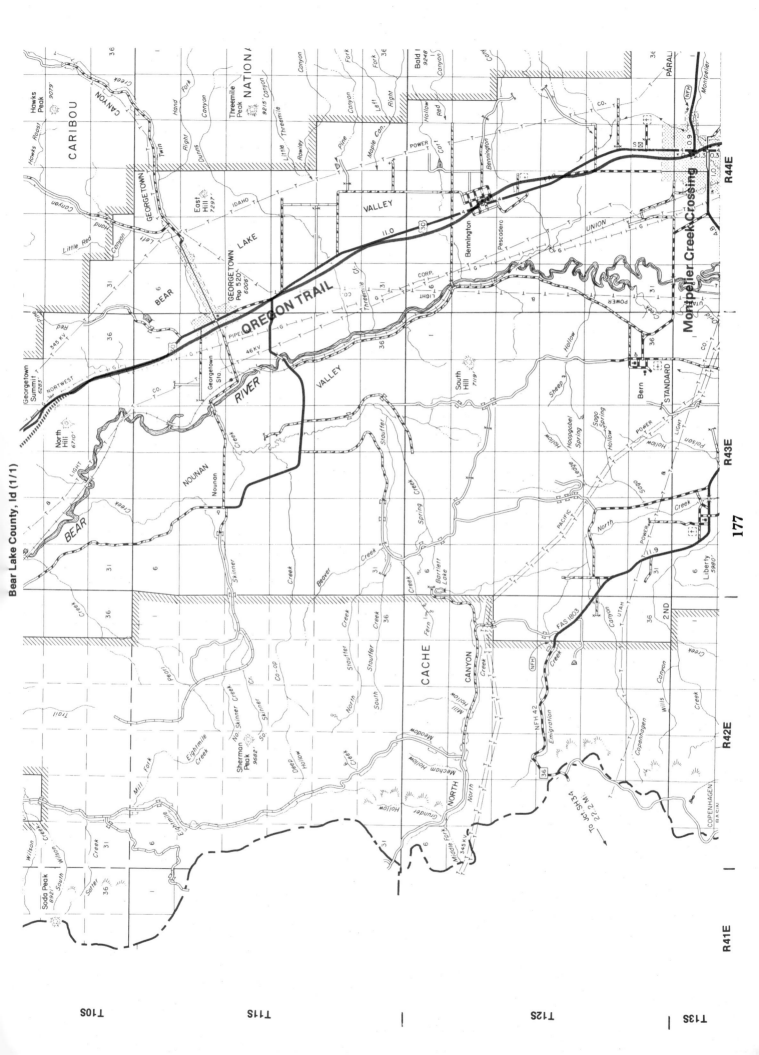

Soda Springs probably was the one most fascinating spot along the Oregon Trail. Only a few of the springs survived the inundation of the Bear. Some California-bound travelers left their Oregon-bound companions here, on the ill-routed Hudspeth Cutoff.

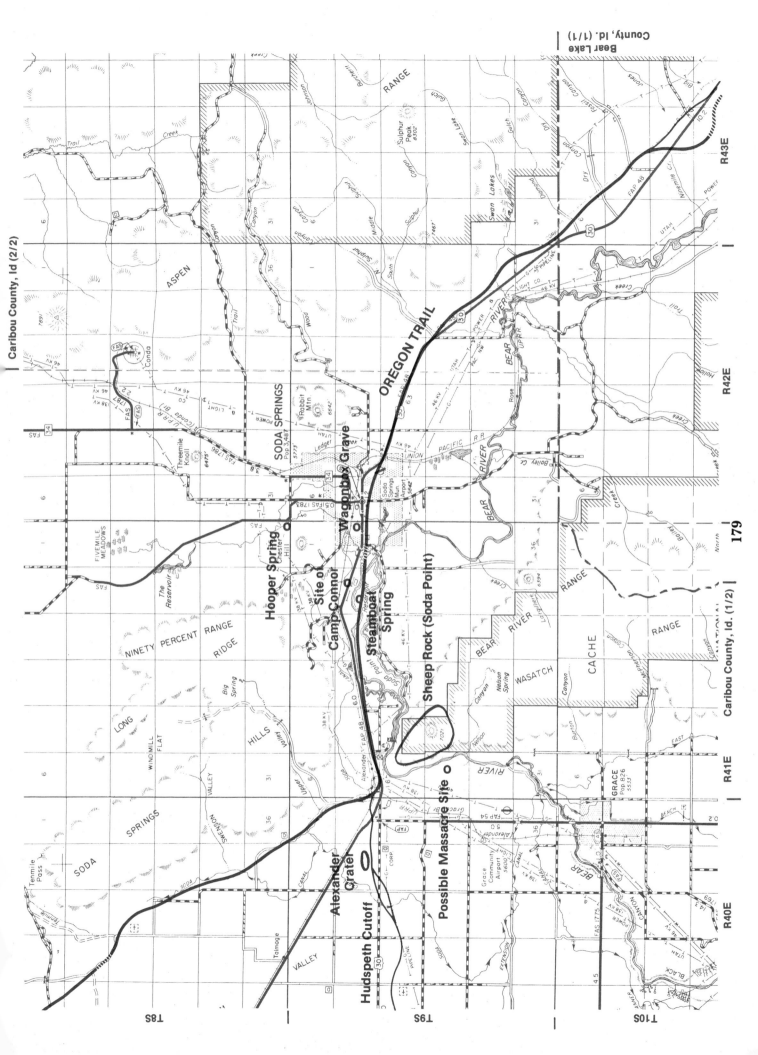

OREGON TRAIL

Hooper Spring

Site of Camp Connor

Wagonbox Grave

Steamboat Spring

Sheep Rock (Soda Point)

Alexander Crater

Hudspeth Cutoff

Possible Massacre Site

SODA SPRINGS
Pop 3,487

GRACE
Pop 826

R43E

R42E

R41E

R40E

T8S

T9S

T10S

The desolation of the Portneuf Valley didn't depress the emigrants, as they knew they were closing in on Fort Hall, a place which was much less disappointing than Fort Bridger. It is rough going along here — the trail is on private property past the reservoir, then turns into the Shoshone-Bannock Indian Reservation, where passage without permission is strictly prohibited. Merle Wells, who is without a peer in his mastery of Idaho's trails, says the ruts shown in the upper left corner of this map are especially noteworthy.

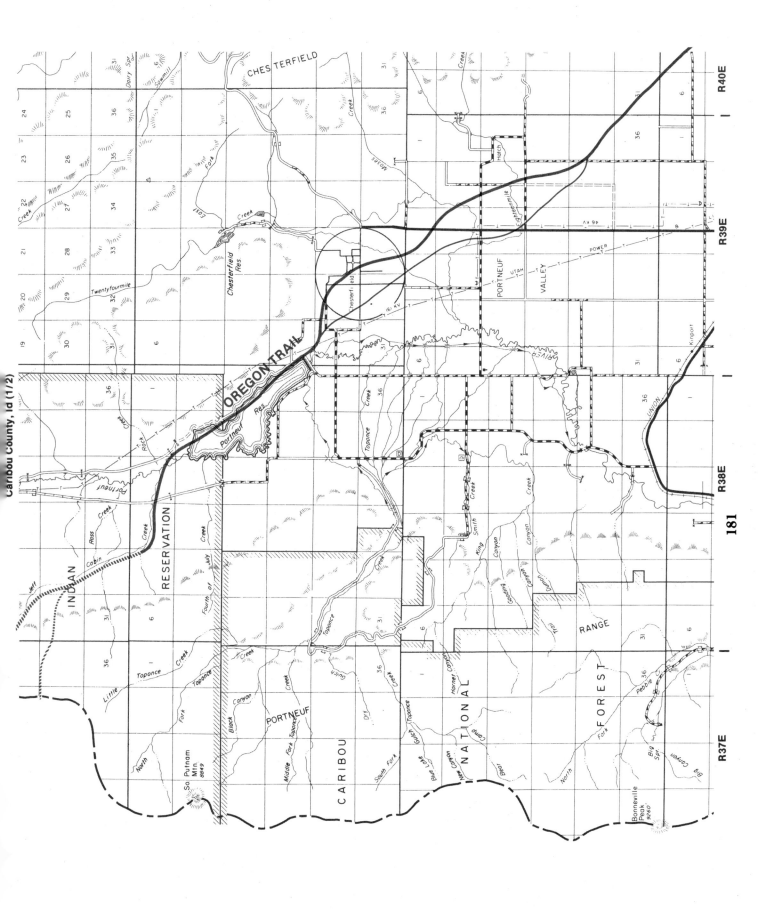

181

182

It is possible to travel on a paved road for a few miles east of the town of Fort Hall to reach the route of the trail, but not possible to travel into the wilderness areas. This is part of the Indian reservation. Visitors who want to visit the site of old Fort Hall must first obtain permission from agency authorities in the town of Fort Hall, and that isn't easy. A full scale replica of old Fort Hall has been built in Pocatello's Ross Park.

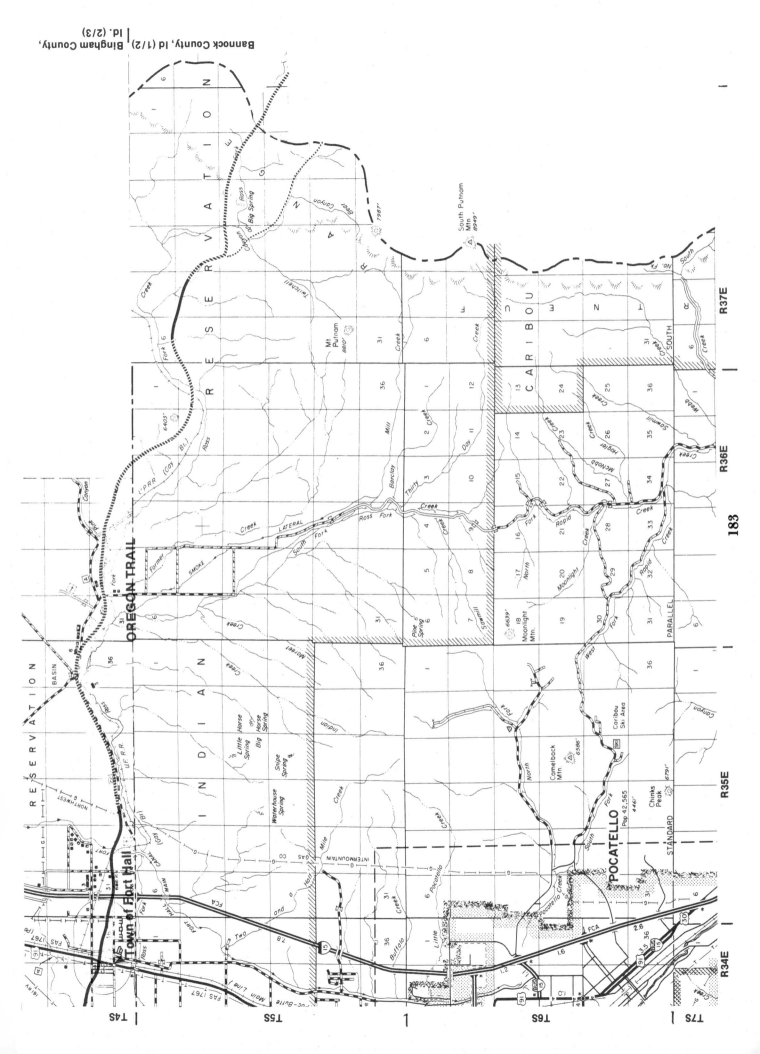

183

The site of Fort Hall probably can be found using this map, but the directions in *The Oregon Trail Revisited* are easier to follow. Haines and his son did a thorough survey of the site, finding the lines of the walls of the old establishment in the tall grass surrounding the monument. The survey is reproduced in his book. Using it and a Boy Scout compass, travelers may walk to the exact sites where history was made.

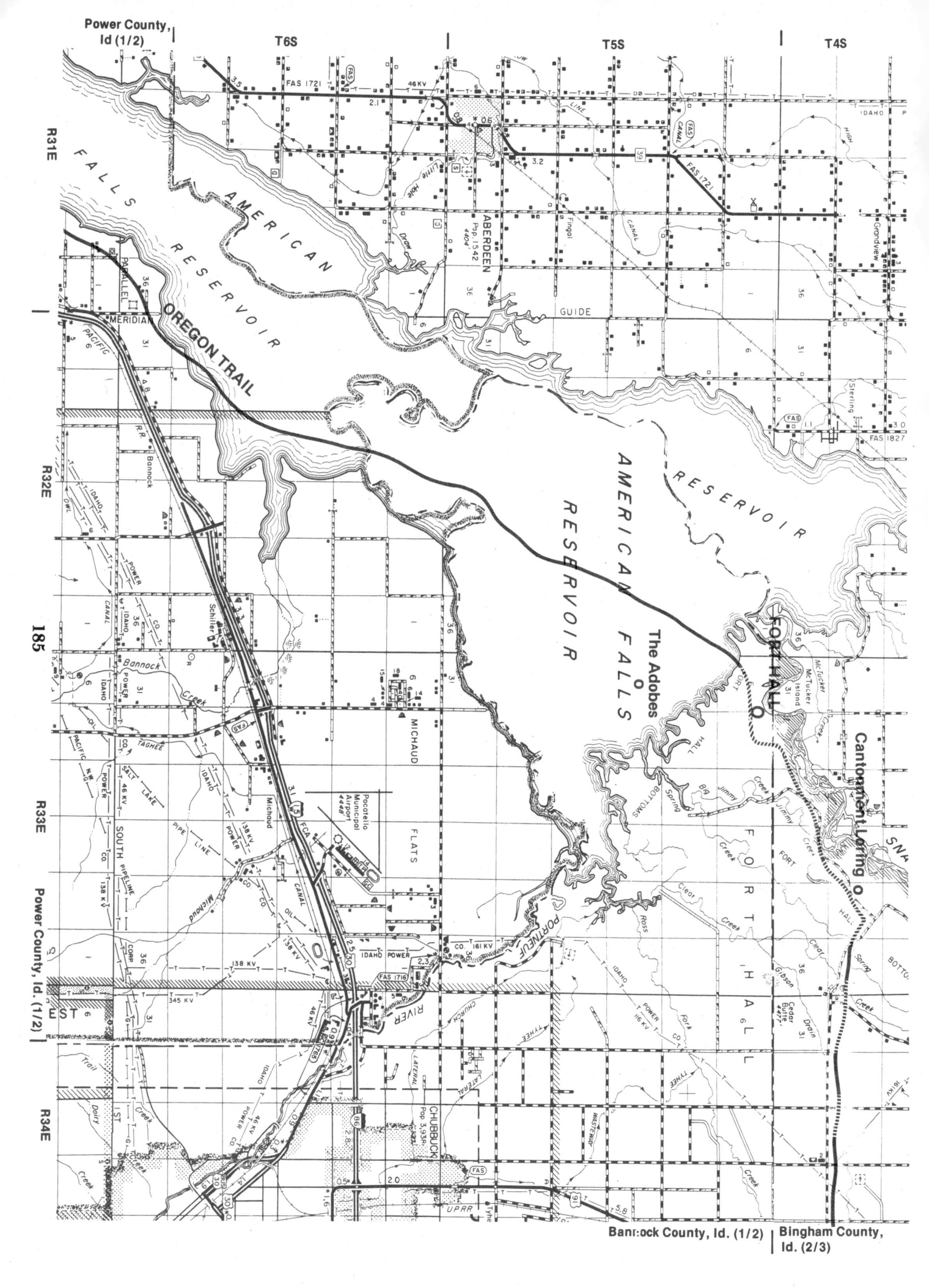

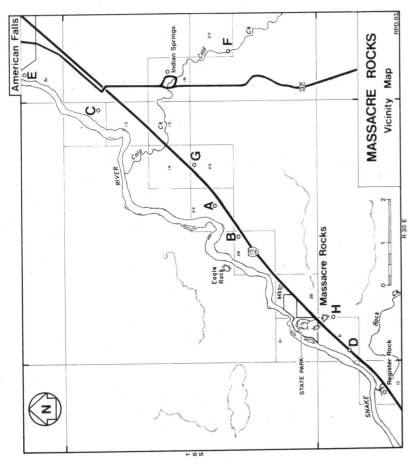

MASSACRE ROCKS
Vicinity Map

RPD.83

Working with interpretive cartography by Aubrey L. Haines plus the diaries mentioned, Reg P. Duffin developed the above map of the events of 1862. On Saturday, August 9, 1862, a train of 11 wagons captained by George W. Adams of Madison, Iowa, was attacked by Indians at (A). Charles Bullwinkle of New York was killed and Miss Elizabeth Adams was severely wounded. The Smart train was also attacked at this time at (B) but managed to make a running fight to a good defensive position at what later became known as Massacre Rocks. The Newman and Kennedy trains were nooning in the vicinity of (C) when they received news of the attack. They moved out and found the Adams train at (A), looted and with one emigrant dead, two wounded and several missing. The wagons were without teams. They took the wagons in tow and moved ahead four miles to camp the night of August 9 with the Smart train and survivors of the Adams train, below Massacre Rocks at (D).

Word of the attack, probably relayed by John Meller of Omaha, also reached the train of a Rev. Bristol just after 4 o'clock. This train was below the American Falls at (E). They hurried forward and camped after sundown where the Adams and Smart train had been attacked. John C. Hillman wrote, "... darkness obliged them to camp on the very ground, ..." H.M. Judson wrote, "... red with blood of innocent men and women ..."

10, 1862, Judson continued, "... by 4 a.m. we are on the road and about 3 miles ahead find Newman and Kennedy and the wrecks of the mule train of 11 wagons and ox trains all together." He was then at (D).

On that morning Captain Kennedy and a party of 30 men tried to retrieve the stolen stock. They encountered the Indians camped on Cold Creek (F). The hostiles were well armed and the Kennedy party was forced to repair three miles to a position on a low ridge, at (G). Here accounts vary but it appears that two men were killed, one being George W. Adams Jr. and the other possibly being G. Luper or Leeker. Two more men were missing and several were wounded, including Captain Kennedy.

Between 4 and 5 p.m. on this August 10 the Walker train arrived at (G). Diarist Jane A. Gould wrote, "We were met by two men, they wanted us to go a short distance from the road and bring up two dead men to this camp five miles ahead...." Continuing, she laments about the death of Bullwinkle, a friend who had traveled with her family until the crossing of the Green River.

On Monday, August 11, 1862, Gould wrote, "The two men that were brought up were buried early this morning with the other three, so they lay five men, side by side, in this vast wilderness...." The site of these graves has been given as about 50 feet south of the Massacre Rocks, about at (H).

On Monday, August 11, the combined trains left the camp at (D). "150 wagons ..."(Gould) "... considerably over 200 making a continuous train near .. three miles long ..." (Judson).

On Tuesday, August 12, 1862, Elizabeth Adams, 26, died from the effects of her wound of August 9 and was buried at the Raft River.

On Friday, August 16, Evans S. McComas of the William Jack train passed the massacre site. He wrote, "Come in the forenoon to where 13 waggons had been attacked and taken by Indians, one man and one woman killed and three more wounded. The man's name was C. Bullwinkle from New York, Aug. 9. Come in the afternoon to where another train had been attacked and found the graves of 5 men, one my old friend Andrew I. Hunter from Iowa City, killed Aug. 9th, '62, one G. Luper from Iowa, Massin O. Liffe Aug. 9, G.W. Adam aged 24 years Killed Aug. 10." We may conclude that Charles Bullwinkle, Andrew I. Hunter and Massin O. Liffe (Massino Lippi, an Italian) were killed in the Adams-Smart attack on the 9th and George W. Adams Jr., and G. Luper (G. Leeker) were killed in the Kennedy foray on the 10th. Others may have been killed and not accounted for. Andrew Hunter had been McComas' friend and prior captain of the McComas party train. The Massacre Rocks State Park has a fine interpretive center relating to these events. The Massacre Rocks defile has been widened to accommo-

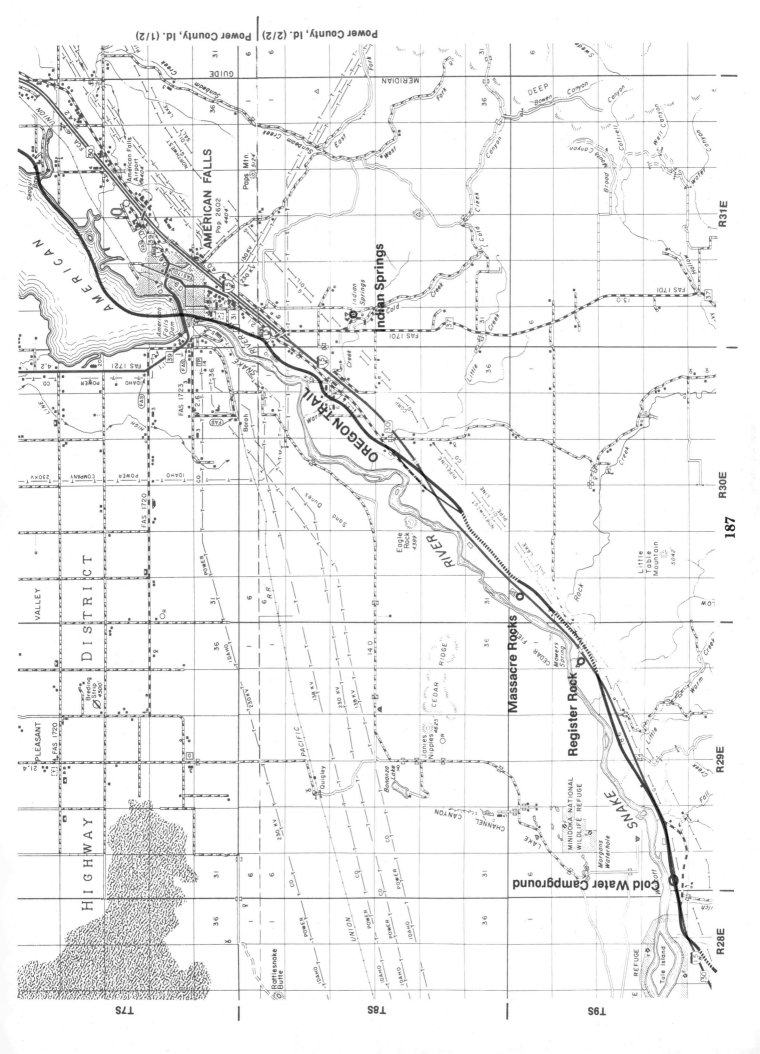

American Falls Airport
American Falls 4404

AMERICAN FALLS
Pop. 2602
4404'

Paps Mtn.
5124

Indian Springs

OREGON TRAIL

SNAKE RIVER

Eagle Rock
4369

RIVER

Massacre Rocks

Register Rock

Cold Water Campground

SNAKE

HIGHWAY

DISTRICT

VALLEY

PLEASANT

Breding Strip
4500

Rattlesnake Butte

Little Table Mountain
5042

Janies Nipples
4625

CEDAR RIDGE

Quigley

Bononza Lake

MINIDOKA NATIONAL WILDLIFE REFUGE

Morgans Waterhole

CHANNEL

DEEP

Bowen Canyon

187

188

All California-bound emigrants had to turn south at the crossing of the Raft River. There were no alternatives beyond that point. The land adjacent to the river is under cultivation, but as seen from the ridge on the west, the trail is in pristine condition and visible almost all the way to I-84. (The interstate highway from here west is no longer numbered I-80N, but I-84.)

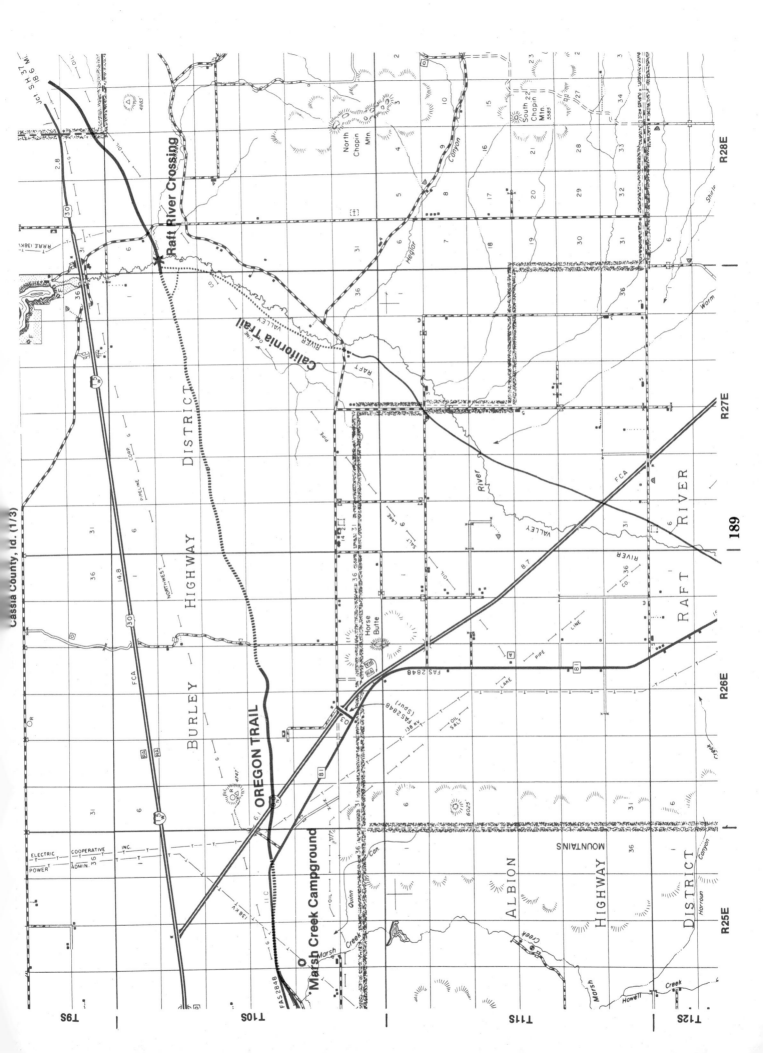

Raft River Crossing

California Trail

OREGON TRAIL

Marsh Creek Campground

BURLEY   HIGHWAY   DISTRICT

ALBION

MOUNTAINS

HIGHWAY   DISTRICT

RAFT   RIVER

RAFT   RIVER   VALLEY

Horse
Butte

South
Chapin
Mtn
5585

North
Chapin
Mtn

Heglar   Canyon

RIVER   VALLEY

SALT   LAKE

ELECTRIC   POWER   COOPERATIVE   INC.   ADMIN.

NORTHWEST

PIPELINE   CORP

Jct SH 37 18.6 Mi.

FAS 2848

FAS 2848

FAS 2848 (Spur)

T9S   T10S   T11S   T12S

R25E   R26E   R27E   R28E

The proximity of the Snake River caused the obliteration of the trail here, for irrigation has converted the rangeland to cropland. The trail is invisible almost all the way across the sheet.

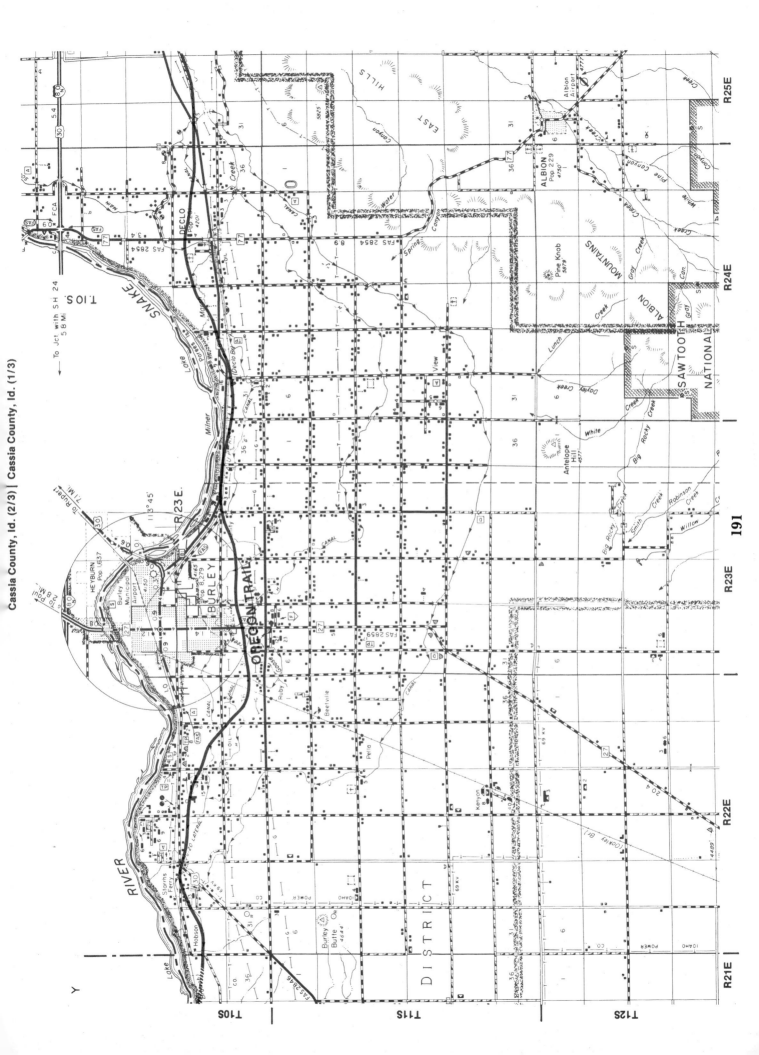

191

The Bureau of Land Management (BLM) has done a fine interpretive job at the Milner Ruts. Hikers may proceed a mile east of the shelter and pass 16 points of interest which are interpreted. Hikers may continue another 3½ miles east before the private lands begin. Both Clappine's Rocks and Caldron Linn relate to the voyage of the Astorians rather than the emigration, but the Idaho State Historical Society museum in Boise has an interesting display of relics of the disaster which occurred there in 1811. The Stricker Store dates to 1863 and still stands. Merle Wells identified a short rut remnant east of Stricker Butte.

SNAKE

Milner Falls

Milner Dam

BURLEY HIGHWAY

Milner Butte 4621

Idaho Power Co 69 KV

Clappine's Rock

Cedron Linn 4280

To Jct I-80N 21 Mi.

Murtaugh Lake

DISTRICT

HIGHWAY DISTRICT

Artesian City

MURTAUGH

MURTAUGH HIGHWAY

ANTELOPE VALLEY

193

Murtaugh Pop 124

Bickel

U.P.R.R.

Hansen Butte

OREGON TRAIL

Rock Creek

Cedar Hill 4296

Twin Falls

To Jct I-80 0.8 Mi.

Echo Lake

Hansen C. Bridge

HANSEN Pop 415 4030'

Stricker Store

Trail Butte

R18E   R19E   R20E   R21E

T10S   T11S   T12S

114°15'

194

Neither the Shoshone Falls nor the Twin Falls, three miles east, are worth visiting in the dead of summer, when reclamation projects have them virtually drained. But in the spring and fall the Snake roars majestically over the precipices as in days of yore, and they are thrilling sights indeed. The wagons had to follow Rock Creek for 11 miles before finding this place to ford, which is now sadly impacted, privately owned and unmarked.

TWIN FALLS

FILER HIGHWAY DISTRICT

OREGON TRAIL

Shoshone Falls

Rock Creek Crossing

Twin Falls Municipal Airport

TWIN FALLS

T9S

T10S

T11S

R15E   R16E   R17E   R18E

196

The scale now changes, and each 2½ inches equals one mile. There is still a short rut swale marking the place where the wagons climbed up out of the chasm cut by Rock Creek.

Rock Creek Crossing

OREGON TRAIL

197

Joins Page 199

City of Twin Falls, Id.

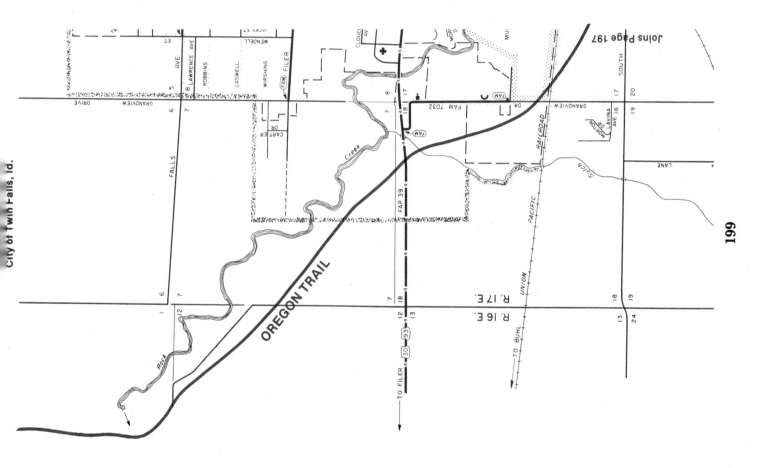

OREGON TRAIL

199

Emigrants welcomed this stretch of the Snake, for here they had their first taste of fresh salmon, caught by the Indians. The bridge shown on the right edge of the map may be taken to reach the overlook area — a worthwhile trip indeed. The Kanaka Rapids, Thousand Springs and Upper Salmon Falls are all considerably depleted by the reclamation program but, like Twin and Shoshone Falls, are fascinating in the spring or fall. Merle Wells advises that the land southwest of Thousand Springs is about to be farmed, meaning another stretch of pristine ruts is about to be plowed under. The Oregon Trail cuts across some of the highway loop at the Upper Salmon Falls overlook area, offering a good stretch of pristine ruts for the short-distance hiker.

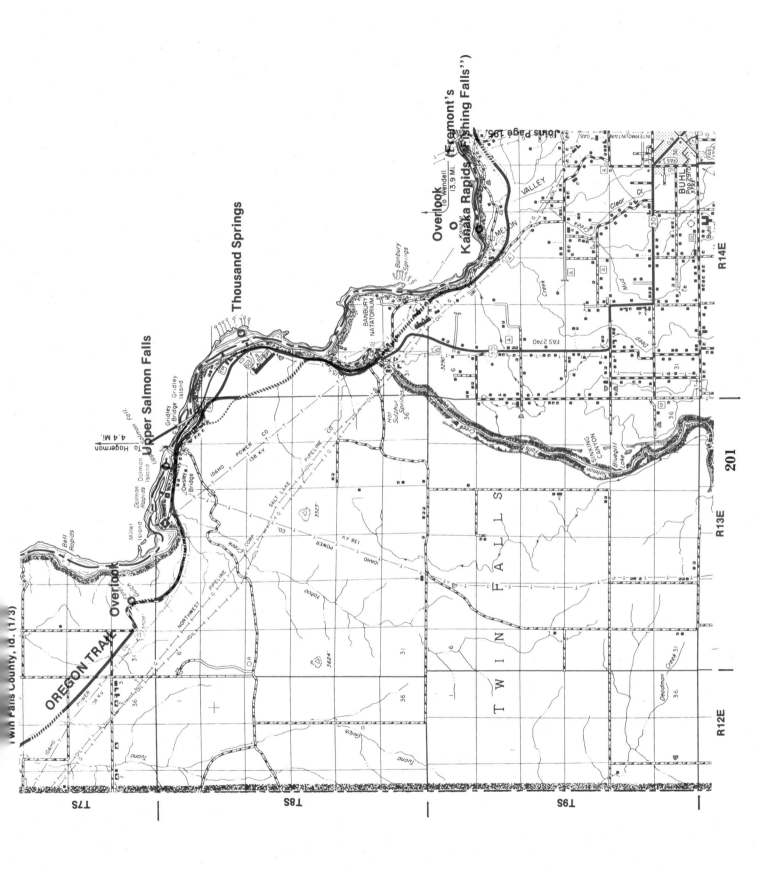

 OREGON TRAIL Overlook

Upper Salmon Falls

Thousand Springs

4.4 MI.
To Hagerman

Overlook
To Wendell
13.9 Mi.

Fremont's
Kanaka Rapids ("Fishing Falls")

Joins Page 195

TWIN FALLS

201

R12E
R13E
R14E

T7S
T8S
T9S

The finest Oregon Trail ruts in the State of Idaho are in the 83-mile North Trail Hiking Segment. The path taken by the emigration across the Snake, as seen from the bluff to the east, is readily apparent in William H. Jackson's 1939 painting of Three Island Crossing. Jackson made the on-site sketch for this painting in 1866, subsequent to the great flood of 1862. Merle Wells feels the flood rearranged the area topography considerably. There is a state park across the river from this site.

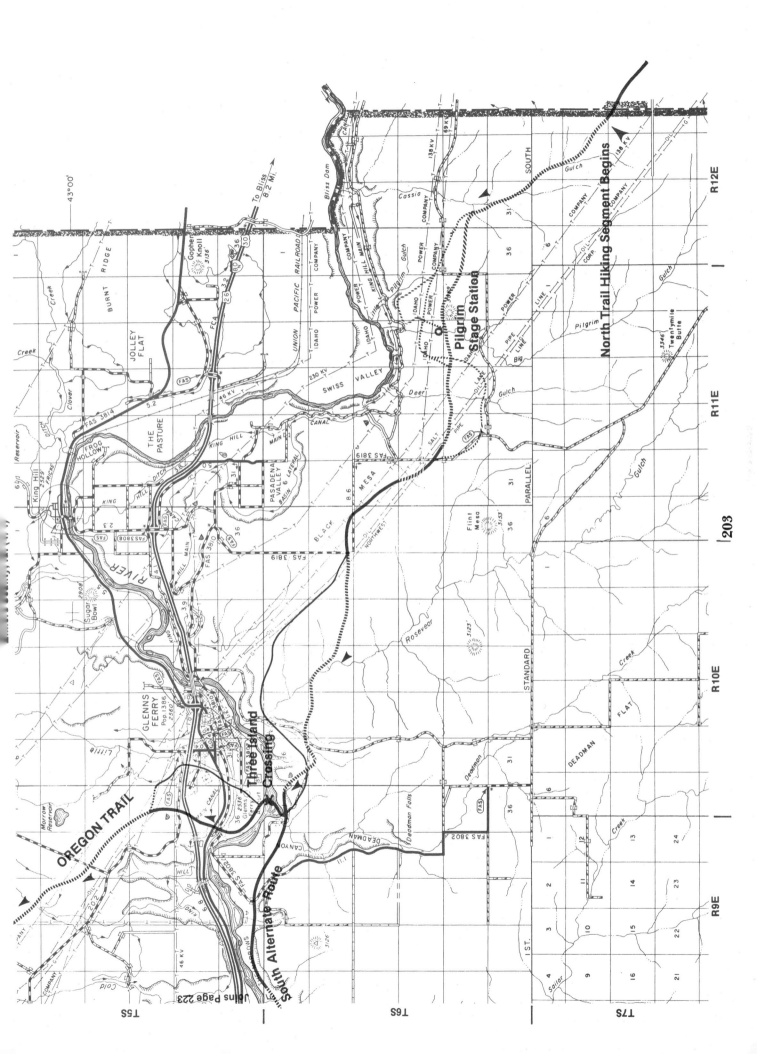

Pilgrim Stage Station

North Trail Hiking Segment Begins

OREGON TRAIL

Three Island Crossing

South Alternate Route

The trail is pristine most of the way along this portion of the hiking segment. The Hot Springs no longer flow during the summer months, victims of the demands of irrigation. The ruin of the old springhouse remains at the site. The stone ruins of two houses are just across the road from **Rattlesnake Station**, the last reminders of the original townsite of Mountain Home.

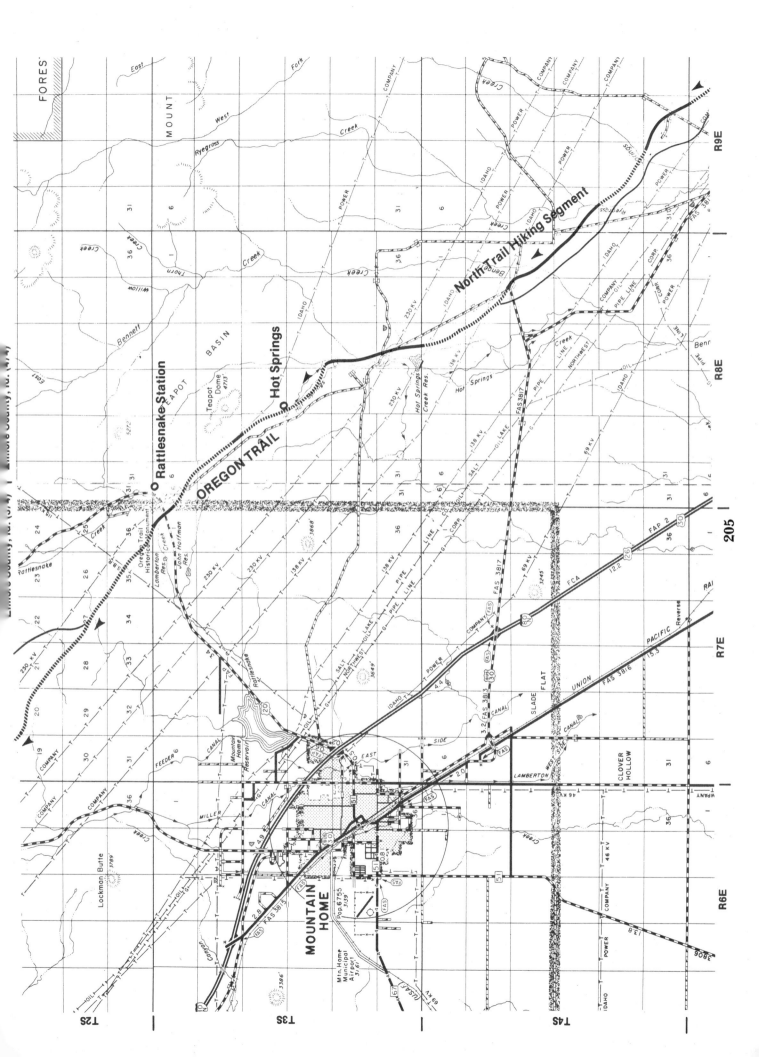

OREGON TRAIL

Rattlesnake Station

Hot Springs

North Trail Hiking Segment

MOUNTAIN HOME

Pop. 6755

Mtn. Home Municipal Airport

FOREST

MOUNT

BASIN

Lockman Butte

Clover Hollow

Slade Flat

Lamberton

R6E

R7E

R8E

R9E

T2S

T3S

T4S

The Canyon Creek stage station, in private use until recent years, was gutted by fire not long ago. The walls still are standing, but they won't be for long without protection.

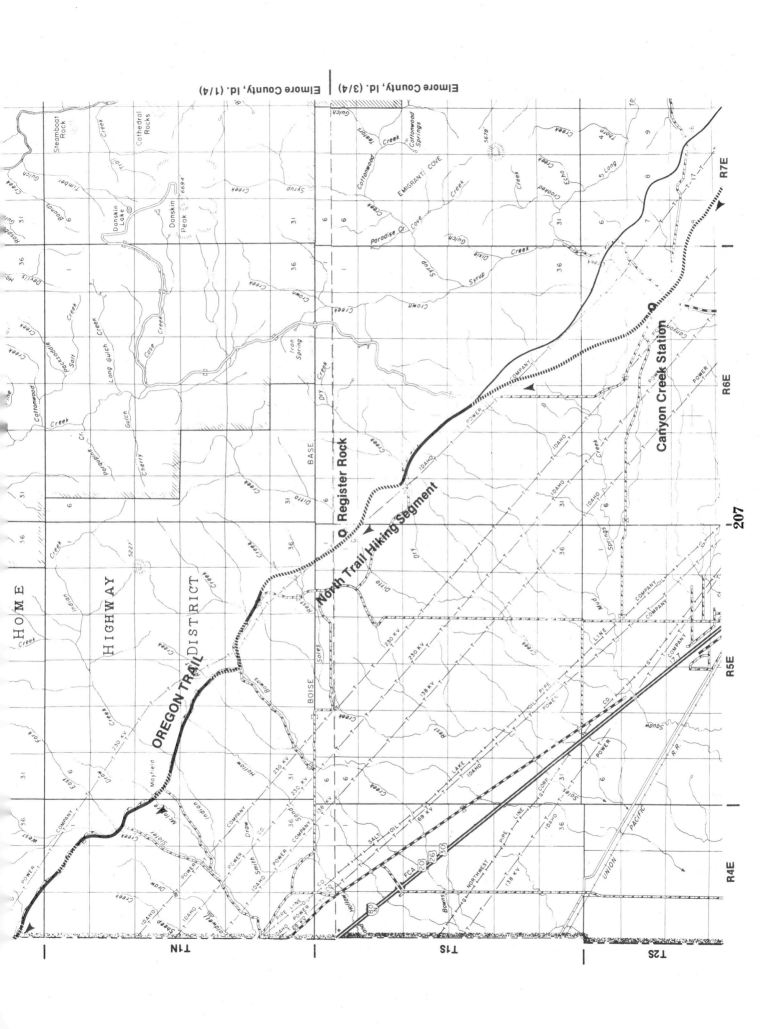

Bonneville Point is adequately marked and accessible by a good gravel road today. There are good ruts to the southeast, but they are on private ground. To the northwest, toward Boise, the ruts have been destabilized by excess latter-day traffic and erosion is now taking its toll.

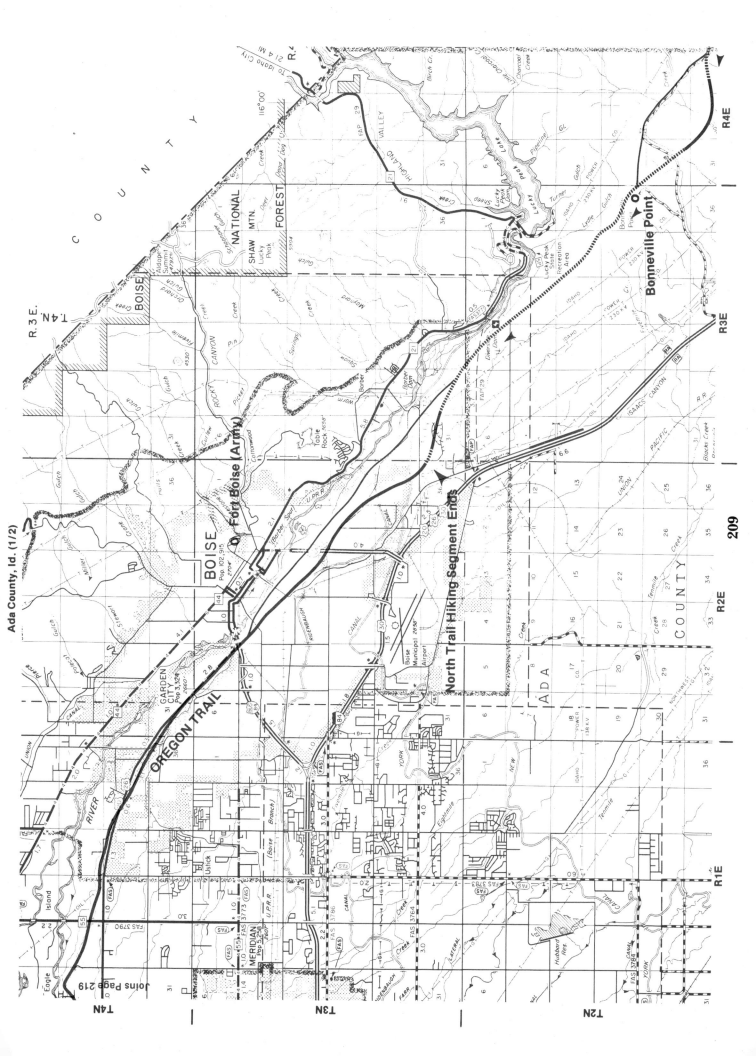

Ada County, Id. (1/2)

209

210

John Latschar and Stanford Young of the National Park Service have suggested the hiking trails marked in this book. The trail shown here uses existing paved roads through the "Oregon Trail" subdivision, then traverses a rut swale to the north. The Idaho Department of Transportation is planning to build a by-pass around the eastern edge of Boise, and the NPS is hopeful that a pull-off or interpretive site can be developed at the western trail head.

Joins Page 213

North Trail Hiking Segment Ends

OREGON TRAIL

RIVER

Flooding of the Boise during the latter part of the 19th century eradicated all traces of the trail through the city. Here are two routes — one probable, the other possible.

OREGON TRAIL

The Army's Fort Boise, 46 miles east of the Fort Boise of the Hudson's Bay Company, was established in 1863 to protect those participating in the Idaho gold rush, as well as the tail end of the emigration. Two of the fort's buildings from that year still stand. The facility is now in use as a medical center for the Veterans Administration.

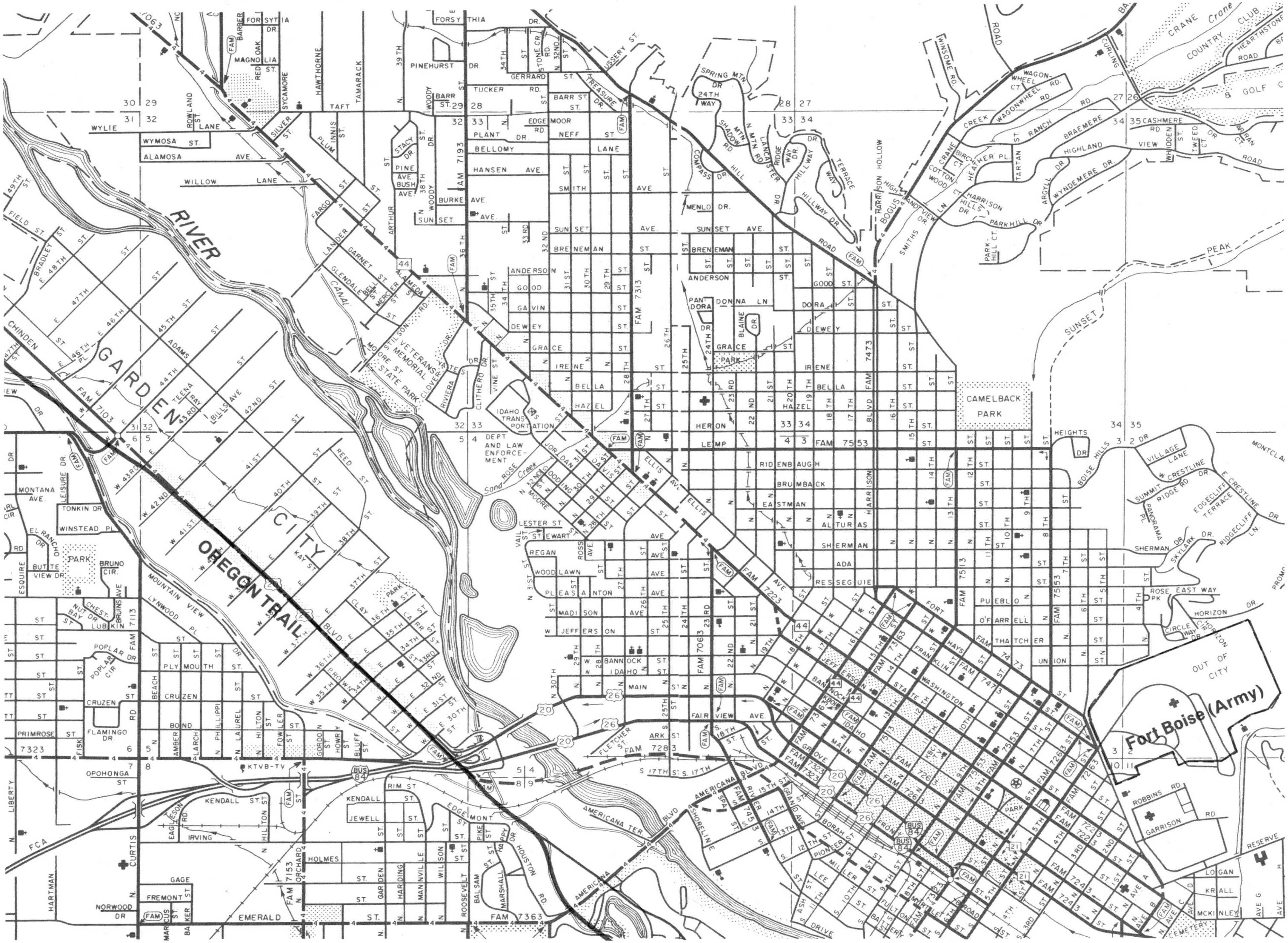
Fort Boise (Army)
OUT OF CITY
CAMELBACK PARK
OREGON TRAIL
GARDEN
CITY
RIVER
VETERANS MEMORIAL STATE PARK
IDAHO TRANSPORTATION
DEPT AND LAW ENFORCEMENT
CHINDEN
AMERICANA
HARRISON
SHORELINE
MOUNTAIN VIEW
CRANE CREEK COUNTRY CLUB

217

Eighteen to 20 persons in a small wagon train were hideously tortured to death during the Ward Massacre of 1854. The aftermath was just as bad, with Indians being the reluctant guests at necktie parties for several years thereafter. Those were bloody times along the trail for both sides. At Canyon Hill some 300 feet of pristine ruts descend a rocky slope to the east bank of the Boise River.

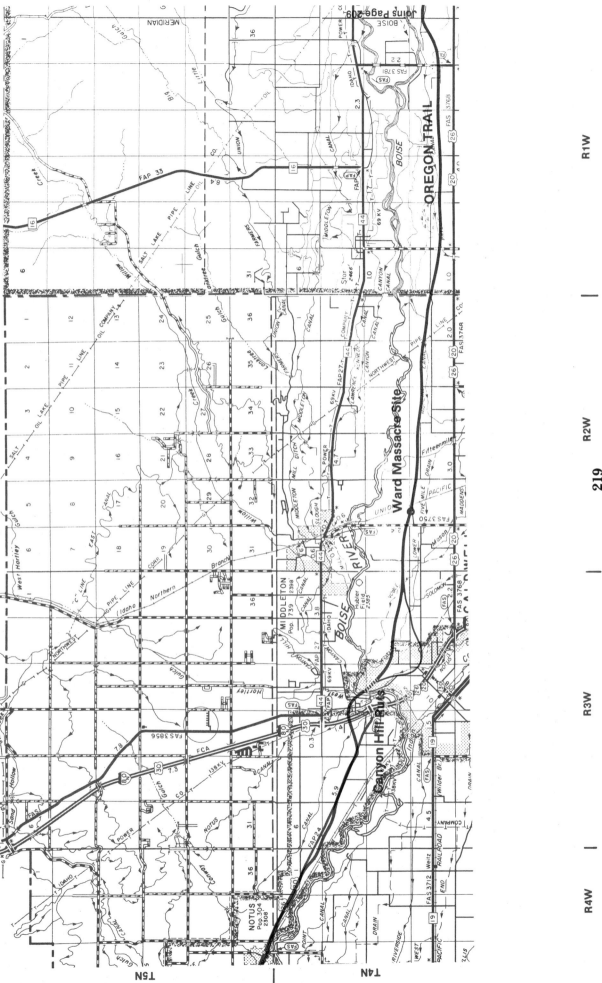

Canyon County, Id. (1/1)

OREGON TRAIL

Ward Massacre Site

BOISE RIVER

MIDDLETON
Pop. 739
2398'

Canyon Hill Rus

NOTUS
Pop. 304
2308'

219

R1W   R2W   R3W   R4W

T5N   T4N

There is nothing at the site of the Hudson's Bay Company's old Fort Boise but a marker erected by a local group in 1972. The ford was a tough one for the emigrants and would be impossible for today's travelers at any time of the year.

Snake River Crossing

Two crossings of the Snake and one of the Boise were avoided by those choosing to follow the south bank of the Snake from the Three Island Crossing site. This is the first of six map pages depicting that route which, despite the lack of big river crossings, was much more difficult than the northern trail. Those who took it rarely had a choice — the high water they found at Three Island rendered a ford there impossible.

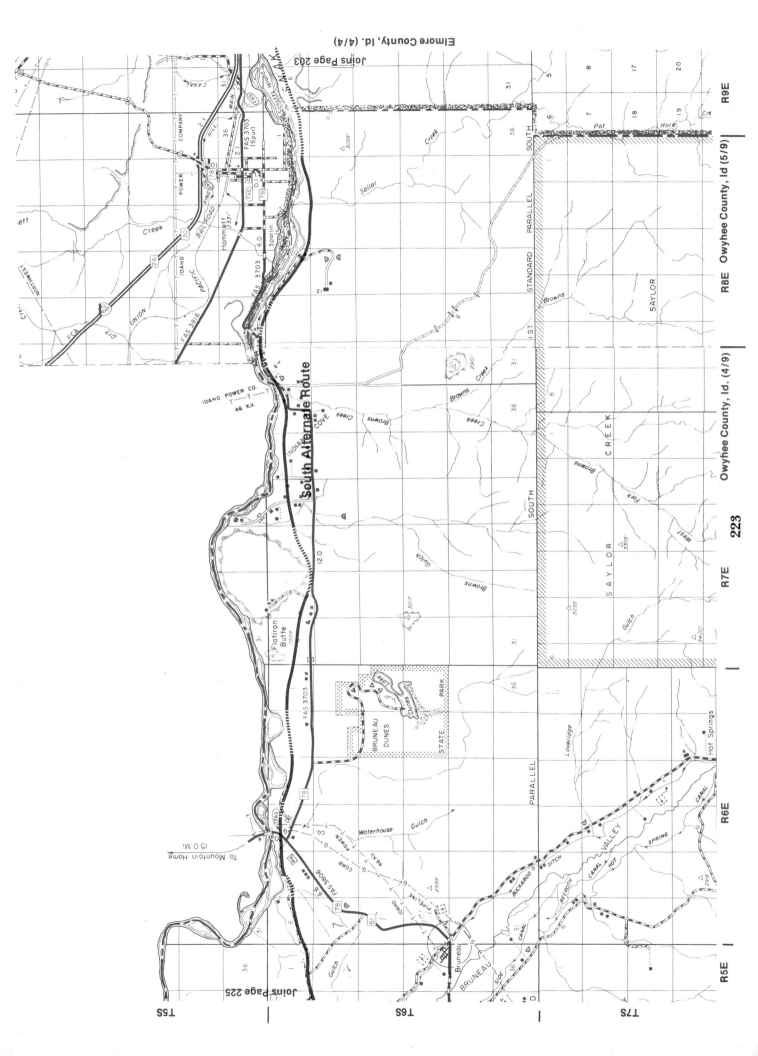

The so-called Strike Ruts are quite evident just southeast of the C.J. Strike Reservoir, which is a much-used recreational area. They are badly eroded in places.

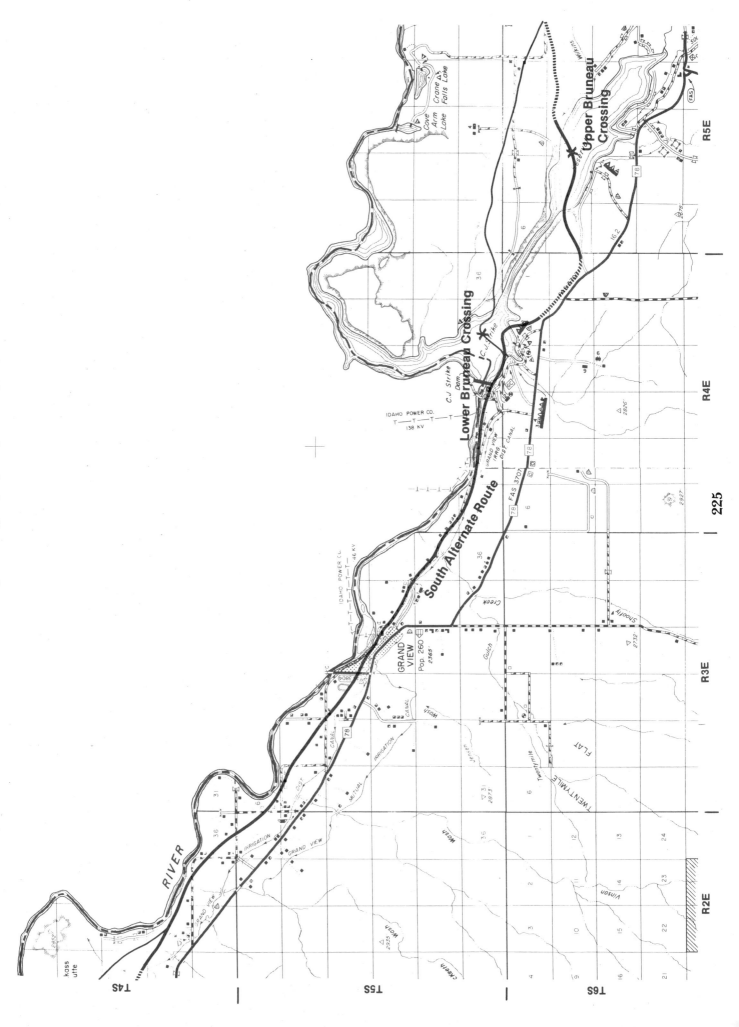

226

The hiker must be either totally dedicated to his sport or a bit daft to take the 18-mile Sinker Creek Hiking Segment. It is hot, dry, dusty and prompted more crabbing by the emigrants than virtually any other similar stretch. Eagles and other raptors love it, however – more than 600 pairs nest along the way. The site of the Otter Massacre traditionally has been pinpointed southeast of Sinker Butte, where there is a cairn of gray sandstone boulders. Two of the stones there have the word "otter," incised in them. Merle Wells has never been comfortable with this location. In 1982 sufficient evidence came to his attention to establish the other location shown on this map. Here is some of the material leading to the conclusions, as drafted by Wells's associate, Larry Jones:

"The encounter of the Elijah Otter Party of 44 emigrants with hostile Indians on September 9, 1860, has evolved into the major documented tragedy inflicted by Indians upon overland-bound travelers. This incident is also one of the rare occasions when Indians not only attempted but sustained a prolonged assault on encircled emigrant wagons. During the seige, several of the Otter party managed to escape, but ultimately faced further deaths and personal hardships before being rescued by a military expedition along the banks of the Owyhee River some weeks following the encounter. Since that time, confusion concerning the location of the site has existed. Some of the 12 survivors were able to give a general description, and subsequent military reports and contemporary newspaper accounts corroborated their recollections. All reports placed the site somewhere below Salmon Falls. The location of the site received a good deal of attention through a series of articles in the Idaho Statesman (July 17-August 21, 1921) written by Miles Cannon. His research placed the site just west of Sinker Creek in Owyhee County. His identification can be found on current United States Geological Survey map publications.

"Recently found evidence now locates the site near Castle Creek, a few miles east of Sinker Creek. Henry M. Judson, an 1862 Oregon-bound emigrant, made the following notes in his diary:

4 Sep 62 About 12 o'clk we reach Castle Creek so called from some singular looking rocks having the appearance of old dilapidated castles and other ruins – soon Capt K's train arrives and Corrals near us – After remaining an hour & a half we are ordered to hitch up & drive on a mile or so for better grass . . . we comply & find grass higher than our heads & just abreast of the Castle rock – on the other side of the corral runs the creek a small crooked stream. . .

5 Sep 62 I should have mentioned yesterday that it is said the Indians two years ago beseiged a party of 30 or 35 men on the very spot on which we were corralled & killed all but 3 after a 3 day fight – some report seeing nearly a whole skeleton on the ground – I myself saw a skull & probably could have found more by searching. . . . [Henry M. Judson, Diary of 1862, Omaha to Oregon. MS 953, Nebraska State Historical Society.]

"Previous to their campsite near Castle Creek, Judson and his group were part of a large encampment of emigrants and military personnel on the Bruneau River. The groups intermingled freely, and it was most likely that the members of Judson's train heard about the 1860 event from the soldiers. In addition, the site not only yielded physical evidence just two years following the incident, but also fits the description of the area given by the survivors.

"Another emigrant in Judson's party, Sherlock Bristol, corroborates a Castle Creek location. Bristol noticed a lot of 'charred remains of wagons, the bones of cattle and horses, and the skulls of murdered men and women' about a mile after crossing Castle Creek. Later he met a Van Zant survivor who told him a tale of horror that he published in 1887. (A founder of Boise, Bristol continued to have a western identification after emigrating to Oregon in 1862.) Aside from G.W. Abbott's Umatilla agency report, October 30, 1860, identifying Elijah Otter's battle site as 'one hundred rods from Snake river,' other contemporary accounts offer little information concerning exact site location.

"Between Indian Cove and a long stretch of trail above Given's Hot Springs, only a few emigrant road segments qualify for Abbott's riverside location. These are a section north of Bruneau sand dunes, another lower Bruneau segment, three points near Grandview, a Jackass Butte segment, and a Castle Creek-Poverty Flat emigrant road bend where Judson and Bristol reported their 1862 evidence. Miles Cannon's Sinker Creek site, while only a mile from Snake River, fails to meet Abbott's specification. On that account, it always was suspect. Since Judson's and Bristol's site is slightly west of Castle Creek, all other possibilities between Indian Cove and Castle Creek are excluded. No other plausible location, aside from a Castle Creek-Poverty Flat site, satisfies Abbott's and Judson's description."

Aubrey Haines, however, wonders if the Otter party was not first corralled at Castle Creek, then moved on after an unsuccessful Indian attack there, to be finally destroyed a mile or so northwest. The jury is still out.

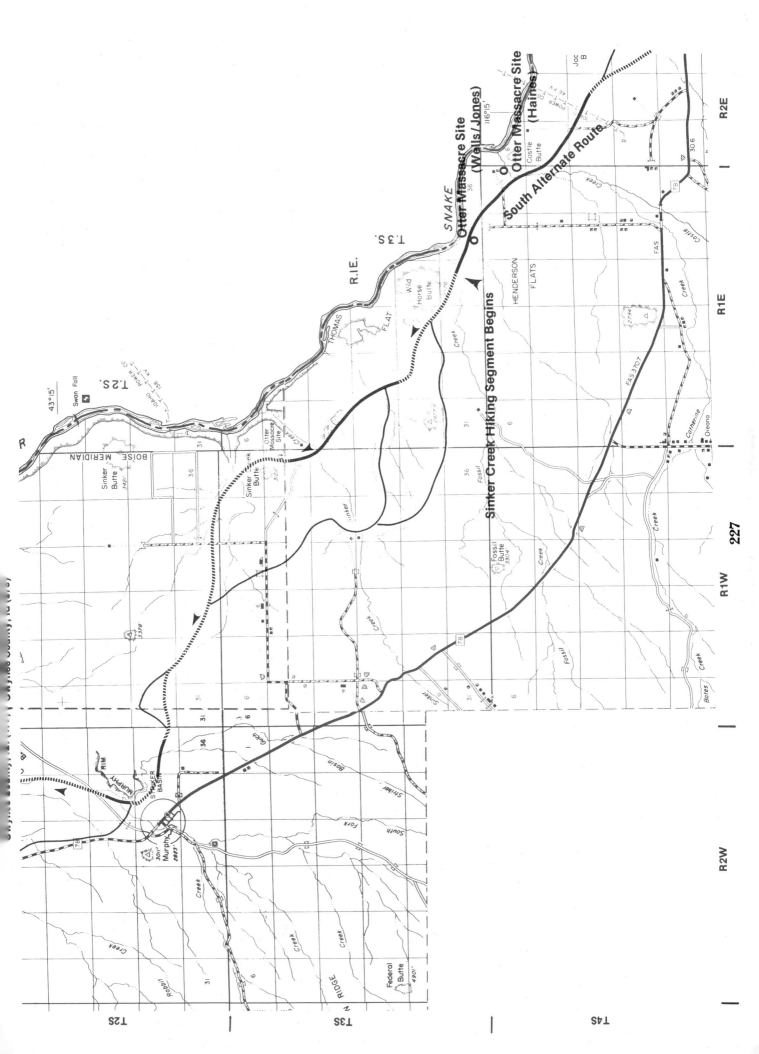

Givens Hot Springs was developed as a resort in 1860. It is still operated as a spa. The water is at a constant temperature of 138 degrees.

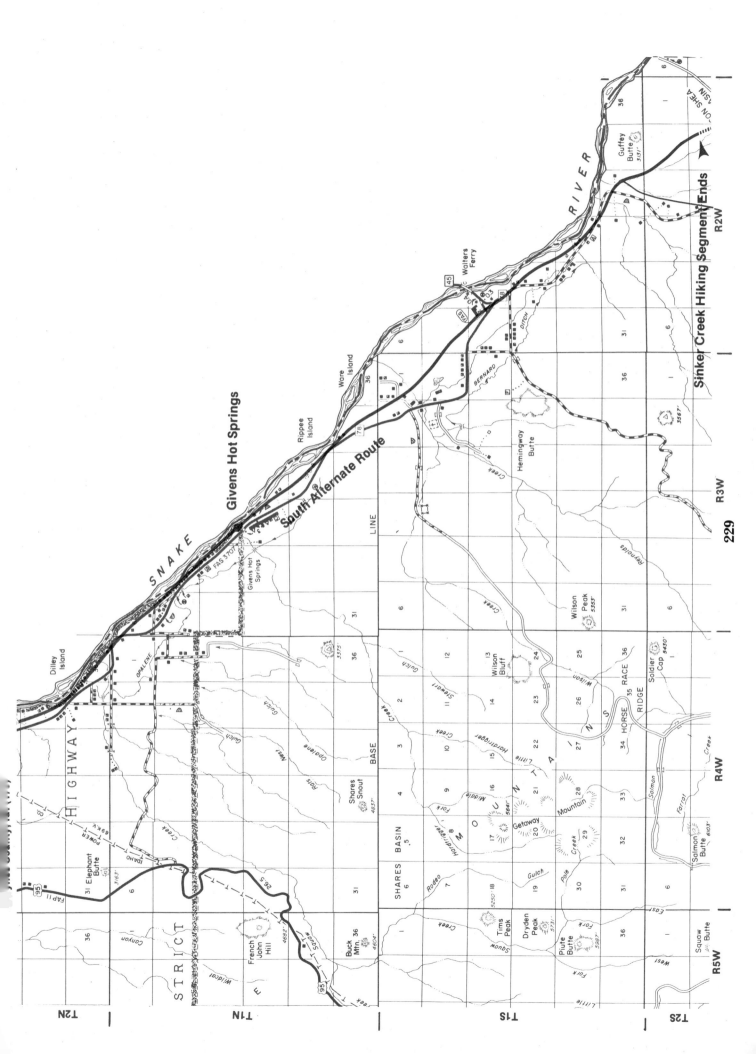

Sinker Creek Hiking Segment Ends

Givens Hot Springs

South Alternate Route

229

The emigrants rarely left the Snake for more than a mile during this stretch of the South Alternate Route, which crosses into what is now the State of Oregon. There is civilization along the way, meaning that there are lots of access roads along the section lines. That also means that practically all rut traces have disappeared.

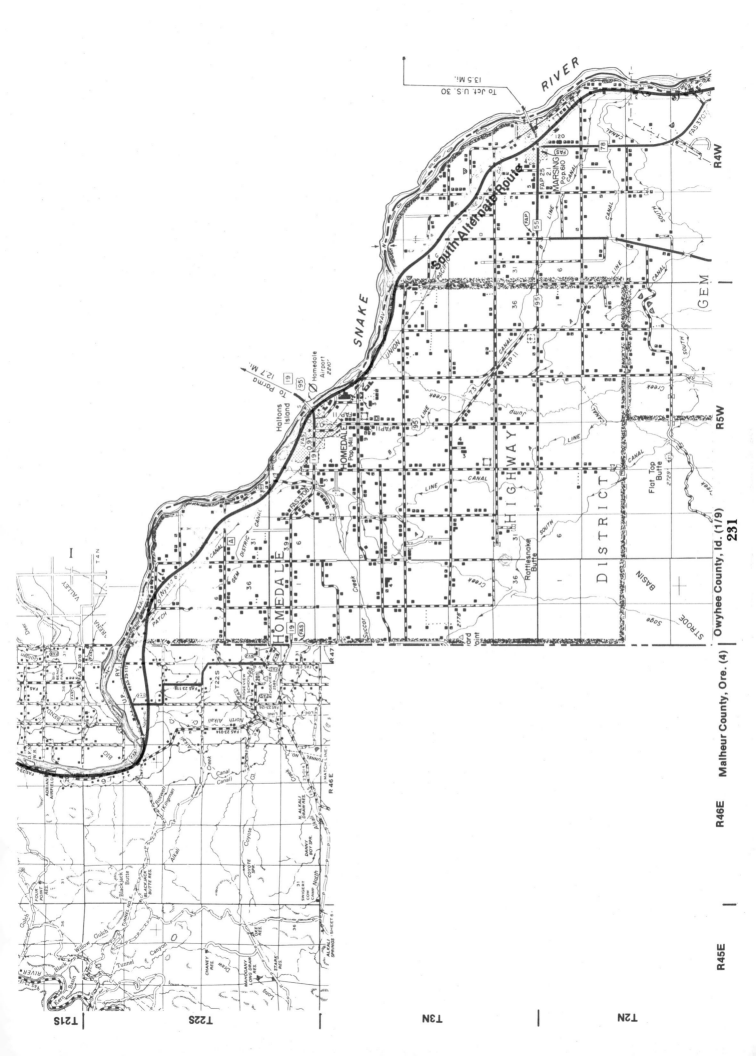

R45E | R46E Malheur County, Ore. (4) | Owyhee County, Id. (1/9)

231

This map overlaps a portion of the map on page 221. Bob and Bertha Rennells of La Grande, Oregon, are the experts on that state. Rennells is retired from the State Highway Department, that same organization which produced Oregon's fine brochure on the Oregon Trail. (A free copy may be obtained by writing to the Oregon State Highway Division, Travel Information Section, Salem, OR 97310). Rennells advises that there is a cedar post and granite marker just west of the Snake River, with a short rut swale barely visible inside the curve of Highway 201. The ruts from Keeney Pass to Vale are intermittent. The BLM has built an interpretive facility atop Keeney Pass, pointing the way to about a mile of the best ruts over the divide between the Snake and Malheur watersheds. The well-marked grave of John D. Henderson is on the left side of the highway entering Vale. The marker indicates that Henderson died of thirst, not knowing he was in sight of the river. That, according to Bob Rennells, is untrue. He has traced the story to the fictional theme of a third grade essayist in Vale.

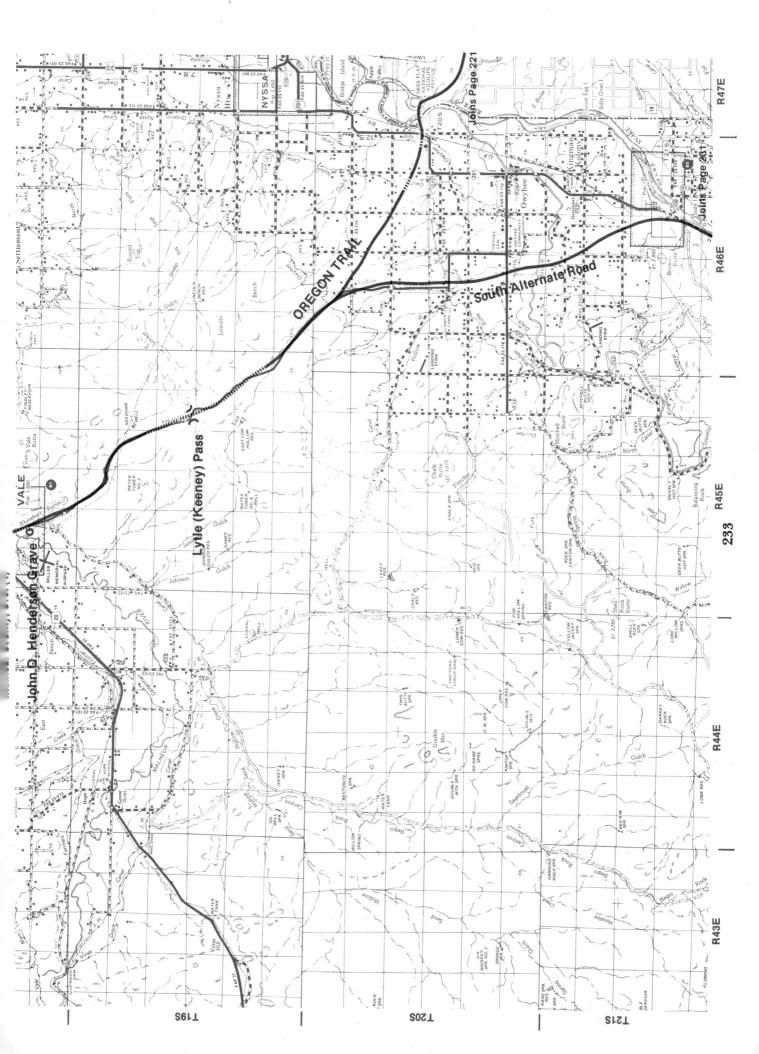

Four or five miles north of Vale, according to Rennells, are some unmarked emigrant graves. The first six miles of the trail north of town is a county-maintained road, and thereafter the ranch roads take over — sometimes over the ruts and sometimes adjacent to them. Some of the ground is private range land, where cattle have the right-of-way, and they damn well know it. A large portion of the route, however, is over BLM ground. There are a number of concrete Oregon Trail marker posts on that property, many of them vandalized. From a point six miles north of Vale to the top of the page, the ruts are good ones.

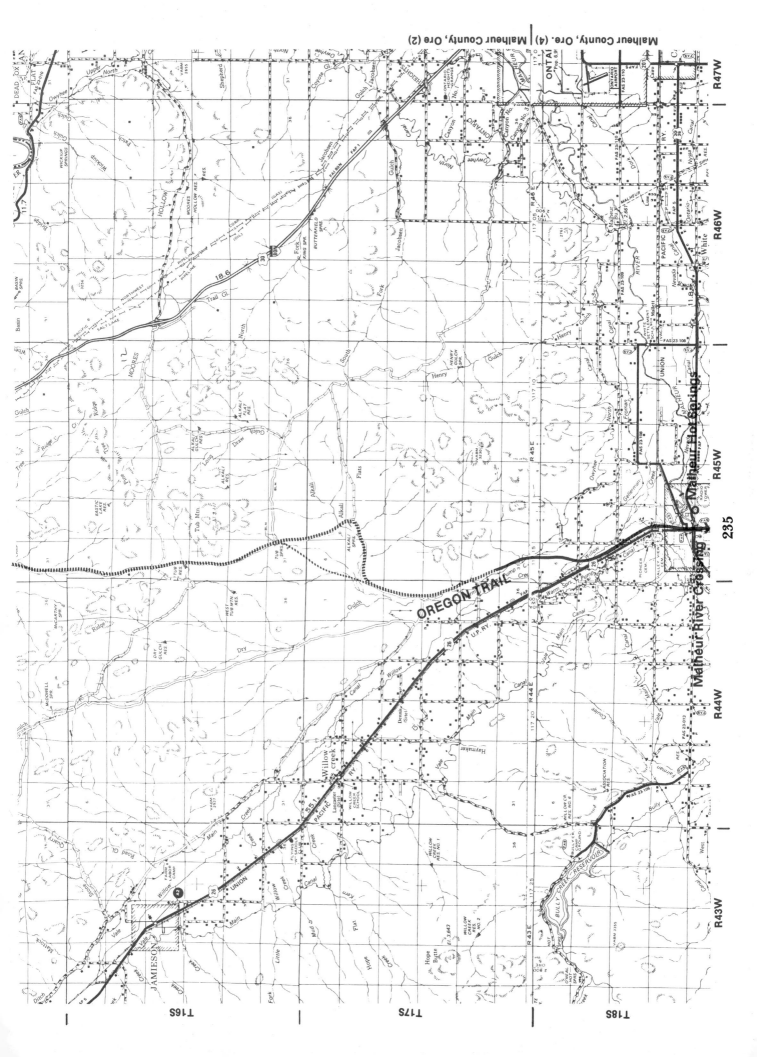

Intercepting the road north of the Love Reservoir is extremely difficult, but it can be done. The Oregon Trail simply disappears in this area, and the automobile traveler then must proceed through dead reckoning navigation to civilization. Oregon has installed a marvelous state park at Farewell Bend — the interpretation is clear and accurate. Both Gray and Duffin call attention to the fine ruts in that vicinity. Bob Rennells says that there are several sets of ruts visible near the Olds Ferry landing, coming off the hill. They are not evident on the site itself but are visible in the grazing areas, when viewed from the freeway. The highway department had to reinter two emigrant bodies — a man and a woman — which were on the site of the I-84/U.S. 30 interchange southeast of Olds Ferry. The new graves are several yards away from the original site. The emigration had a tough pull north of Huntington, where they unwittingly passed through country laden with gold. The trail is virtually impossible to follow through the canyon there, where railroad construction has wiped out all but a few rut remnants.

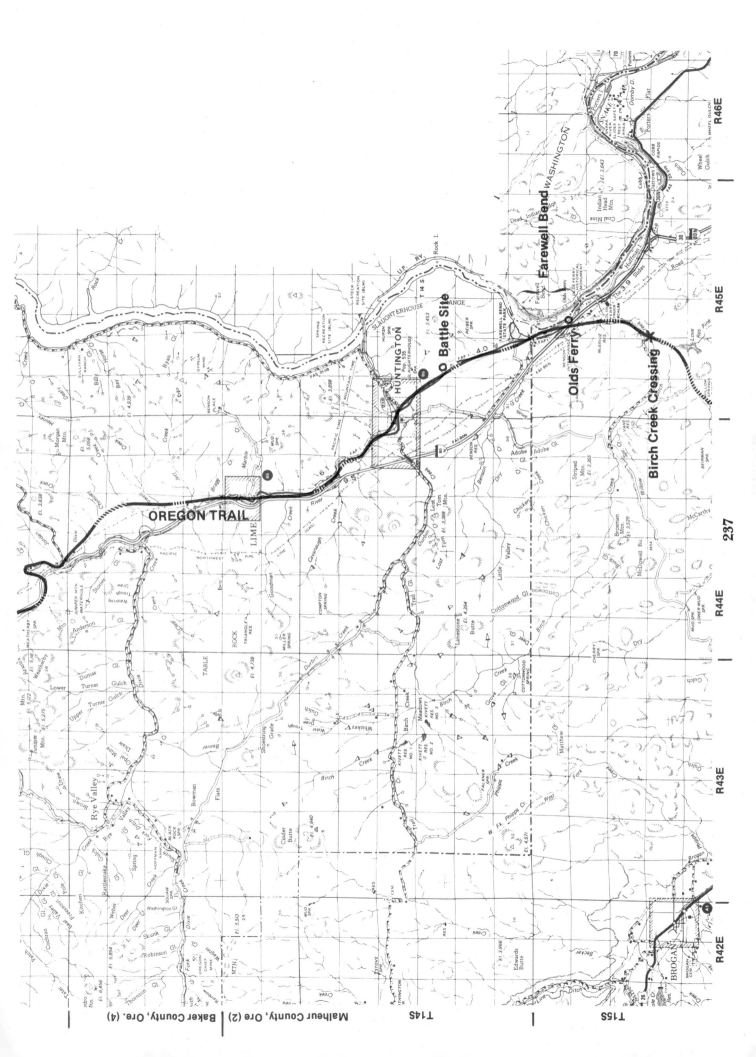

The Weatherby rest area was built on an old emigrant campsite, but highway construction has eradicated all rut traces there. The Burnt River was followed for some 15 miles north of Huntington, through a region described by John C. Fremont as being one of the worst stretches of the emigrant road. Charred debris observed in 1862 was then described as the remains of a wagon train which had burned two years earlier. The site is on private land, but most of the ruts indicated to the north are on BLM ground.

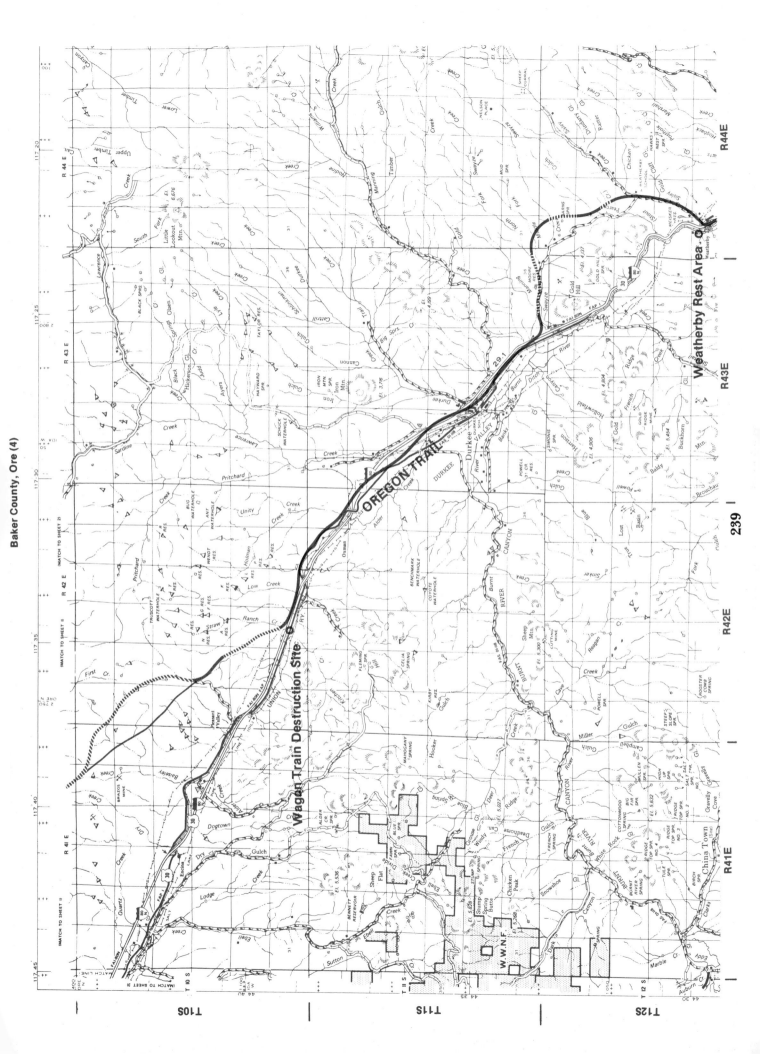

240

The Virtue Flat swarmed with gold seekers in the 1860s, but Oregon Trail travelers thought only of the Blue Mountains. The magnificent obstacles finally appeared as the emigration rounded Flagstaff Hill and descended into the pastoral Baker Valley. The BLM has erected a visitors display at Flagstaff Hill, and the ruts may be seen there descending almost to the valley floor. The Lone Pine, mentioned in many early diaries, was felled in the 1840s.

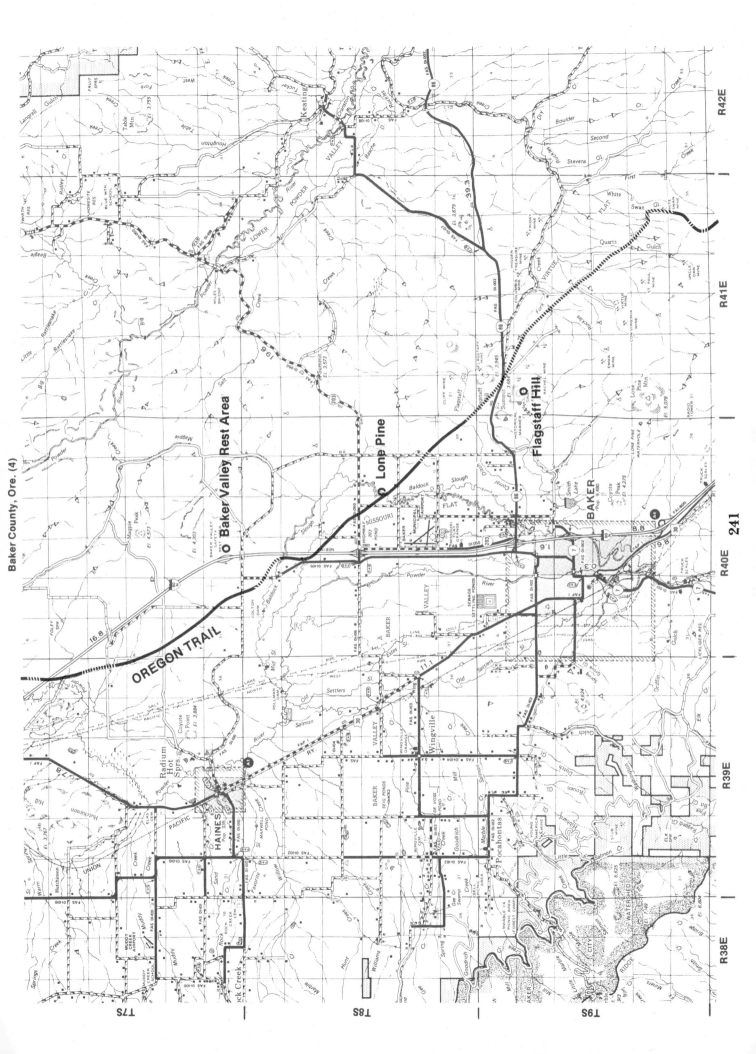

Baker County, Ore. (4)

241

The 15-Mile House is in bad shape and getting worse. New pipeline construction has devastated much of the rut segment atop Ladd Canyon Hill, but the descent swale into the Grande Ronde remains pristine. Some of the rut segments may be viewed from the I-84 safety rest area.

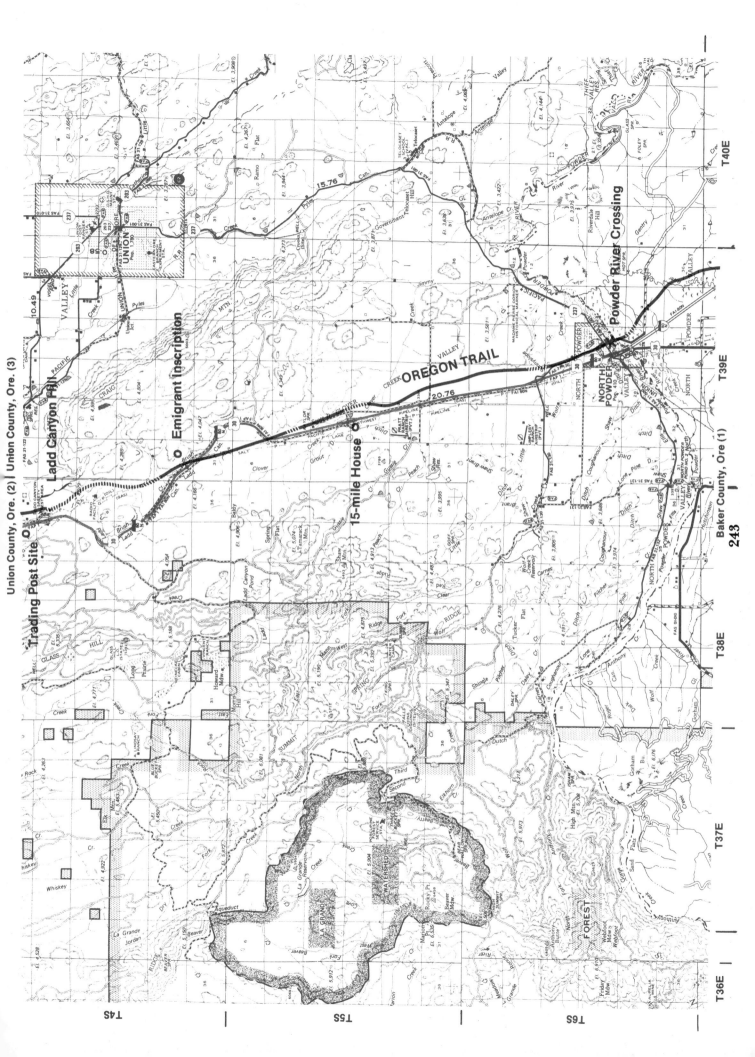

Union County, Ore. (2) | Union County, Ore. (3)

Trading Post Site

Ladd Canyon Hill

Emigrant Inscription

15-mile House

OREGON TRAIL

Powder River Crossing

NORTH POWDER

Baker County, Ore (1)

243

T40E T39E T38E T37E T36E

T4S T5S T6S

A good hiker could make the 18-mile Blue Mountain Hiking Segment in one day without puffing, but there are some problems there: both ends are on private land and are closed to the public. At this time hiking may begin at Hilgard and continue no further than the point where the Wallowa-Whitman National Forest ends, as shown on the map. This section of the trail traverses a forest which was seen with wonder by the midwesterners who came by a century and a half ago — it was their first close-up glimpse of a western coniferous forest. There is a fine rut swale south of the river in the Hilgard Junction State Park, but that portion of the area has yet to be developed for visitors. The Rennells have never found proof that the grave supposedly occupied by the body of Emily Doane really is, but they feel it is "very likely." There are three other graves in the vicinity.

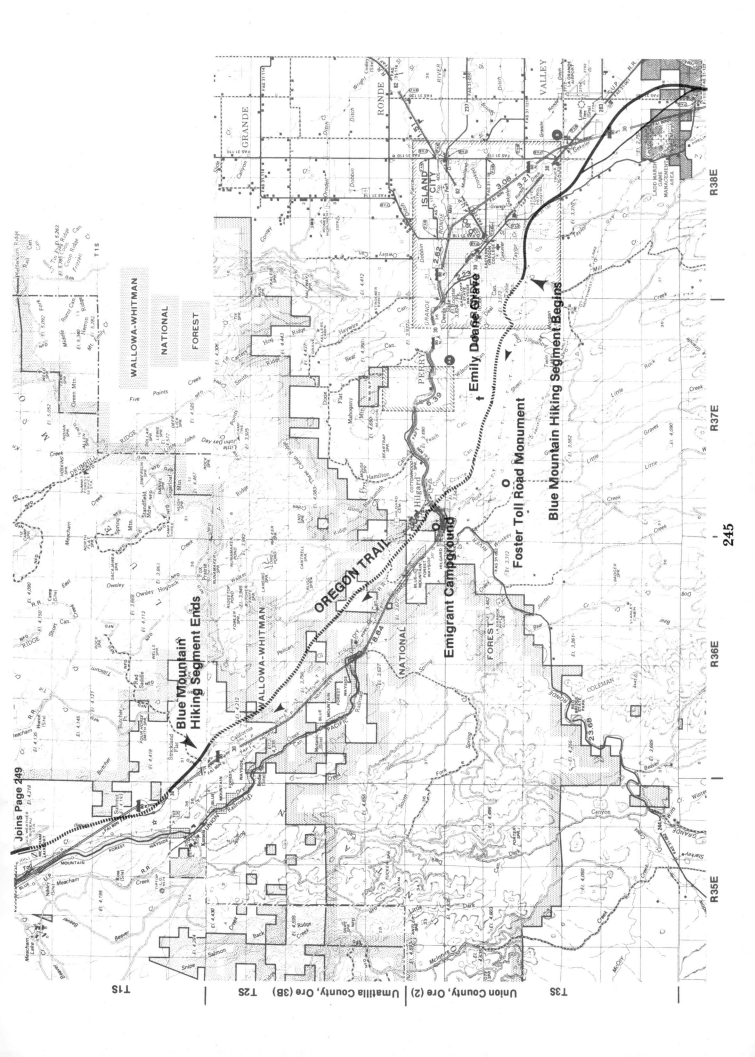

245

246

Emigrants were enthralled with the Grande Ronde when they passed through it, but there was no settlement there in the early years so they continued ahead to Oregon City. The present city of La Grande is one of the most beautiful in the West, and its citizens — especially Bob and Bertha Rennells — seem especially aware of their Oregon Trail heritage. A visit to "Old Town" is rewarding. The hiking segment to the west starts out on private property, and trespassing is absolutely forbidden in the first half mile. The full mile through section 12 is owned by a friendly rancher who occasionally opens it to visitors. There is absolutely no trespassing on the land to the west of there, where the owner has armed riders on patrol.

City of La Grande, Ore.

OREGON TRAIL

Blue Mountain
Hiking Segment Begins

"Old Town"

TABLE MTN

T 2 S T 3 S R 38 E
WILLAMETTE MERIDIAN

248

Emigrant Springs is another sylvan state park. The springs which attracted the 19th century travelers became victims of pipeline construction many years ago, but several smaller springs still rise within the park. Deadman Pass marked the end of the climb out of the Grande Ronde, and the last stretch through the Blue Mountains. From the summit, a mile northwest of the rest stop, the emigrants were able to view the valley of the Umatilla — a thrilling sight indeed. At the bottom of the slope a branch of the trail turned northeast to the Whitman Mission, west of present Walla Walla, Washington. The route has long since been lost, since it was abandoned after the brutal Whitman massacre in 1847. The National Park Service has done a superb job of interpretation there, and a half-day visit is urged.

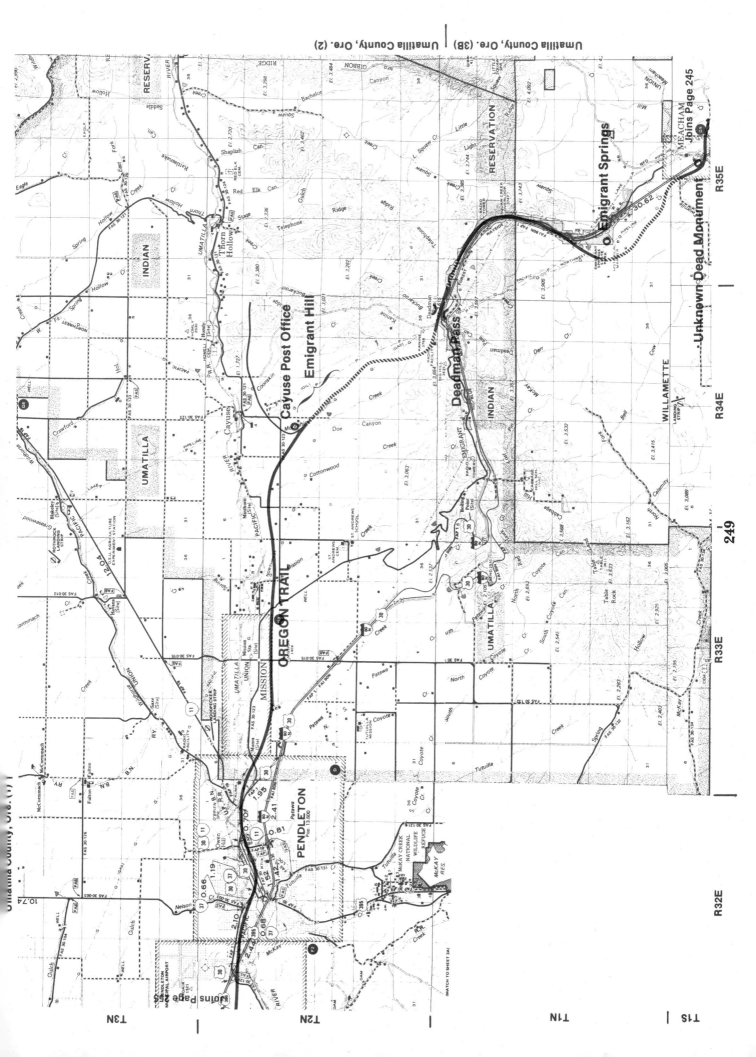

Emigrant Springs

Unknown Dead Monument

MEACHAM
Joins Page 245

RESERVATION

INDIAN

UMATILLA

Cayuse Post Office

Emigrant Hill

Deadman Pass

OREGON TRAIL

MISSION

PENDLETON
Pop. 13,500

McKAY CREEK
NATIONAL
WILDLIFE
REFUGE

McKAY
RES.

Joins Page 245

R32E | R33E | R34E | R35E

T3N | T2N | T1N | T1S

The route through the city of Pendleton today is largely conjectural, as all trace of the old trail has long since disappeared. Even the location of the Umatilla crossing is debatable.

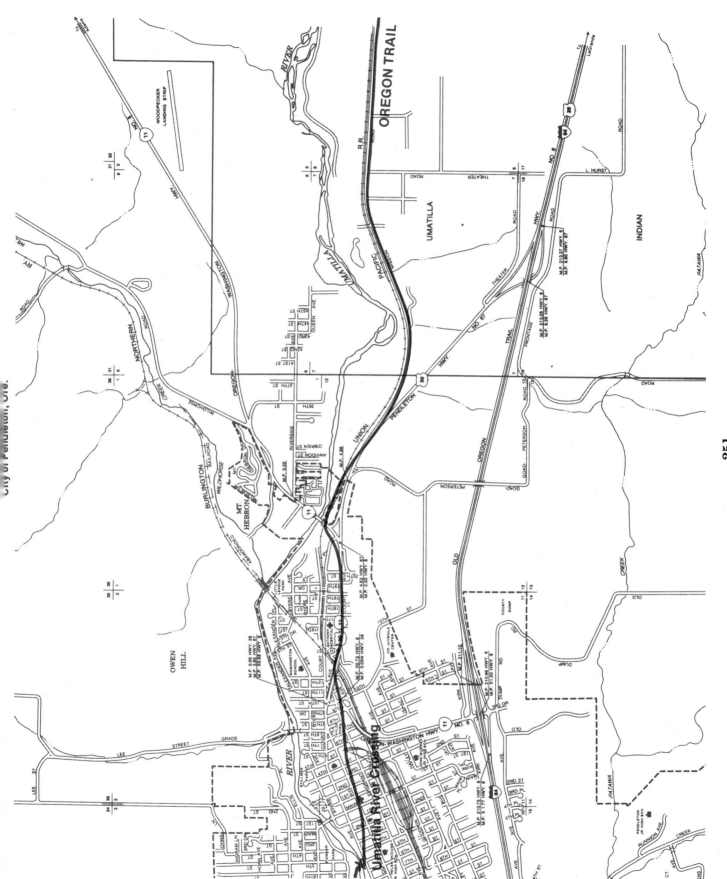

OREGON TRAIL

Umatilla River Crossing

There is a commemorative marker on Highway 30 a quarter of a mile southwest of Blue Mountain Community College, just west of the state hospital.

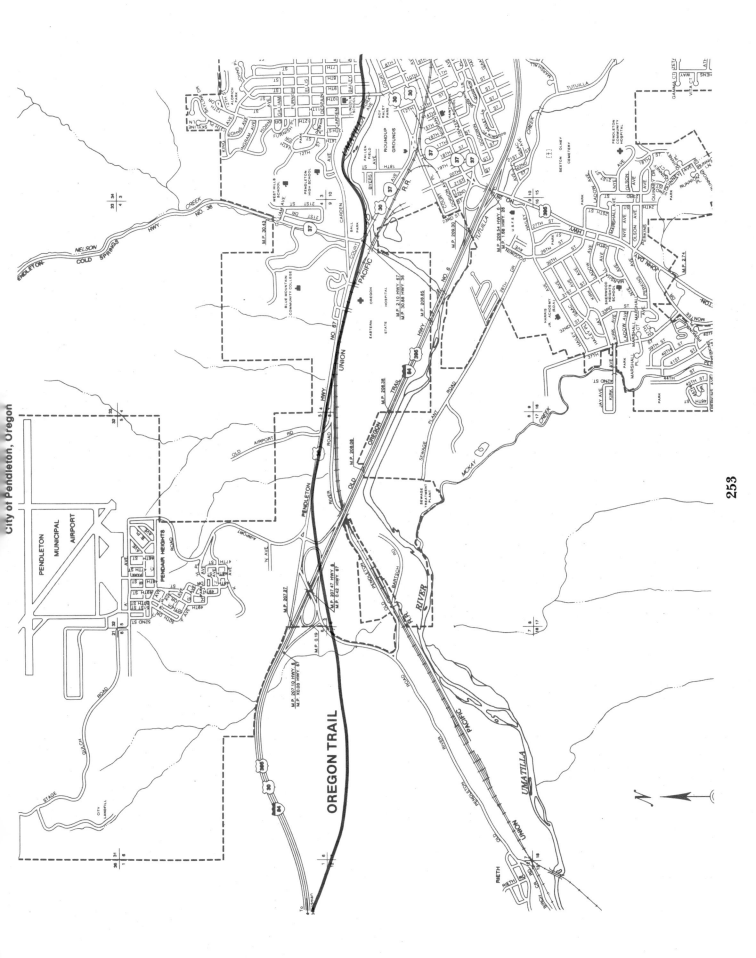

City of Pendleton, Oregon

253

There couldn't be a more meaningful presentation of the case for education about the Oregon Trail than can be found in Echo Meadows. A few years ago this rut segment from "A" to "Z" was absolutely pristine. It has since been plowed and is now in grain. In the early spring and at maturity, just prior to harvest, the swale of the Oregon Trail is barely discernible. Would the farmer have reacted favorably had he been asked to donate a hiking easement through his land? Had he been offered a modest sum for this purpose? Greater efforts must be made toward preservation while there is still something left to preserve.

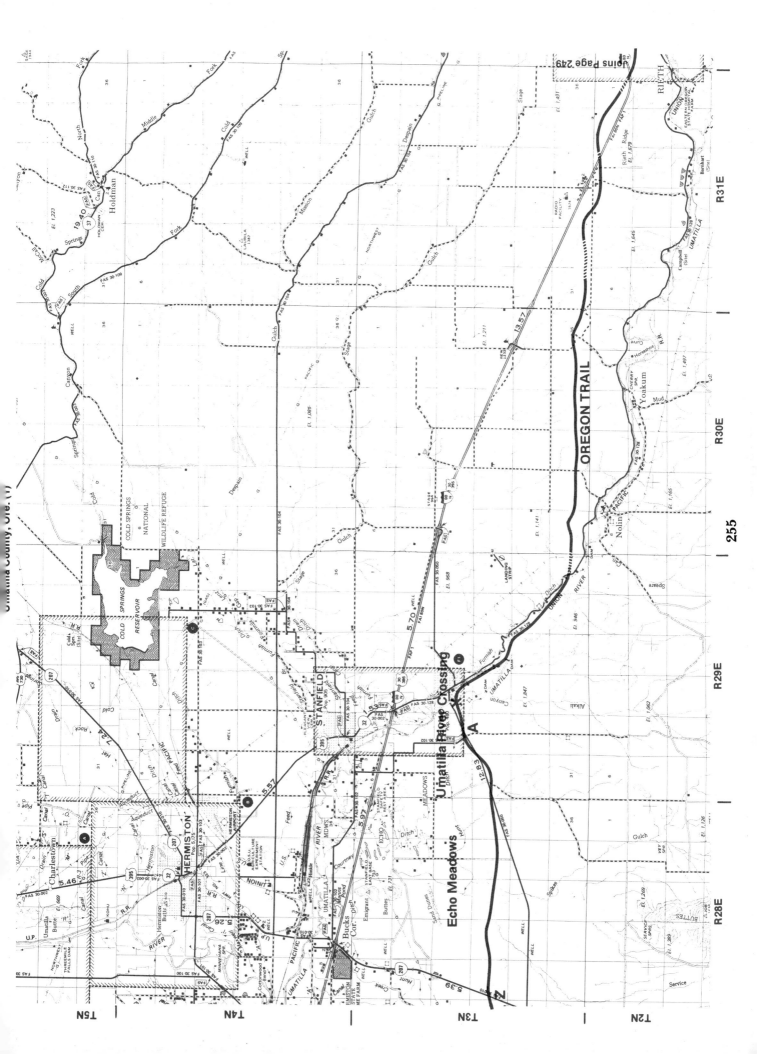

Umatilla County, Ore. (1)

OREGON TRAIL

RIETH

Umatilla River Crossing

Echo Meadows

STANFIELD
Pop. 905

HERMISTON
Pop. 5,175

Charlestown

COLD SPRINGS
RESERVOIR

COLD SPRINGS
NATIONAL
WILDLIFE REFUGE

Holdman

255

R28E   R29E   R30E   R31E

T5N   T4N   T3N   T2N

256

The Boardman Bombing Range is owned by the U.S. Navy. Part is leased to Boeing Aircraft Company and part to ranchers for grazing purposes. The land from Butter Creek Road, on the right edge of the map, west to the bombing range is also private. The Navy occasionally uses the northern portion of the bombing range for gunnery practice, so it would be a good idea to stay on the trail — if they don't shoot the cattle, then theoretically at least they won't shoot the hikers. There are several well-springs along the southern boundary of the range. The site shown here is the principal one, located adjacent to the foundation and other ruins of the old stage station.

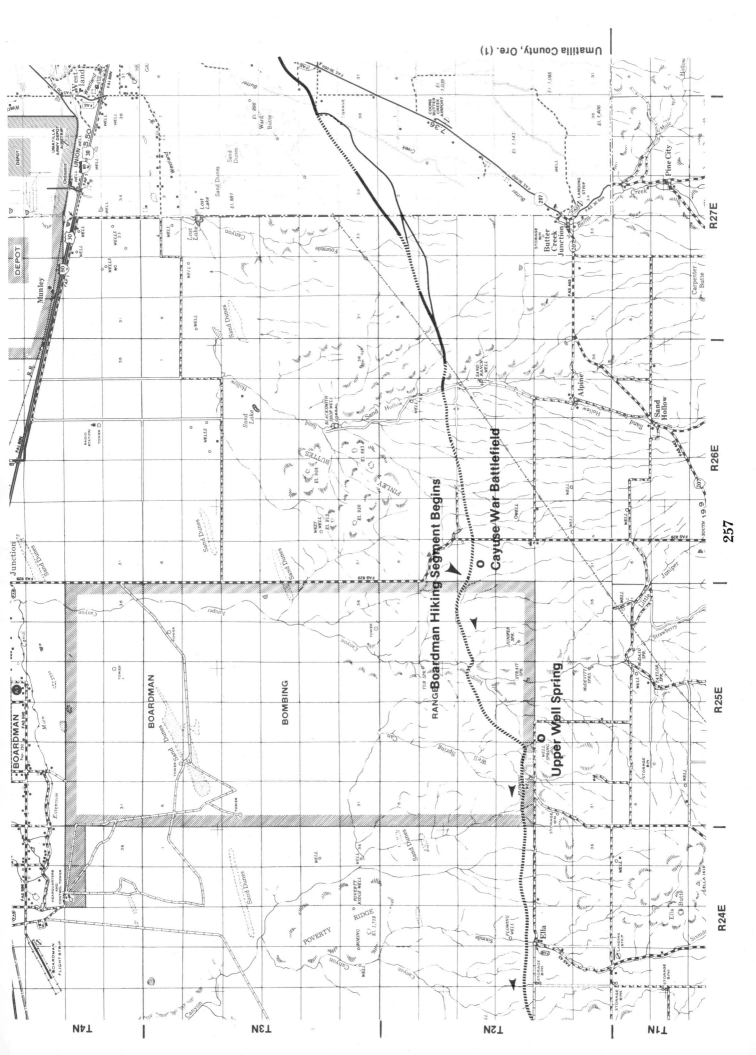

Umatilla County, Ore. (1)

258

The BLM has established a fine little interpretive site where the Oregon Trail ruts pass through Fourmile Canyon. They are on both sides of the gravel road. It was along here that the emigrants first caught sight of the snowy tip of Mount Hood.

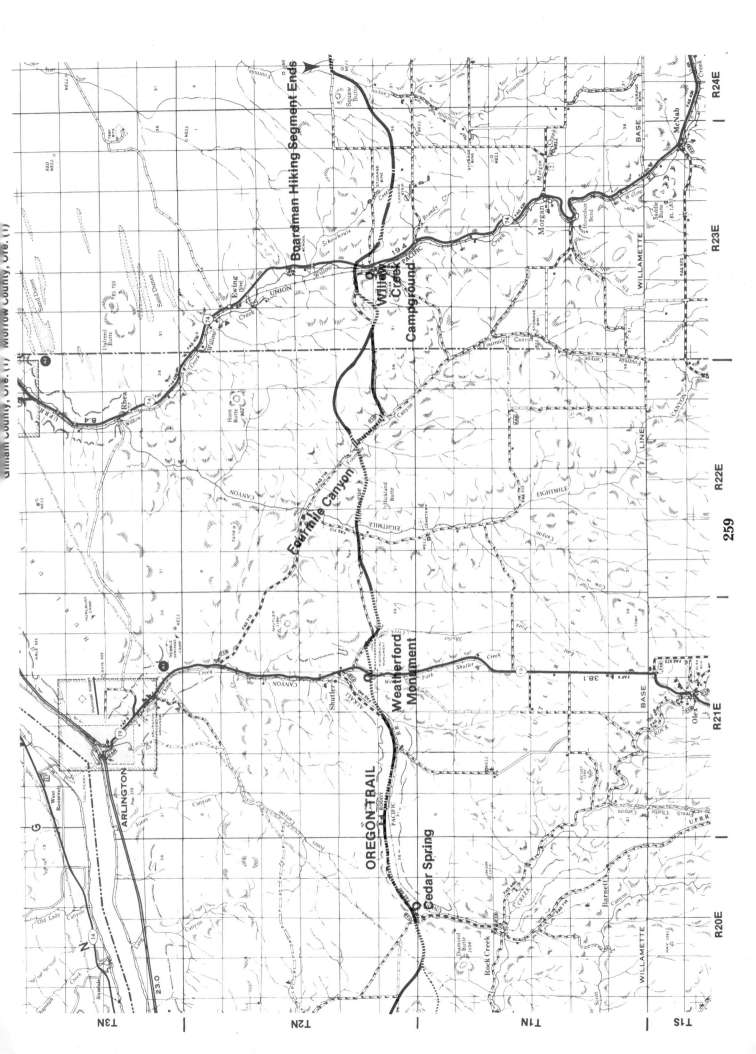

259

Today's traveler may experience a great 19th century thrill by crossing the John Day River at McDonald Ford. This is BLM land, but there is private land all around it — it is a good idea to stick to the county roads. The ford ranges in depth from 6 to 12 inches during midsummer, negotiable by high-slung vehicles but lots more fun for hikers. The trail is visible both leading down to and emerging from the ford, but not right at the ford on either bank.

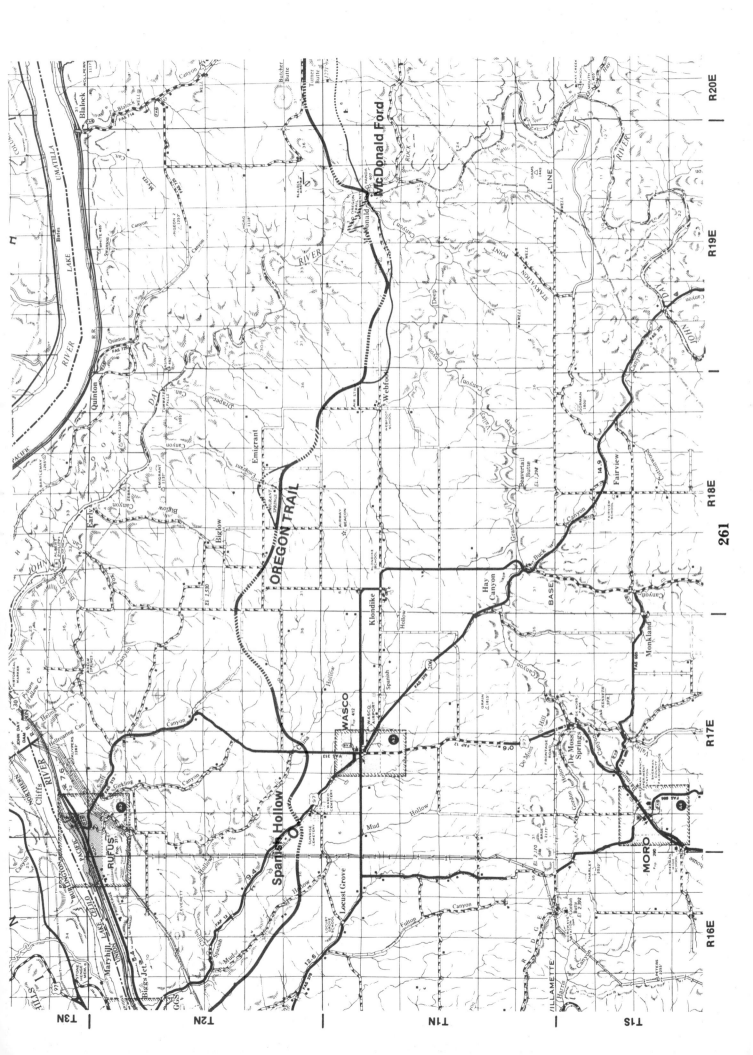

Certainly one of the most thrilling vistas of the emigrant route was seen from the crest of the hill near Biggs Junction, when the travelers caught their first view of the broad Columbia River, then turned to see the snow cone of Mount Hood towering over their left shoulders. The "first view" monument is located along old Highway 30 just west of town. Wherever possible, visitors should drive along that old highway west of here, rather than the interstate highway. At the Deschutes River the trail up the west side is quite evident from either Highway 30 or I-84, particularly in early morning or late evening light.

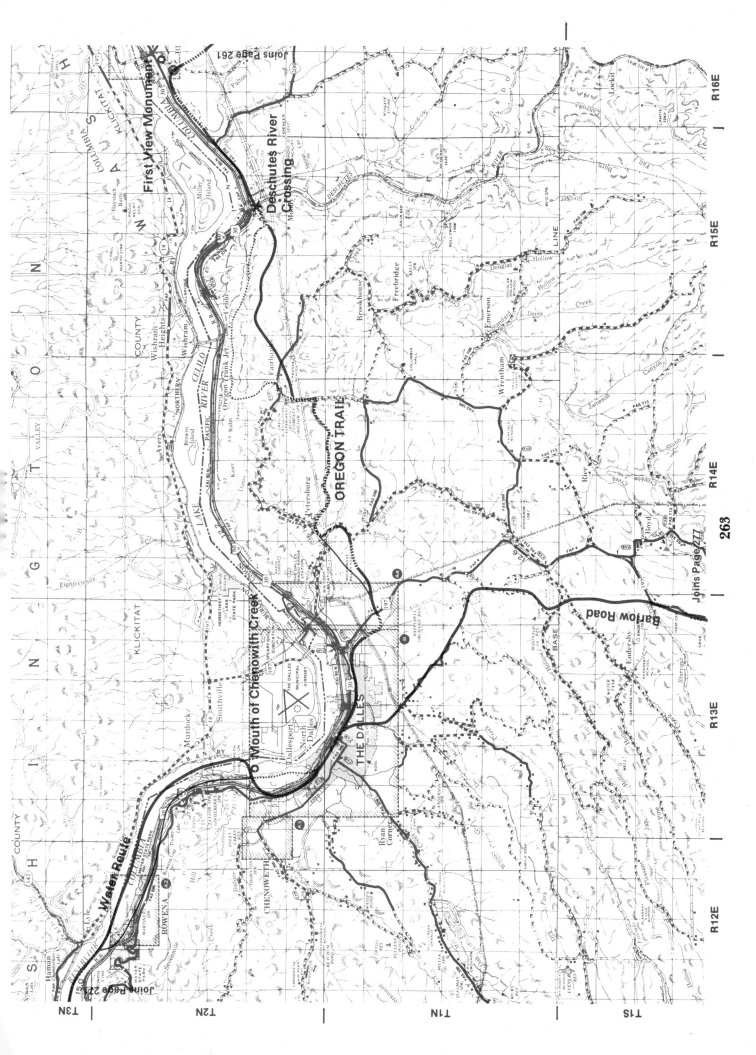

Joins Page 261

First View Monument

Deschutes River Crossing

OREGON TRAIL

Mouth of Chenowith Creek

THE DALLES

Water Route

ROWENA

Barlow Road

Joins Page 277

Joins Page 217

The Dalles is considered to be the end of the land route to Oregon City, but Jim Weeks of that city reminds readers that this was strictly true only for three years — 1843 through 1845. The Barlow Road became an extension of the trail in 1846. Furthermore, water travelers sometimes had to proceed a few miles downriver to the Rowena area for timber to use in their rafts.

COLUMBIA

RIVER

C E L I L O   L A K E

THE DALLES MUNICIPAL AIRPORT

DALLESPORT

BURLINGTON

RY.

KLICKITAT — COUNTY
WASCO — COUNTY

HESS PARK

THE DALLES DAM

VICTORS BLDG

COVINGTON PT.

SEUFERT PARK

GRAVE ISLAND MEMORIAL CEM.
CUSHING FALLS
M.P. 87.79

VIEWPOINT

FIFTEENMILE CREEK

ROAD

FAS B411

RADIO TOWERS

SUBSTATION

BIG EDDY SUBSTATION

SUBSTATION

MICROWAVE RELAY STATION

31 32
6 5

36 31

CITY RES.

NO. 4
To Dufur
FAP 4

CALIFORNIA

HAZELDELL ORCHARD RES.

CREEK

FIFTEENMILE

LAMBERT

THIRTEENMILE

SUMMIT RIDGE DR. E.
ROYAL CREST DR.
CREST VIEW DR.
BRENTWOOD
COLUMBIA VIEW DR
M.P. 1.28

DRIVE-IN THEATER

STATE HIGHWAY STATION

INDIAN RD

UNION

COLUMBIA DR

PARK RD

THE DALLES

SEVENTH DAY ADVENTIST SCHOOL

13TH

ST.

RICHMOND ST.

MORTON

2
11 12

DIST. 12 RAM

11TH ST.

14TH PL.

15TH

18TH

E. 17TH ST.

THOMPSON ST.

16TH

E. 17TH ST.

MONROE

FREMONT ST.

10TH

OLD DUFUR

MOSIER

E. 9TH ST.

E. 11TH ST.

12TH

SHEARER ST

RESERVOIR

THOMPSON ATHLETIC FIELD

OREGON

QUINTON

E. 14TH ST.
E. 16TH ST.

NEVADA ST.

THE DALLES GENERAL HOSPITAL

MINNESOTA ST.

CLAUDIA CT.

VIEW CT.

ATHLETIC FIELD

ROBERTS ST

E. 14TH ST

12TH ST.

DRY HOLLOW RD.

VIEW CT.

HAZEL PL.

14TH ST.

LEWIS ST.

CLARK ST.

E. 15TH ST.

DRY HOLLOW SCHOOL

LEWIS

10 11
3 2

MONROE

UNION

BREWERY

GRADE

9TH

JOS G. WILSON SCHOOL

HARRIS PARK

THE DALLES CITY

RIVERVIEW

E. DRY STATION

JOINS PAGE 267

COLUMBIA

ROAD

FAP 4

CALIFORNIA

M.P. 0.00

M.P. 9.41

THE DALLES

TYE

LOCKS

M.P. 86.81

BOAT BASIN

TRAILER PARK

TRAILER PARK

E. ON AMN. 101.8
E. ON HWY. NO. 585
M.P. 0.00
M.P. 8.99 HWY. NO. 2

HWY. NO. 1

STATE NO. 292

30

197

CALIFORNIA

THE DALLES PACIFIC HWY.

COLUMBIA RIVER

84

M.P. 18.74

FAI 84

MADISON

30

NO. 2

UNION

MONROE

STATE STA.

M.P.

OREGON TRAIL

Barlow Road

FAS B413

RD.

One of the most interesting cities along the trail is The Dalles, where the residents have carefully marked their points of interest. Visitors to The Dalles are encouraged to stop at the Original Courthouse. Wendy Bradley, who is in charge of the visitor center there, helps the author with his books and if she'll help him she'll help anybody.

Joins Page 269

OREGON TRAIL

Rock Fort (Lewis & Clark)

Original Courthouse

Olney's Store

Barlow Road

Joins Page 265

Joins Page 265

Mission Monument

End of the Trail Monument

Parade Ground

Fort Dalles Building

Wascopam Springs

Mission Site

Pulpit Rock

DRY HOLLOW

RYAN CORNER

267

The rafts were boarded at the mouth of Chenowith Creek (the spelling has been corrupted from the original "Chenoweth"). The river route is shown here. Impoundment of the Columbia makes water passage much easier today, because the rapids now are covered and the Corps of Engineers will open the Bonneville locks for any craft. Highway 30 west of The Dalles is a beautiful drive. The River Road dead-ends at the mouth of Chenowith Creek, where the Mountain Fir Lumber Company operates a pulp mill. Travelers of the 19th century sometimes continued on land for another six or seven miles to an area near present Mayer State Park. There the Rowena Bluffs closed in on the river and stopped all further wagon passage by land.

City of The Dalles, Ore.

GOOSEBERRY

CHENOWITH

COLUMBIA RIVER

OREGON TRAIL (Whitman Route)
WASCO CO.

RIVER

COLUMBIA

FAI 84

30

RIVER HWY

COLUMBIA

NO. 292 (FAI)

TAYLOR FRANTZ RD

The Dalles Country Club

TRAILER COURT

TAYLOR LAKE

SQUAW ISLANDS

ROCKY ISLAND

POND

UNION NO. 2

CREEK

VALLEY

HIDDEN

FOLEY LAKES RESERVIOR

BADGER

SEVENMILE RD

FAS 8A17

HILL

DR

MURRAY

CREEK

WHITMAN CT W

MAPLE ST W

OAK ST W

PINE ST W

HILAND ST

STARWFLDT CT W

FAS 8A18

CHENOWITH

BURLINGTON

WASHINGTON
OREGON

Mouth of Chenowith Creek

KLINDT POINT

CHENOWITH SUBSTATION

THE DALLES HWY

CREEK

MOSIER

M.P. 82.37

CRATES

PACIFIC

MOSIER ST W

COLUMBIA

THE DALLES ST

ALUMINUM PLANT

Joins Page 267

269

CHENOWITH
LOOP

NW COLUMBUS

CASCADE

COLUMBUS ST W

IRVINE WAY W

LEE WAY W

DAWSON

DRIVE THEATER

CHENOWITH PRIMARY GRADES

CHENOWITH
HIGH SCHOOL

CHENOWITH W

LORENZEN ST W

CHENOWITH MIDDLE SCHOOL

FOREST ST W

W. 14TH ST

OCCI-MID-COLUMBIA EDUCATIONAL CENTER ADMIN. BLDG.

GRANGE

ATHLETIC FIELD

13TH

EMERSON

10TH

11TH ST

W. 12TH ST

W. 13TH

GARDEN

PLEASANT

CASCADE CT W

HOSTETLER

RICHLAND

FLORAL CT W

HOME CT W

LYNDHURST

7TH CT W

ROAD

CHENOWITH ST W

CHENOWITH

Hood River is one of the most scenic towns in Oregon, largely because of its proximity to the peak for which it was named. Highway 35 will take today's traveler around the cone in utmost comfort.

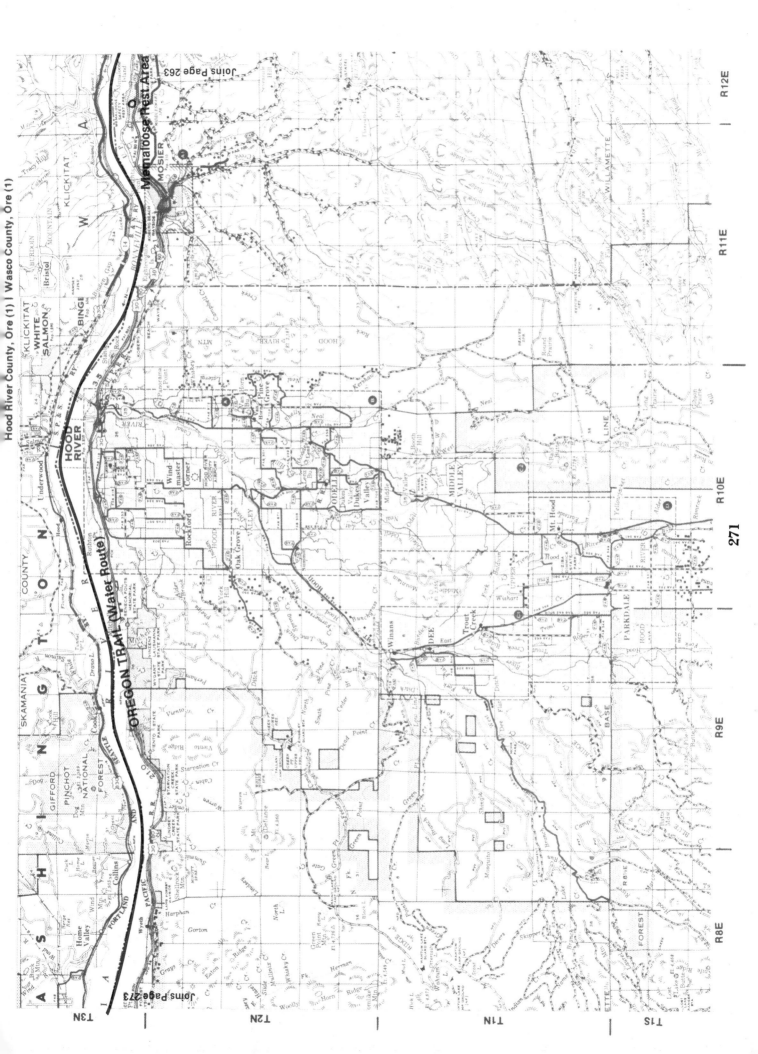

272

A great deposition of rocks caused by a prehistoric landslide forced the rafts ashore in the vicinity of Cascade Locks, for a portage of from three to five miles. (The obstacles are still there, now inundated completely by the waters behind Bonneville Dam.) Afloat again, the emigrants stared agog at the beautiful falls and canyons among the forested hills of the south bank. Old Highway 30 here offers one of the most magnificent drives in the United States, and it's free.

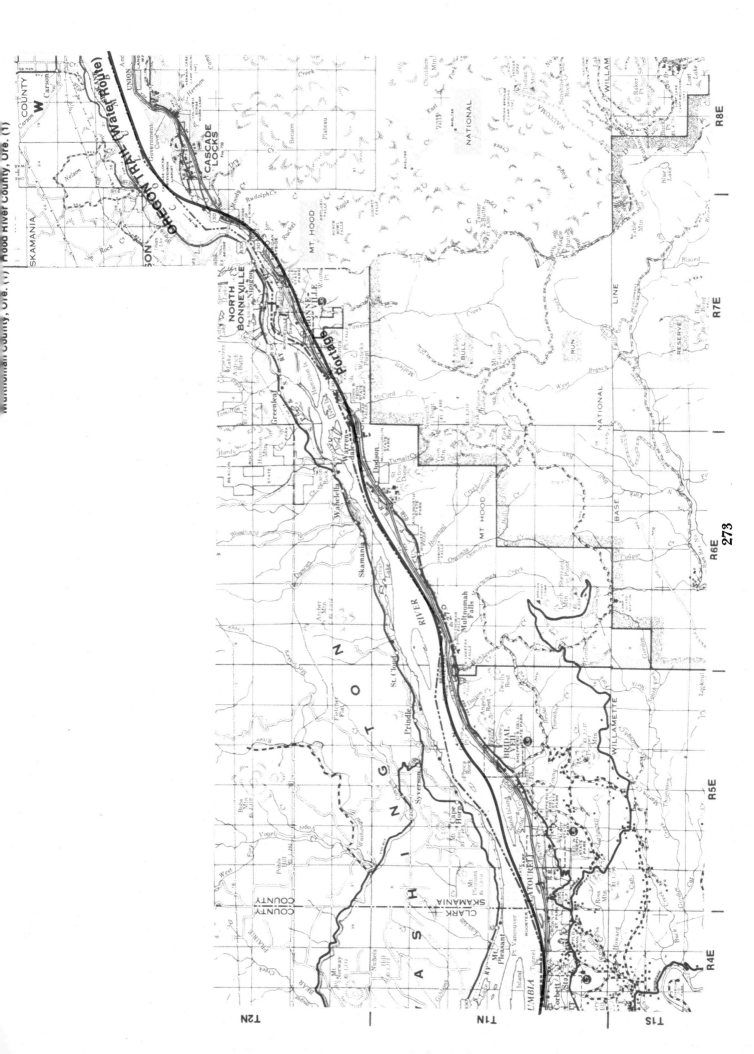

Some of the emigration stopped off at Fort Vancouver but most of the water travelers continued on to the mouth of the Willamette. They proceeded up that river to Oregon City. Fort Vancouver is now in the midst of a restoration program by the National Park Service. The stockade wall and five of the buildings have been reconstructed following an intensive archaeological investigation. (The maps on pages 285 and 287 complete the water route to Oregon City.)

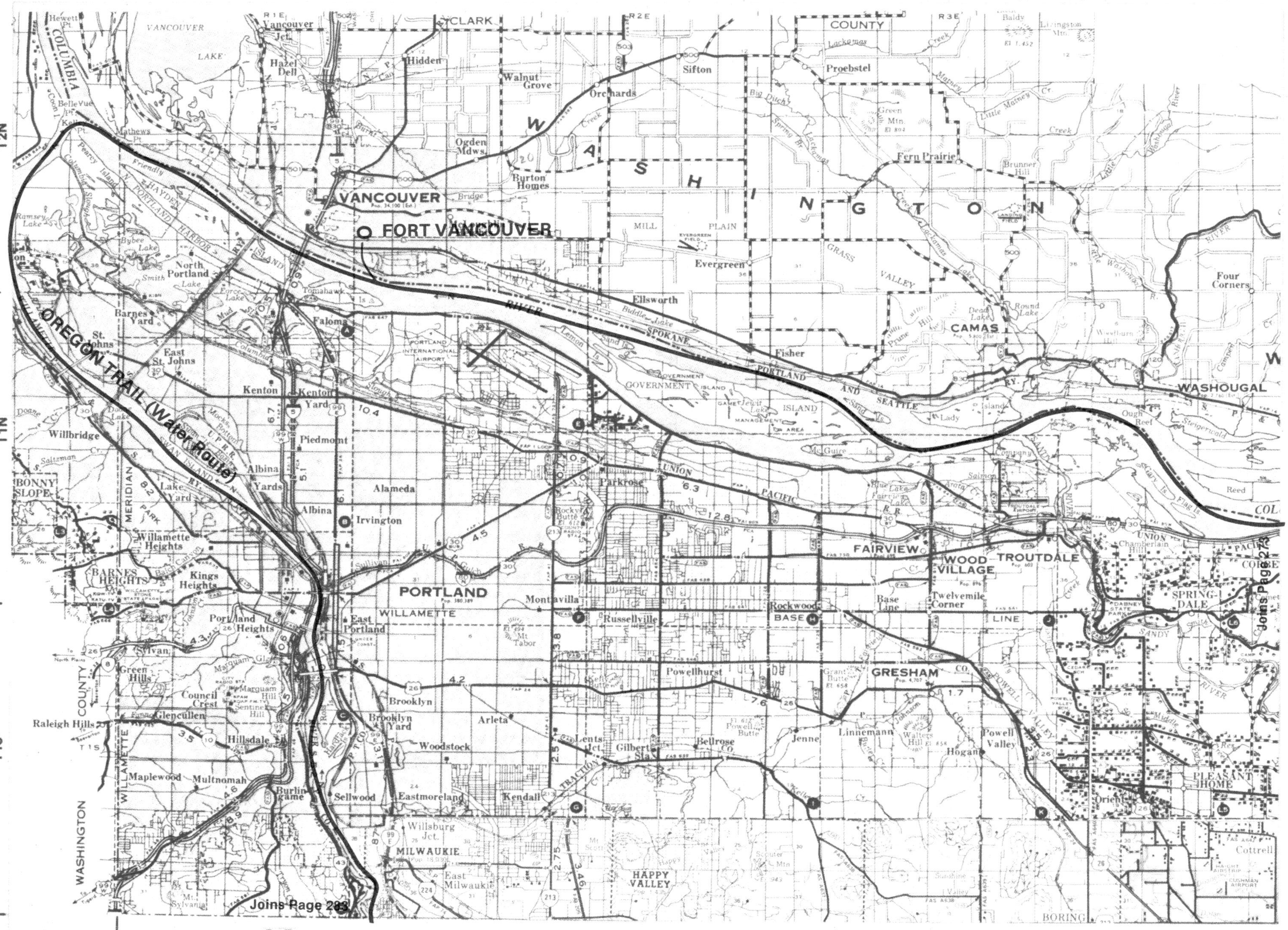
VANCOUVER
FORT VANCOUVER
OREGON TRAIL (Water Route)
PORTLAND
WASHINGTON
CLARK
COUNTY
COLUMBIA
RIVER
WASHOUGAL
CAMAS
FAIRVIEW
WOOD VILLAGE
TROUTDALE
GRESHAM
MILWAUKIE
HAPPY VALLEY
Sifton
Orchards
Walnut Grove
Hidden
Hazel Dell
Vancouver Jct.
Proebstel
Fern Prairie
Brunner Hill
Four Corners
Evergreen
Ellsworth
Fisher
Burton Homes
Ogden Mdws.
North Portland
St. Johns
East St. Johns
Barnes Yard
Kenton
Piedmont
Alameda
Irvington
Albina
Parkrose
Montavilla
Russellville
Rockwood
Powellhurst
Brooklyn
Arleta
Woodstock
Sellwood
Eastmoreland
Kendall
Lents Jct.
Gilbert Sta.
Bellrose
Jenne
Linnemann
Hogan
Powell Valley
Pleasant Home
Orient
Cottrell
Boring
Spring-Dale
Twelvemile Corner
Base Line
Willbridge
Bonny Slope
Willamette Heights
Barnes Heights
Kings Heights
Portland Heights
Sylvan
Green Hills
Council Crest
Glencullen
Raleigh Hills
Hillsdale
Maplewood
Multnomah
Burlingame
Mt. Sylvania
Willsburg Jct.
East Milwaukie
East Portland
Portland International Airport
Government Island
McGuire Is.
Union Pacific R.R.
Spokane Portland and Seattle Ry.
Joins Page 283
Joins Page 273
T2N
T1N
T1S
R1E
R2E
R3E
R4E

Jim Weeks feels that the Tygh Valley, not The Dalles, should be considered the start of the Barlow Road. Barlow was able to travel there over established trails from near The Dalles in a single day. Cultivation south of The Dalles is believed to have wiped out all traces of the Barlow Road. Just west of the town of Tygh Valley, where emigrants frequently camped, there are intermittent ruts climbing out of the valley floor. Those, according to Weeks, are not remnants of the Barlow Road, as many believe, but early versions of the road to Wamic. "The Barlow Road went up a swale direct to the top of the hill," he said.

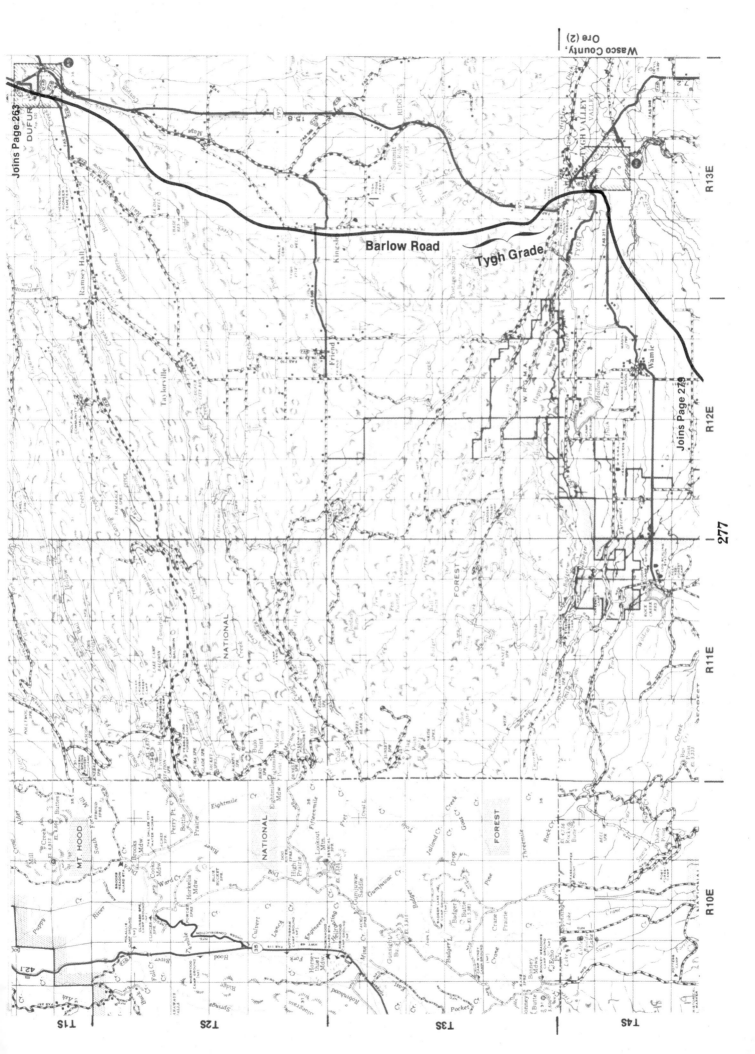

Joins Page 263

DUFUR

Barlow Road

Tygh Grade

TYGH VALLEY

Friend

Wamic

Joins Page 249

277

NATIONAL

FOREST

MT. HOOD

NATIONAL

FOREST

R10E   R11E   R12E   R13E

T1S   T2S   T3S   T4S

The exact location of the east tollgate of the Barlow Road is lost, but it is believed to have been in the meadow at the indicated point. Traces of the old road may be seen leaving that meadow to the south. The Barlow Road Hiking Segment extends for 32 miles between the east and west tollgates. The eastern half, to Barlow Pass, is over primitive dirt roads but may be traversed with a normal automobile. The dirt road follows the Barlow for most of the way, but in places it takes a shortcut, leaving pristine ruts in between. Vehicles travel the road, but the Forest Service wisely refuses to grade or improve it in any way. That means it is very rough. The only way to do it right is to hoof it, just as the emigrants did. "Fort Deposit," where Sam Barlow left his wagons while he packed out to the settlements during the initial use of the road, has never been lo-

cated. Troy Gray prefers the westernmost of the two possibilities shown. Weeks feels it was located at or close to Devil's Half Acre: "Many of us who have researched the Barlow story do not think the cabin was located on the White River but rather on Barlow Creek — and not far from the summit. This may or may not be important to this discussion, but William Barlow, Sam's son, says in his noted *Reminiscences of Seventy Years* that a visitor who spent the winter of 1845-46 with the caretaker of Fort Deposit: '. . . In the spring he got up his horses that he had kept **down on the creek** on good grass all winter and went back to The Dalles.' I don't think anyone would refer to the White River, a sizable stream, as a 'creek.'" The passage through Devil's Half Acre and Barlow Pass is incredibly beautiful.

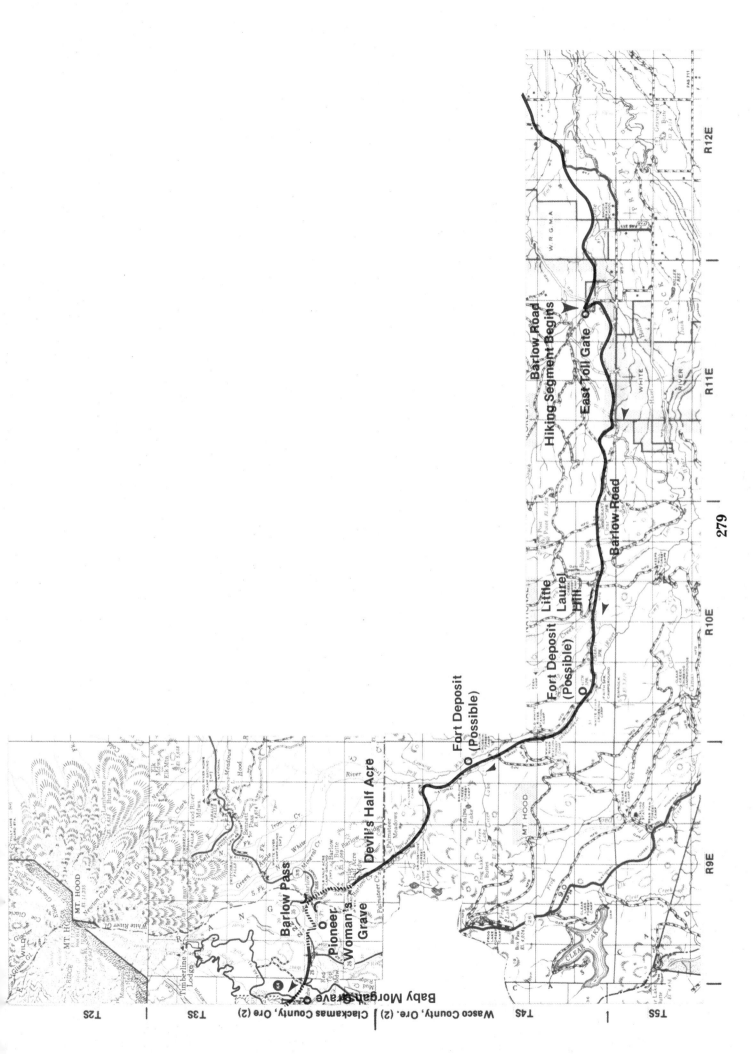

MT. HOOD

Barlow Pass

Pioneer
Woman's
Grave

Baby Morgan grave

Devil's Half Acre

Fort Deposit
(Possible)

Fort Deposit
(Possible)

Little
Laurel
Hill

Barlow Road

Barlow Road
Hiking Segment Begins

East Toll Gate

Wasco County, Ore. (2) | Clackamas County, Ore (2)

T2S

T3S

T4S

T5S

R9E

R10E

R11E

R12E

Traces of the trail vanish about a mile west of the Pioneer Woman's Grave, but may be picked up by following the paved roads to Summit Meadows, where Vicker's Summit House stood. (It was a later facility.) Laurel Hill was the most difficult passage of the entire Oregon Trail. Several tree stumps near the top of the chute bore evidence of rope burns, cut when the wagons were eased down with restraining ropes. The last of the stumps rotted away in the 1970s. The last tollgate on the western end of the Barlow Road, which also is the end of the hiking segment, was abandoned in 1915. The gate presently at the site is a reconstruction.

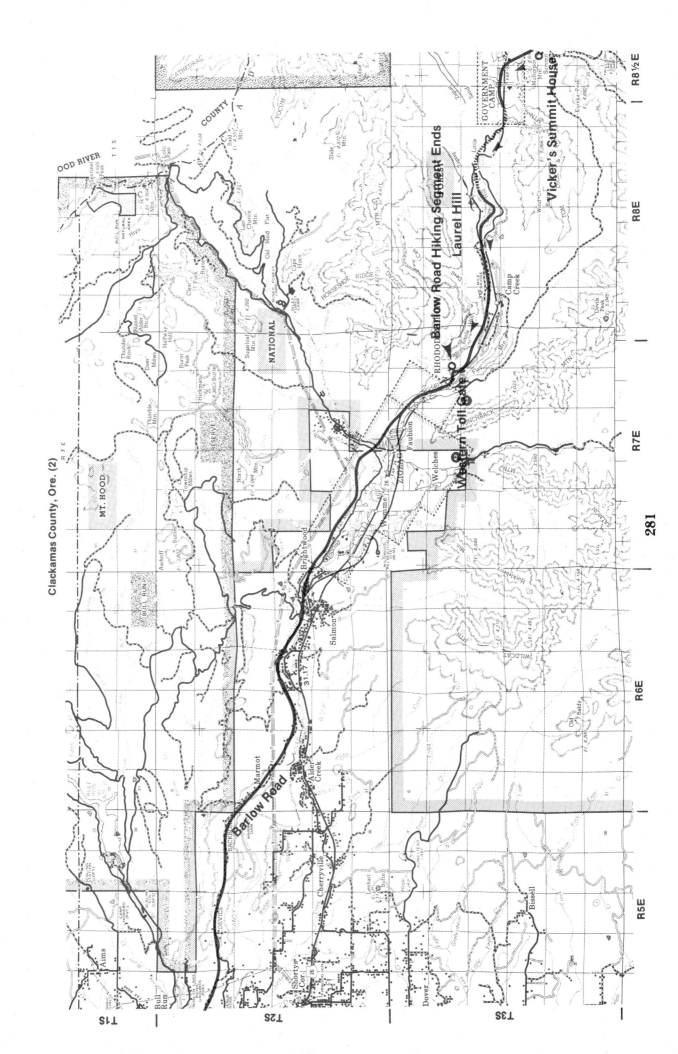

Clackamas County, Ore. (2)

281

There probably was more excitement along this portion of the road than there was just west of Independence, which the emigrants had left 20 to 24 weeks earlier, for they now were within a day or two of their destination.

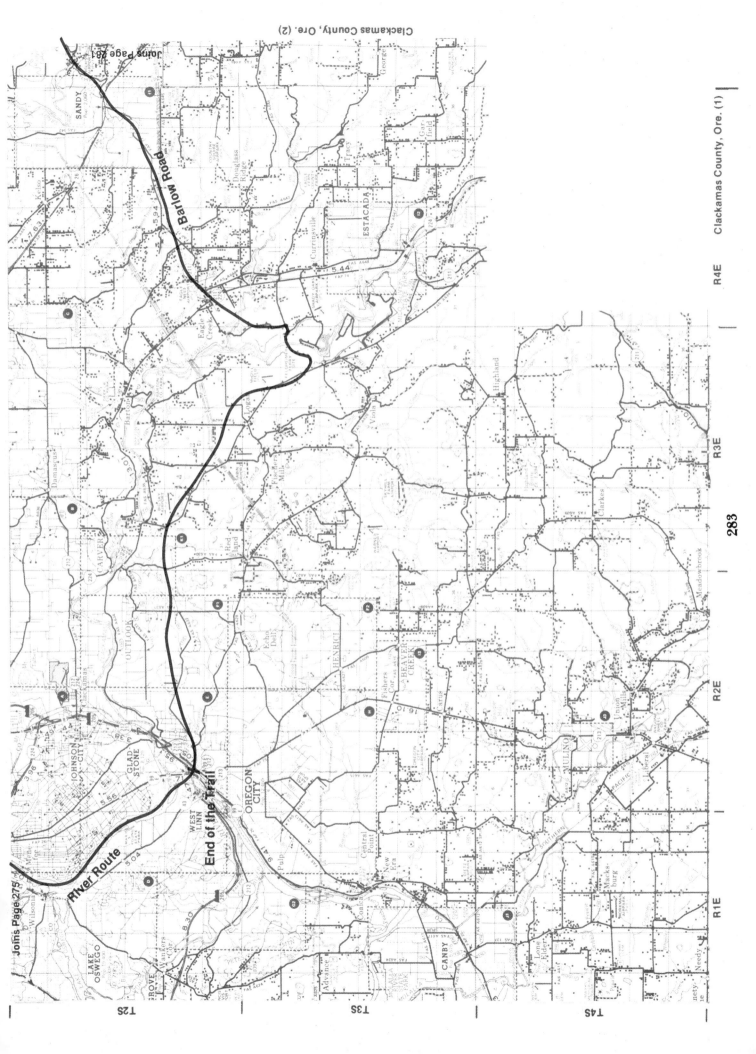

284

The water-borne emigrants probably felt the same elation as those coming in from the Barlow Road, as they hugged the bank downstream from the Falls of the Willamette.

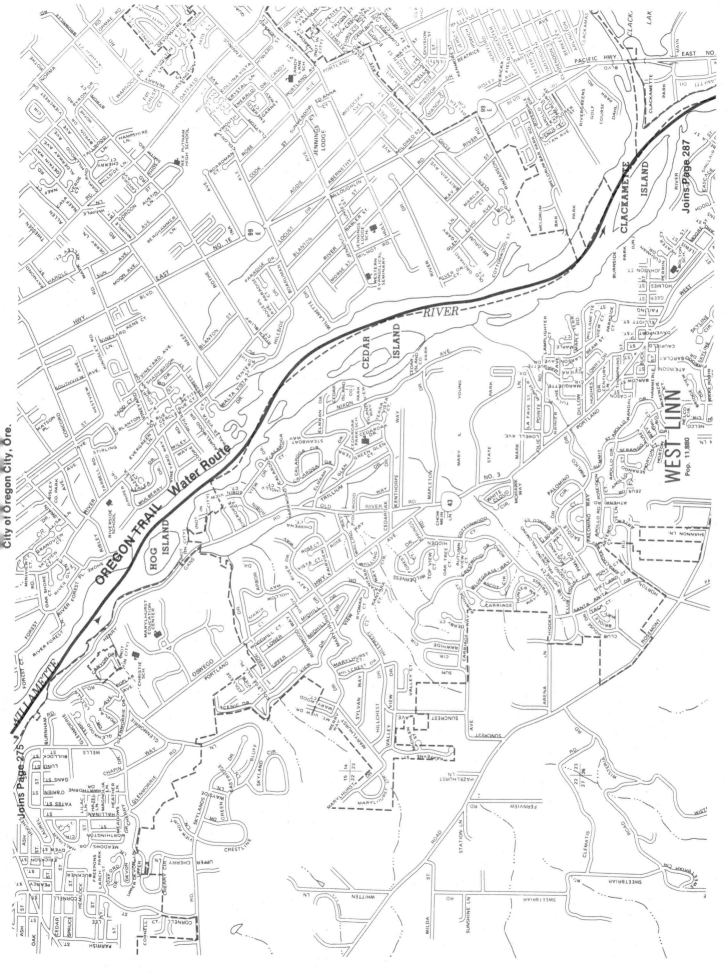

286

The McLoughlin House, the Falls of the Willamette, and the End of the Trail monument in Kelley Field are all worth visiting while the traveler is in Oregon City. The crown jewel, however, is their fine "End of the Trail" interpretive center, completed in 1983 by the citizens and city government of the community, at no cost to the federal government. Here the emigrants, moving by land or by water, reached the end of their journey. They had been engaged in hard labor for 16 to 22 weeks, and through that effort they secured a new way of life for themselves. More important, they bonded the Pacific Northwest to the United States, and for that reason they will never be forgotten.

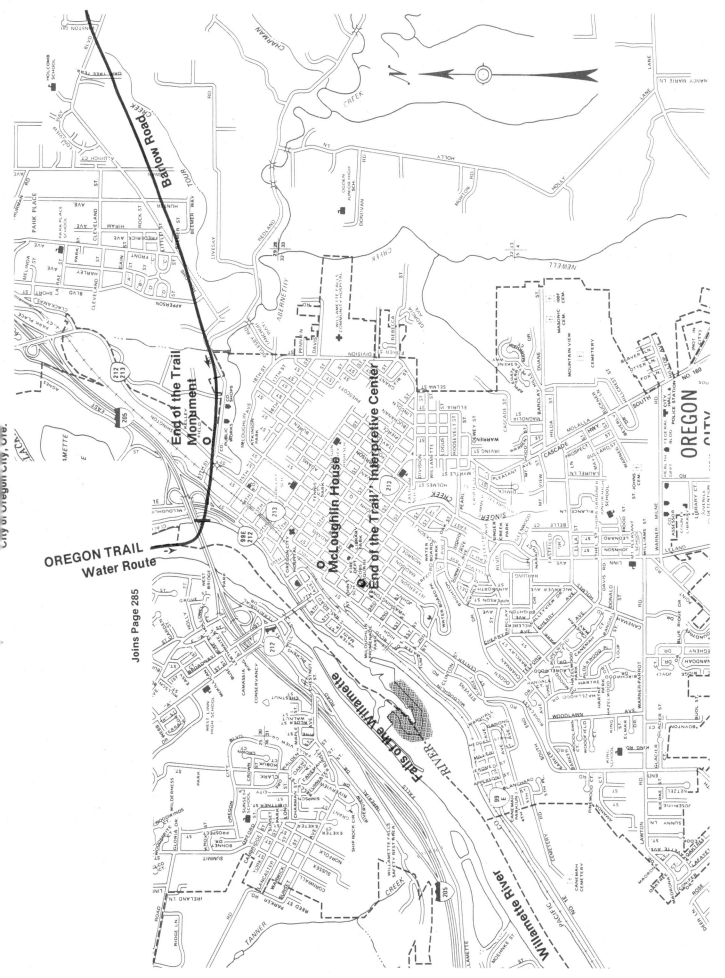

Barlow Road

End of the Trail Monument

OREGON TRAIL
Water Route

Joins Page 285

McLoughlin House

End of the Trail Interpretive Center

OREGON CITY

Falls of the Willamette

Willamette River

287

INDEX

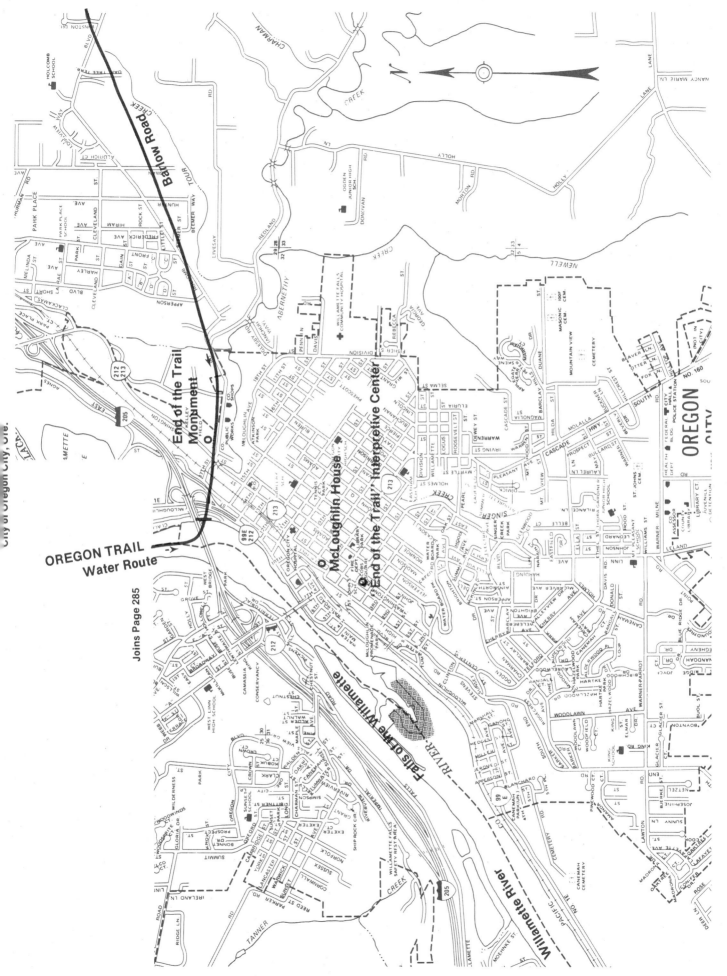

City of Oregon City, Ore.

Barlow Road

CREEK

CHARMAN

HOLLY

NEWELL

WILLAMETTE FALLS COMMUNITY HOSPITAL

MASONIC IOOF CEM.

MOUNTAIN VIEW CEMETERY

ST. JOHNS CEM.

OREGON CITY

End of the Trail Monument

OREGON TRAIL
Water Route

Joins Page 285

McLoughlin House

End of the Trail Interpretive Center

OREGON CITY HOSPITAL

WEST LINN HIGH SCHOOL

Falls of the Willamette

RIVER

CREEK

Willamette River

CANEMAH CEMETERY

287

Explore the Oregon Trail

BY AUTOMOBILE OR ARMCHAIR, WITH THE AWARD-WINNING GUIDEBOOK,

THE OREGON TRAIL REVISITED

Now available: Deluxe Hardbound Edition!

1984 Retail Prices:

Cloth, $12.95, plus $1.35 mailing. (Mo. residents add 60¢ sales tax.) ISBN: 0-935284-07-9 (Second Edition Only)

Paper, $6.95, plus $1.35 mailing. (Mo. residents add 32¢ sales tax.) ISBN: 0-935284-29-X (Third Edition Only)

by
Gregory M. Franzwa

This 436-page book, with 140 illustrations, tells the story of the Oregon Trail as it stretched from the roaring square at Independence, Mo., to the valley of the Willamette River.

Included are detailed instructions guiding the vacationer to or over the trail, wherever it may be reached by the family automobile. The back of the book guides the traveler on a two-week "speed trip" along the route of the trail via the nearest major highways.

This book is recommended by author David Lavender in *The Overland Migrations*, commissioned by the National Park Service and published by them in 1980. The NPS, in its official brochure on the Oregon National Historic Trail, published in 1982, recommends this book as "An indispensable travel guide for those who wish to follow the trail by automobile."

Frank Peters, Pulitzer Prize-winning critic for the *St. Louis Post-Dispatch*, said this about the book: "A more appetite-whetting slice of history, either for armchair types or for students eager to get the feel of American reality with their own feet, would be hard to find."

Foreword by George B. Hartzog Director, National Park Service (in year of initial publication)

See your favorite bookseller

THE WORLD'S MOST
COMPREHENSIVE CATALOG OF

Historic Sites Along THE OREGON TRAIL

PRECISELY LOCATES 394 SITES — PHOTOS, MAPS & DIARY REFERENCES!

by Aubrey L. Haines

Now, in this single volume, the reader may obtain complete information on virtually all sites of historic importance along the Oregon Trail, from Independence, Missouri, to Oregon City, Oregon. Each site description includes the name, location (to a tolerance of 200 yards), distance from Independence, a general summation, material extracted from the journals of the 19th century emigrants, then the 20th century revisitors. Haines usually has remarks of his own to add, and closes with the name of the map on which that particular site may be found. Included are many historic sites not necessarily related to the covered wagon movement — stage stations, Pony Express buildings, graves and battlefields of the Indian Wars. 453 pages, 104 photos, 24 maps, a 411-unit bibliography, index to sites and map list.

Second Edition!

Foreword by
Russell Dickenson
Director, National Park Service

1984 Retail Prices:

Cloth, $24.95
plus $1.75 mailing.
(Mo. residents add $1.15 sales tax.)
ISBN: 0-935284-21-4

Paper, $12.95
plus $1.75 mailing.
(Mo. residents add 46¢ sales tax.)
(ISBN: 0-935284-28-1

See your favorite bookseller

Relive Irene Paden's Fascinating Visits to the Oregon Trail –

THE WAKE OF THE PRAIRIE SCHOONER

"The first time you come across this book you have the sensation of meeting an old friend — you feel as comfortable with this chatty account of a life and of history as you do with a pair of old shoes. The book is witty, gossipy and filled with wisdom and insight. It makes today and it makes yesterday easier to understand and accept.

"Mrs. Paden makes the life on the old trails — primarily the Oregon Trail — come into vivid focus, and yet there are no melodramatics, no exaggerations, no romance for its own sake in this account. But it is not a straightforward and dull recounting, either. It is lively, informative and as much fun as a visit with your favorite raconteur. Every page of this book is effervescent with human emotion — and yet the book is free of cant and tall-tale episodes.

"It is one splendid book and will be a life-long companion to the reader."

– Don H. Peterson
Rawlins (Wyo.)
Daily Times

Now Marketed By THE PATRICE PRESS

1984 Retail Price:
Paper only, $5.95 plus
$1.35 mailing. (Mo. residents
add 28¢ sales tax)
ISBN: 0-8093-0462-7

Irene D. Paden studied the Oregon Trail exhaustively for eight years, making her first field trips in 1935 and concluding her study in 1943 with the publication of this remarkable book. Here is a rare personal literary exposition of the trail as it appeared a half-century ago. The solid, deep and continuous ruts which she describes in Kansas and elsewhere have long since disappeared. Her observations are spiced with her family's trials and tribulations as they searched out the highlights of the old trail. They inquired of local farmers, combed county courthouse records, and studied countless diaries. This facsimile edition was published in 1969.

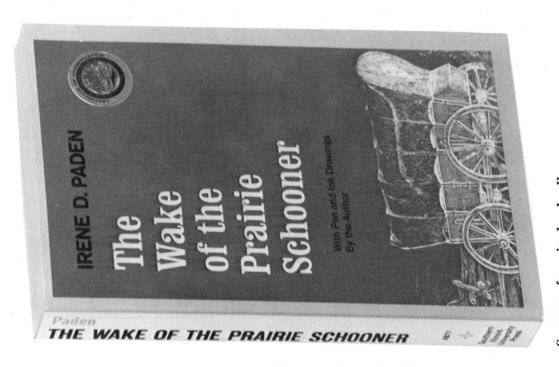

See your favorite bookseller

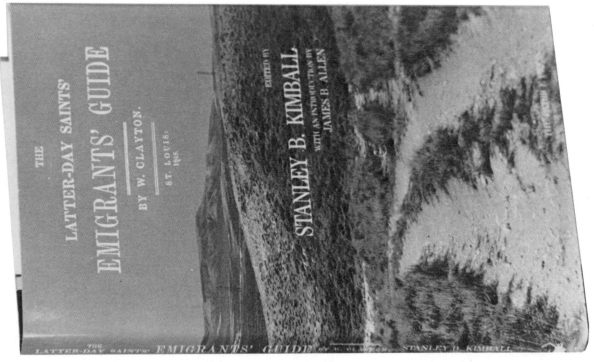

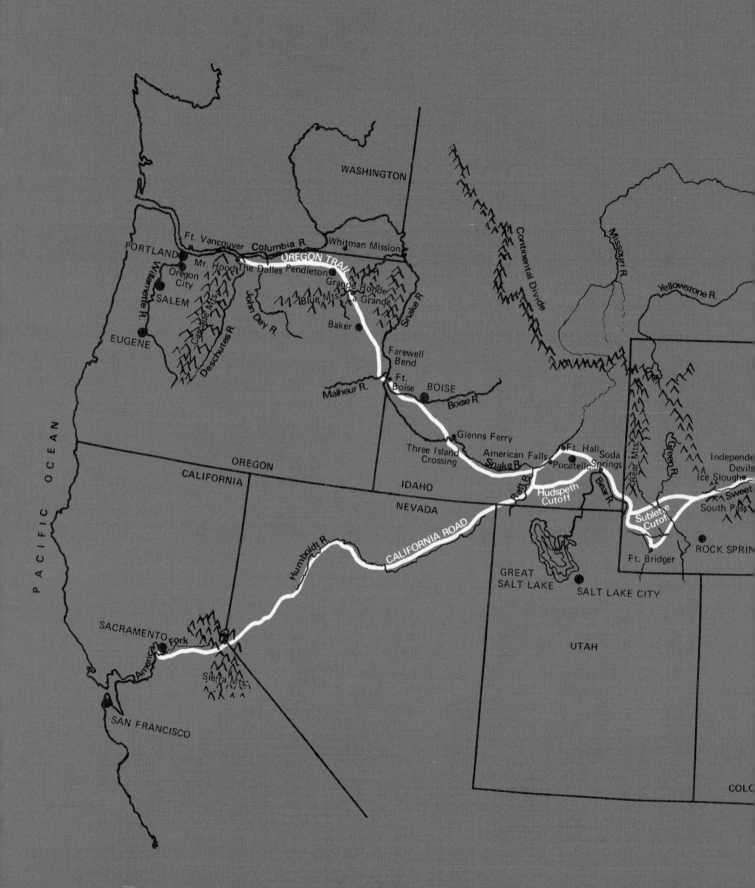